Reign of Appearances

The public sphere, be it the Greek agora or the *New York Times* op-ed page, is the realm of appearances – not citizenship. Its central event is spectacle – not dialogue. Public dialogue, the mantra of many intellectuals and political commentators, is but a contradiction in terms. Marked by an asymmetry between the few who act and the many who watch, the public sphere can undermine liberal democracy, law, and morality. Inauthenticity, superficiality, and objectification are the very essence of the public sphere. But the public sphere also liberates us from the bondages of private life and fosters an existentially vital aesthetic experience.

Reign of Appearances uses a variety of cases to reveal the logic of the public sphere, including homosexuality in Victorian England; the 2008 crash; antisemitism in Europe; confidence in American presidents; communications in social media; special prosecutor investigations; the visibility of African-Americans; violence during the French Revolution; the Islamic veil and contemporary sexual politics. This unconventional account of the public sphere is critical reading for anyone who wants to understand the effects of visibility in urban life, politics, and the media.

Ari Adut is Associate Professor of Sociology at the University of Texas at Austin. He holds graduate degrees from the University of Chicago and the École des Hautes Études en Sciences Sociales, Paris. He is also a former member of Institute for Advanced Study. He is the author of *On Scandal: Moral Disturbances in Society, Politics, and Art* (Cambridge University Press, 2008). Adut's research has been featured in the *New York Times* and on the BBC, and it has received support from the Social Science Research Council and the American Council of Learned Societies.

Reign of Appearances

The Misery and Splendor of the Public Sphere

ARI ADUT
University of Texas

CAMBRIDGE
UNIVERSITY PRESS

One Liberty Plaza, 20th Floor, New York, NY 10006, USA

Cambridge University Press is part of the University of Cambridge.

It furthers the University's mission by disseminating knowledge in the pursuit of education, learning, and research at the highest international levels of excellence.

www.cambridge.org
Information on this title: www.cambridge.org/9781107180932
DOI: 10.1017/9781316848395

© Ari Adut 2018

This publication is in copyright. Subject to statutory exception and to the provisions of relevant collective licensing agreements, no reproduction of any part may take place without the written permission of Cambridge University Press.

First published 2018

Printed in the United States of America by Sheridan Books, Inc.

A catalogue record for this publication is available from the British Library.

Library of Congress Cataloging-in-Publication Data
Names: Adut, Ari, 1971– author.
Title: Reign of appearances : the misery and splendor of the public sphere / Ari Adut.
Description: New York : Cambridge University Press, 2017. |
Includes bibliographical references and index.
Identifiers: LCCN 2017034621 | ISBN 9781107180932 (hardback)
Subjects: LCSH: Political sociology. | Civil society. | Social psychology. | Habermas, Jhurgen. | BISAC: SOCIAL SCIENCE / Sociology / General.
Classification: LCC JA76.A353 2017 | DDC 306.2 – dc23
LC record available at https://lccn.loc.gov/2017034621

ISBN 978-1-107-18093-2 Hardback

Cambridge University Press has no responsibility for the persistence or accuracy of URLs for external or third-party Internet Web sites referred to in this publication and does not guarantee that any content on such Web sites is, or will remain, accurate or appropriate.

For Nicole

All significant truths are private truths. As they become public they cease to become truths; they become facts, or at best, part of the public character; or at worst, catchwords.

T. S. Eliot
Knowledge and Experience in the Philosophy of F. H. Bradley

And [Sosicrates] adds that [Pythagoras] used to compare life to a festival.

"Some people came to a festival to contend for the prizes, and others for the purposes of traffic, and the best as spectators."

Diogenes Laertius
The Lives and Opinions of Eminent Philosophers

Contents

Preface		*page* ix
Acknowledgments		xiii
1	A Critique	1
	Civicness and Civility	4
	Citizenship	7
	Egalitarian and Widespread Participation	8
	Public Events	12
2	A Realistic Perspective	15
	Types of Access	15
	Private and Public	23
	Physical and Virtual Public Spaces	35
	Levels of Visibility	36
3	Publicity	43
	Publicity and Common Knowledge	45
	Collective Effects	57
	Social Status Effects	59
4	Politics in Public	69
	Use of Publicity	70
	Discontents for Political Actors	75
	American Presidents	78
	Scandal and Politics	83
	Liberal Democracy and Publicity	86
	Visible Citizenship	90
5	Content Regulation	94
	Censorship	94
	Expansion	108
	Contraction	111

6	Visibility in Society	118
	Groups	118
	Surveillance	132
7	Justice and Morality in the Public Sphere	136
	Law	136
	Moral Ambiguities	142
8	A Defense of Spectatorship	146

Endnotes   159
References   177
Index   201

Preface

The public sphere is one of the most popular terms – indeed buzzwords – in our contemporary political and intellectual culture. It does not only describe a central phenomenon; it has a heavy normative load as well. Hence the common wisdom that a vibrant public sphere – and by this one means the whole society dialoguing in a civil fashion about the common good in town halls, the streets, the media, and on the internet – is essential to a well-functioning liberal democracy. Hence the appeals that we hear everywhere about the virtues of actively, openly participating in these spaces.

Yet the conventional thinking about the public sphere is unrealistic. As is the standard talk on its close synonyms, such as "the public realm," "the public domain," or "the public square" – often used interchangeably. Civic, civil, egalitarian, widespread dialogue among simple citizens, seen as the raison d'être of the public sphere, is elusive, if not unverifiable. In any case, consequential and engrossing public events, and public life in general, don't assume the form idealized by those who speak and write about the public sphere. More important, the public sphere, by subjecting all its contents to the gaze of anyone, can pose a threat to liberal democracy and citizenship – just as it can undermine law and morality.

The public sphere is faultily glorified because most commentators miss its essence. They miss the very notion, the very experience of "being in public." What makes the public sphere (a town square, the *New York Times* op-ed section, or a television show) public is that its contents are open to general sensory access. In effect, the public sphere is simply any space where we are visible. What characterizes it is not what exists or happens in it: all sorts of things exist and happen in it, not just enlightened debate. A public is not a body of active citizens talking or deliberating about the common good. It is a rather more prosaic, pedestrian entity: an audience, a collection of silent spectators faced with the same spectacle. This is why the public sphere is mostly an inegalitarian institution, producing a steep hierarchy of attention, marked by an ineradicable asymmetry between the few who act and the multitude who watch. The more important a public event or public discourse, the more marked the asymmetry will be.

The public sphere is not the realm of civic dialogue, a deliberative order in which citizenship is exercised. It is simply a space of appearances. Its central event is not dialogue, which is fundamentally something spoken, egalitarian, and symmetrical. Public dialogue, the fixation of so many intellectuals and activists, is but a contradiction in terms: the moment there is an audience, a dialogue will inevitably mutate into a spectacle. In effect, the main event of the public sphere is spectacle, which is fundamentally something visual, inegalitarian, and asymmetrical. The public sphere, because it abandons all its contents to the gaze of anyone, cannot but objectify anything that appears in it. The widely lamented maladies of the contemporary public sphere – lack of participation, spectacle, inauthenticity, and objectification – constitute the very nature of the phenomenon. What many seek in it – reciprocity, dialogue, authenticity, and intersubjectivity – can only truly, without denaturalization, survive in the confidential cocoon of the private sphere. Some citizenship takes place in public – but not its single most important act, which is voting. And the effects of publicity on citizenship are anything but unequivocally positive.

In the pages that follow, I propose a realistic account that emphasizes the sensory – and especially the visual – core of the public sphere. This account is not predicated on imponderable motivations or habitually breached dialogue etiquettes. By contrast, I seek to understand public life as it is, as it is lived both on the street and through media – and not just as civic talk. The account that I propose is couched in the lived experience of being in and of attending to things in public. It considers not only participation, but also spectatorship. It covers both exceptional occurrences and routine events in public.

What makes events in the public sphere potentially consequential is that they have the possibility of getting publicity. This highest form of visibility is not, as the common wisdom says, the wide dissemination of information. Nor is it, as many philosophers and economists argue, something that simply produces common knowledge. Rather, publicity is attention on a focus by a collectivity consisting of spectators who think or know that others are watching the same thing. Much of this book is about the fateful effects that publicity has on information, meaning, people, politics, law, and morality. Illustrations come from a wide array of cases: homosexuality in Victorian England, the 2008 stock market crash, anti-Semitism in Europe, confidence in American presidents, electoral and congressional voting, communications in social media, the court of Louis XIV, special prosecutor investigations, the visibility of African Americans, the Reign of Terror during the French Revolution, the Islamic veil, sexual politics in America, public executions, and pricing in contemporary art.

Another aim I pursue is to capture the relationship between politics and the public sphere: political actors exploit, but are also constrained by, the public sphere, which is both regulated and transformed by politics. Political power shapes the private-public distinction by determining what can appear in public spaces, especially in those receiving high levels of publicity. Much of political conflict revolves around the same issue as well. Censorship – the quintessential content regulation in the public sphere – is an integral part of all governance and politics. Their common lip service to free speech notwithstanding, political actors of all sizes and stripes persistently attempt to restrict what can be attended to in society. Censorship, because of its pejorative connotations, but equally because of its unacknowledged rampancy, is a murky topic. Its logic is indissociable from that of publicity.

Very frequently visibility is equated with surveillance, by which one means the visibility of information about individuals to governments and corporations. Yet this phenomenon, the vertical and often stealthy observation of individuals who are not visible to one another, is a different beast from general visibility. The public sphere is where a huge portion of surveillance in society happens, but such surveillance is horizontal or bottom-up, with its proper phenomenology. Unfortunately, the consequences of the visibility of individuals to one another, as well as that of the government to individuals, are not well understood. A common yet unquestioned assumption is that top-down surveillance is bad; governmental transparency and open citizen participation in the polity, good. But, as we will see, horizontal and bottom-up transparency has far from always beneficial effects on social, political, and moral life. A good deal of what follows is, then, about the misery of the public sphere.

Yet the public sphere has also its pleasures, allures, freedoms – for both those who access it and those who appear in it. These are altogether different from what most commentators praise about the public sphere, though. Most thinking on the issue, while glorifying the civic participant, belittles, even pathologizes the spectator. But spectatorship is the very essence of public life, which is largely a visual experience involving distance. And there is a unique and very much unappreciated transcendence to spectatorship too: one that liberates us from the bondages and burdens of the private sphere and endows us with an aesthetic orientation toward the world. This orientation is not inferior to civic participation; it is in fact the very core of urban experience as well as of culture in general. So what follows is also about the splendor of the public sphere, a splendor that is at once all shallow appearances and existentially indispensable – a splendor that is not without a certain grandeur.

Acknowledgments

I am grateful to Nicole Adut, Jeffrey Alexander, David Ciepley, Paul DiMaggio, Ivan Ermakoff, Neil Gross, Ann Swidler, Diego von Vacano, Michael Walzer, Michael Young, and Ezra Zuckerman for their comments and corrections. Ideas from this book were presented at the École des Hautes Études en Sciences Sociales, Paris, where I benefited greatly from the reactions of Marc Breviglieri, Louis Quéré, Laurent Thévenot, and the other members of the Groupe de la sociologie morale et politique. For editorial support, I am indebted to Robert Dreesen and Gail Naron Chalew. I adopted some material from an article that I published elsewhere: "A Theory of the Public Sphere," *Sociological Theory*, 30 (5): 236–260. The manuscript was completed at the Institute for Advanced Study, Princeton. I am thankful for the hospitality I received from this warm community of scholars – and especially from Michael Walzer.

I

A Critique

Reflections on the public sphere have been mostly oriented by the writings of Jürgen Habermas. Despite certain disagreements with some parts of his theory, most commentators have followed the German philosopher. Here is his understanding:

> By 'public sphere' we mean first of all a realm of our social life in which such a thing as public opinion can be formed. Access to the public sphere is open in principle to all citizens. Citizens act as a public when they deal with matters of general interest without being subject to coercion.[1]

Public opinion can be formed only in physical or virtual spaces where citizens can partake in conversations regarding the common good, according to Habermas. So *The Transformation of the Public Sphere*, his groundbreaking work, traced the history of the phenomenon from the eighteenth-century coffeehouses to contemporary television.[2] In the communications that are to take place in these spaces, the eminent thinker claimed, the particularities of the speakers – their social class, economic interests, passions and prejudices, ethnicity, religion, etc. – need to be bracketed out for the public sphere to function as it is supposed to: universalistic discourse is a necessity. Access should be universal as well. There ought to be widespread and informed participation; the presumed outcome of dialogue is rational consensus.

Habermas claimed that these conditions were not satisfied before the eighteenth century.[3] It was, above all, he argued, thanks to the commodification of news and culture and to the rise in literacy during the early modern period and the Enlightenment that the European bourgeoisie could organize itself as a deliberating public in the eighteenth century by discussing general matters in coffeehouses, newspapers, salons, and reading clubs. The hierarchical and fragmented feudal world had not allowed for such an organization. Neither did the Greek agora (the market place) nor the pynx (the venue of the Athenian legislature) do any better by Habermas's lights: these were simply competitive arenas for recognition and not fora for rational deliberation. While literary matters were the original discursive objects of the public sphere, soon politics became its cynosure. Censorious of secrecy and arbitrariness, the national bourgeoisies challenged their own governments. The principle of publicity regarding matters about the common good was held against the doctrine of *arcana imperii*, just as, in the same breath, truth and rationality were pitted against *raison d'État*. Deprived of participatory citizenship, the bourgeoisie demanded to critically discuss in physical spaces as well as in print matters pertaining to administration and economics. And eventually this rising class would seize political rights with the ascendance of the constitutional state, in part by dint of the opposition gathered in the coffeehouses and the press.

At this point, Habermas's narrative grows glum, though. The public sphere started to deteriorate in the 1870s, as competitive capitalism succumbed to the sway of monopolies. From then on, states took to intervening regularly in political conflicts, and economic interests invaded the public sphere – a paradoxical upshot of the extension of suffrage. In the course of the twentieth century, industrial capitalism transformed citizens into selfish consumers, democracy into masses, sensationalistic media into emotional dupes, public relations experts into subjects, and the welfare state into clients. Particularistic concerns, emotional irrationality, voyeurism and exhibitionism, technocratic reason all combined, conspired to vitiate civic communication. The content of the public sphere, now mostly supplied by mass media, was depoliticized, manipulative publicity superseding rational dialogue in print as in television.[4] "The world fashioned by the mass media is a public sphere in appearance only,"[5] wrote Habermas with undisguised disdain.

The Habermasian approach to the public sphere has been very influential, spurring countless studies, typically with an explicit concern to broaden civic participation, in the absence of which democratic decision-making processes are expected to suffer. According to the political theorist Seyla Benhabib, for instance, the public sphere entails anonymous conversations in civil society by and among associations, networks, and organizations. Such communications are "the embodiment of discursive democracy in practice."[6] For sociologists, too, the emphasis is on civic discussion in public spaces.[7] Similarly, those who study social capital in the wake of Robert Putnam's *Bowling Alone* search for ways to reverse the decline of civic participation in America.[8]

Now, *The Transformation of the Public Sphere*, while a watershed, set off a flurry of criticism as well.[9] Historical research has questioned its timing. A full-fledged political public sphere – one with explicitly religious concerns, which are slurred over by Habermas – was already afoot during the English Revolution in the form of petitions.[10] Habermas has also been taken to task for his class reductionism: the enlightened public of the eighteenth century displayed little class unity; many of its leading lights were in fact liberal aristocrats.[11] And because of the repressiveness of the absolutist state, in several European countries the enlightened bourgeoisie politically operated within the secretive world of Masonic lodges, not open coffeehouses.[12] The substance of their discourse was not nearly as empyrean as the German thinker imagined; their motives were far from disinterested. There are, in effect, multiple ways of exercising citizenship other than the cerebral template championed by Habermas: the nineteenth-century American public sphere was at times quite carnivalesque, coarse, and even corruptible, a world where political allegiance could be openly traded for money.[13]

Habermas posited a public sphere with a unitary public in his original formulation. By contrast, numerous scholars have pleaded for a multiplicity, for counter-publics contesting the hegemony of dominant ones.[14] According to such left critics of Habermas, the universalism of the public sphere is a chimera, if not a chicanery: the actual public sphere privileges the discourses of the mighty and sets normative standards that discriminate against and mute the downtrodden.[15] Critics have maintained that historical public spheres have frequently been erected upon ethnic and racial exclusion. Feminists have, in a similar fashion, argued that the private and public distinction that Habermas takes for granted is, in fact, a gendered and gendering institution with iniquitous impact, that it equates the female with the private and the emotional – thereby barring half of humanity from public life.[16] They have objected to the banishment of personal and sexual matters, along with issues like childcare which predominantly affect women, from public discourse – a banishment that both disguises and actuates the dominium of men over women. At the same time, distinctly female forms of public action that do not square with the model stipulated by Habermas have been uncovered by feminist historians. Craig Calhoun has claimed that identities are often formed in the course of public debates, as opposed to preceding them.[17] Others have thrown into doubt the superiority of rationality over narrative knowledge and personal experience.

These criticisms have yielded incisive insights about debate in civil society. Still, Habermas and his followers, but also his critics – along with many who write about the "public realm," "public square," "public space," or the "public domain" – all operate in broad strokes within something that I will refer to as the conventional perspective. Commentators in the media have equally, by and large, adopted it. The focus here is the civic or civil dialogue that is supposed to take place in physical and virtual public spaces. Public space is not treated in its own right. I will get to this very problematic – indeed damning – omission in the next chapter, but before doing that let us see how the conventional perspective suffers from three problematic elements: i) the condition of civicness or civility, ii) the conflation of the public sphere with citizenship, and iii) the ideal of widespread, egalitarian participation. There are scholars who have addressed some of these problems. Yet studies that escape one are usually marred by the others.

Civicness and Civility

Barring important exceptions,[18] the scholars adopting the conventional perspective posit a close link between the public sphere and the normative orientation of its inhabitants. Public does not only qualify the space that we are in, but also the group we constitute as well as the moral telos of our action. When we are not oriented to the common good, when we are not plentiful the public sphere deteriorates, loses its raison d'être. According to Habermas, this is what happened when, as a result of capitalism, economic interests came to govern communications in public. For some, the public sphere is even contingent on a civic attitude. Nina Eliasoph writes that the public sphere "comes into being when people speak public-spiritedly."[19] Jeffrey Alexander's "civil sphere" – an offshoot of the concept of public sphere – is equally defined by a universalistic morality: "a solidary sphere in which a certain kind of universalizing community comes to be culturally defined and to some degree institutionally enforced."[20]

Yet concern for the common good, far from being a self-evident social fact, is more of a will-o'-the-wisp, very hard to verify objectively by scholars or laypeople. The public-spiritedness that one spots in the world is frequently simply a reflection of one's ideological biases: hence the proclivity of public sphere scholars, most of whom are openly liberals or radicals, to key in on left-leaning movements and their overall silence on nonprogressive groups – except to denounce them.²¹ Opponents in public discussions and controversies attribute selfishness to each other as a matter of fact. Indeed, how can we exclude that there can be a whole kaleidoscope of self-serving interests in our minds while we are marching in demonstrations, participating in parent-teacher association meetings, signing petitions, or sending off op-ed pieces? One can obviously attend a local meeting not only to reflect on public matters, but also to socialize, to meet prospective mates, to project a reputation for being smart, to signal a righteous concern to neighbors, to deny housing to immigrants, to prepare for a lynching, to kill time. Those who lead these events – community leaders – will typically have self-regarding political ambitions. Or it can reasonably appear that way to observers. Of course, from the National Rifle Association to the ACLU to anti-abortion organizations, most politicized groups, or rather their spokespeople who intone in public, dress up their discourse in universalist nomenclature – with terms like equality or freedom.²² Few would write a publishable letter to a newspaper without a pretension to speak in the name of some general, grandiose principle. But there is no reason for us to take these claims at their face value. High-minded rhetoric in public is not uncommonly found by its addressees to be ritualistic, hollow, not to say devious. The motive behind such discourse cannot be easily pinned down, and public-spiritedness in public rarely goes without instigating ethical assaults aiming to debunk it. Those who participate heavily in public affairs are typically recognized as partisan; they will not fail to be perceived by their opponents as selfish or brainwashed. Arguments in a supposedly civic debate are difficult to distinguish from the standard ideological positions in a society; it is hardly surprising that such situations get heated in no time.

What if we relax the discursive conditions and say that the public sphere is where people – whatever their intentions – engage in civil debate? But then we are still left with very little: it is difficult to find interesting and consequential public events, discursive or otherwise, that don't feature disruptiveness, ad hominem attacks, malice. It is a rare – and usually boring – debate, one that solely involves issues. The more a politician disquisitions impersonally, logically, professorially in public, the more, the linguist Michael Silverstein points out, the "message being conveyed is, in actuality, [his] rigidity, narrowness, and myopia."²³ In political life, the more important the debate, the nastier it tends to get. Consider how both Donald Trump and Hillary Clinton cruelly cudgeled each other's character in each of the three presidential debates in 2016.

Further, the one who receives attention from a multitude will be automatically aggrandized; personality, thus, cannot but be an integral part of any public debate. Even, or especially, when the stakes are low, public debate almost always induces grandstanding, if not in reality then in perception, which then instigates moral assaults on the grandstanding of the grandstanders. And public debate, no matter its civil genesis, will usually end up fomenting partisanship and polarization.[24] Parties routinely complain of each other's incivility, and the worst hidden agendas are ascribed to one's opponent in the press, on television, at the town hall. This holds as much as for today as it did for the golden age of American associational life touted by Tocqueville. Michael Young has found that the antebellum evangelical sin societies and fraternal associations charged one another unremittingly for being uncivil and anti-democratic.[25] The same goes for the voluntary organizations of the Reconstruction and Progressive Eras, whose antagonisms compounded the ethnic and religious rifts in the United States.[26] Consider as well the acrimony that dictates any debate about gun laws in the American public sphere, where each side habitually, hatefully holds the other responsible for untold homicides.[27] In a broader sense, the more people talk in public and the more public their talk becomes, the cheaper their talk gets – and, as Frank Knight's first Law of Talk posits, "cheaper talk drives out of circulation that which is less cheap."[28] At the same time, public positions in controversies tend to turn increasingly radical and noncompromising. The ease with which one can respond to discourse in the public sphere will only make things more uncivil. On Twitter, for instance, any public tweet – in its original or retweeted form – can be responded to by anyone. Responses, particularly to controversial tweets, are very often abusive, bordering on harassment.[29]

Last but not least, most speech and action that succeed in changing society are rarely civil. The primary aim of civil disobedience, the paradigmatic example of effective public contestation, is to provoke violence by authorities. The public that most commentators write about is a collection of rational, well-behaved citizens. It is the opposite of a mob, which is irrational, rowdy, feverish, and manipulated by ill-intentioned politicians. Yet the referents of these categories cannot be easily agreed upon. Groups one likes are publics; those that one doesn't, mobs. In the United States, conservatives thought that the Occupy Wall Street protesters were a mob; predictably, liberals characterized the Tea Party members exactly in the same way.

Citizenship

The conventional perspective identifies the public sphere – for example, the town square or the media – as the site where citizenship is or ought to be exercised,[30] whether this entails rational dialogue or discursive struggles between dominant and subordinate groups. The public sphere is "a theater in modern societies in which political participation is enacted through the medium of talk," in the words of Nancy Fraser.[31] Such a conflation of the public sphere with citizenship is problematic on multiple grounds.

First, while the darlings of most public sphere commentators are associations discoursing in the open, the very essence of citizenship is indubitably something else. It is voting: the only political act that a majority of citizens ever engage in. Even more devastating, voting in modern societies is a solitary act carried out in secret – that is, outside the public sphere. After all, the secret ballot is the sine qua non of contemporary liberal democracy. The rationale is that voting should not take place in public because its visibility can discourage good citizens from expressing their true preferences, while encouraging the venal ones to sell their votes – both of which would pervert citizenship.[32] And most people who actively engage in politics in the town square or the media are not simple citizens but elites of some kind. It is often some kind of an intellectual – whom Sartre defined as "he who meddles with things which are none of his business."[33] Or it is some kind of a political actor – in other words, someone who has an apparent gain in meddling. Simple citizens, even when they genuinely care about public matters, would rather hide their names or positions, especially if they think they may not be in the majority; open, sincere engagement is imprudent, perilous. This is why the hallmark of a liberal society is not widespread political participation in the open, which is rarely voluntary and is more of a feature of totalitarian states, but its opposite: the right given to citizens to not engage with political matters in public, and the liberty to peacefully lead private lives free as much as possible from societal and governmental surveillance and interference.

Second, there is ample elevated public discourse (which relate to truth, God, art, etc.) that has little to do with citizenship. Even in Habermas's narrative, the origin of the bourgeois public sphere was in literary matters: discussions of eighteenth-century bestsellers such as Samuel Richardson's *Pamela*. This problem, already noted by several scholars,[34] is not necessarily an insurmountable one; nevertheless, the emphasis on citizenship would leave out many significant communications – but also events – from the public sphere.

Finally, there is here a dubious motivational distinction among political activity within civil society, the political system proper, and state institutions. Public sphere is usually situated within civil society – the site of autonomous social organization outside the ambit of the state. Political behavior here is celebrated by a romanticized, universalist conception of citizenship, particularly when undertaken by leftist or minority groups, whereas politics outside the civil society is relegated to unscrupulous power-grabbing. Yet many citizens and civil associations defend narrow interests, their discourses notwithstanding.[35] And those who claim to act in the public sphere in the name of some common good however defined (neighborhood groups, LGBT activists, professional organizations, National Rifle Association, immigrant associations, churches, labor unions, etc.) tend to be collectivities often benefiting from connections to political parties. Frequently receiving funding or subsidies from the state, these actors, for all their windy rhetoric and alpine pretensions to be above the profane world of institutional politics, are objectively indistinguishable from interest groups or lobbies. Besides, there is no evidence that private citizens – singly or collectively – are more public-spirited in their words or deeds than professional politicians, or that community activists are bereft of self-regarding ambitions.

In any case, civic life can seldom be carried out independent of political structures. The antebellum American associational life that Tocqueville praised so much sprang from political party networks and was enabled by the national postal system, canals, and turnpikes built by the government.[36] Policy decisions at critical moments in history have vastly shaped the nature and organization of the American media.[37] Marking off a pristine space of citizenship from a contaminated political society and state administration is too naïve: there are robust financial, ideological, and organic links between actors in civil society and institutional politics.

Egalitarian and Widespread Participation

The conventional perspective envisions the public of the public sphere as a discursive community. It assumes the possibility of – it indeed prescribes – widespread, egalitarian, and consequential dialogue about important general matters. The norm is a hyper-politicized world where we are all community organizers or *intellectuels engagés* – or at least enthusiastic joiners. A gloom-and-doom tenor is adopted when this stringent proviso is all too often not obliged by reality, and the tone turns denunciatory. As we saw, Habermas argued that the public sphere degenerated during the nineteenth and twentieth centuries, as citizens were degraded into listless, manipulated spectators. Others maintain that capitalism, neoliberalism, racism, patriarchy, or some other social evil makes the public sphere exclusionary.[38] But a paramount assumption here is that absent systemic domination and exclusion, egalitarian civic dialogue in public spaces should – almost naturally – flourish.

It is, however, again quite naïve to expect that everybody can or will be equally interested in public affairs and take part equally in the critical debates about them. Pace Aristotle, only so many men – and women – are political animals; those who are, are only so part of the time. Political indifference and lethargy in social life are widespread across time and space, a fact we cannot chalk up to domination or exclusion. Participation in public life is a source of personal fulfillment for some, sheer drudgery for others. According to Albert Hirschman, when we do steer toward participation, we do it mainly because of the ineluctable disappointments in our private lives, and only temporarily so, as the public arena will never ultimately not foster frustrations of its own – all this making interest in the polis cyclical.[39] For quite a few, it is escapism, a search for distractions that generates occasional, yet rarely sustained, interest in public matters. When asked about them, citizens' attitude is ambivalent; most don't have strong feelings or fixed opinions and give contradictory responses.[40] Only 5 to 10 percent of Americans are active participants in local or national politics.[41] In effect, interest in politics seems to be a minority taste. With the advent of cable television in the United States, 10 percent of all viewers watched more news; 30 percent stopped tuning into news altogether, simply concentrating on entertainment.[42] Further, cable television executives realized quickly that those who wanted political content wanted it unapologetically partisan.

At any rate, deliberation about public issues is contingent upon knowledge, if not expertise, and we are ignorant about the most elementary facts.[43] A poll found that in 1964, at the height of the Cold War, only 38 percent of Americans were aware that the USSR was not a member of NATO.[44] Half of contemporary Americans don't know the names of their elected representatives or the major political issues of the day.[45] A recent poll found that only 36 percent could name all the branches of the US government.[46] If you find this shocking, consider that the figure was even lower, less than 20 percent, in the 1960s.[47] Ignorance expectedly erodes interest. There is thus substantial evidence showing low levels of civic participation in the contemporary United States.[48] The federated membership organizations of the first half of twentieth century (such as fraternal societies like the Masons, religious organizations like the Women's Christian Temperance Union, and veterans' groups like the American Legion as well as labor organizations, business groups, and the PTA) have given way to professionally managed advocacy groups since the 1960s.[49] The latter are operated by paid staffs of professionals, whose principal worry is getting donations to support their lobbying efforts rather than recruiting members.

"America's new civic universe is remarkably oligarchic," bemoans Theda Skocpol.[50] But have Americans ever been very civic? Contra the common wisdom legated by Tocqueville, a number of historians has marshaled evidence that the image of an antebellum America with a rich associational life is a hyperbole.[51] And things were not much better in the early sixties, either. In 1961, Robert Dahl observed that most people were uninterested in politics; what they cared about mainly, he said, were "food, sex, love, family, work, play, shelter, comfort, friendship, social esteem, and the like."[52] Michael Schudson has contended that all these issues have been politicized since then.[53] Maybe. Nonetheless, it is not any less true that those who have politicized them are a tiny minority of politicians, activists, and intellectuals. Most of us seldom experience these issues in our everyday lives, especially when they involve us personally, as political matters.

Obsession with civil society associationalism is peculiar to American intellectuals. Yet are European democracies, much less concerned with voluntary organizations, inferior? In fact, voter turnout, welfare functions, social services, and political literacy are superior on the other side of the Atlantic – with lower crime rates, to boot. Tocqueville, the sacred reference of America's pride in its supposedly exceptionally vibrant associational culture, was far from uncritical of it; he saw that voluntary associations could engender standardization, conformism, intolerance. A researcher has found that those who join voluntary associations are more likely to interact with people like themselves.[54] And a long tradition in political science has argued that apoliticism is not necessarily bad. Civil society activism in the absence of stable political structures can yield anarchy, radicalism, and eventually authoritarianism.[55] Contemporary Egypt in the wake of the Arab Spring is an example. There is also evidence that fascism in Germany was fueled by an ever-politicizing civil society.[56] Waxing civic participation in a society can indeed be both a symptom and an aggravating factor of waning institutional politics. It is often because institutional politics has stopped working adequately that people take to the streets; but, in doing so, they may also frequently make it all the harder for politicians to do their job.

In any case, public communication rarely takes the form of a debate with widespread, egalitarian dialogue. Not even among intellectuals: as any academic would have to concede, it is ordinarily a handful of professors who dominate – thanks to taste, ability, ambition, or narcissism – faculty meetings; others, if they show up at all, remain, for the most part, spectators, simply spectating their colleagues perform, when they are not daydreaming or furtively checking their smart phones. We don't find a very different situation in the colonial New England town meetings, which commentators who are censorious of modern American apathy wistfully remind us with. Turnout was apparently very low in these gatherings.[57] Agenda was set and the discussions were led by local notables, who were much more comfortable with and fond of public speaking. Action or discourse that is putatively civic is produced by ambitious elites in front of nonparticipating, nonresponding audiences. Even during times when there is growing participation in polity, the passive citizenry remains the overwhelming majority.

Nowadays, technology allows all of us to participate in the public sphere; yet we don't. Most people who read news stories or blogs on the internet don't write anything in the comments section. Usually that section is empty; should there be any comments, we are unlikely to read them. Twitter, which makes it extremely easy for anyone in theory to have an audience, is not more egalitarian. Most of those on Twitter have fewer than 10 followers; a very tiny few like celebrities have millions of them. Those you follow on Twitter typically don't follow you back. It is a rare tweet that obtains a response or a retweet. Few people get any attention at all.[58]

The conventional perspective is blind to, reluctant to acknowledge, or given to denounce away the constitutive asymmetry of the public sphere between the few who receive attention and the numerous who give it, between those who speak and those who listen, between those who do and those who watch. There is such an asymmetry in all the spaces where Habermas and others labor to track down public-spirited discourse. Not only in the media, but also in small-scale settings – where people encounter one another face to face, where status differences are modest, and where formal roles allocate egalitarian speaking rights – an asymmetry between participants and spectators will nevertheless emerge swiftly, spontaneously. This asymmetry will be sharp to the extent that attention from others is profitable – hence scarce, and subject to competition. Few are visible in places that receive high publicity; even fewer are noticed; and a miniscule minority is ever heard in public. And those who seek attention are not only out to convey ideas but at least equally to acquire reputation and fame – which are at once gratifying to those with a penchant for public life and indispensable to all political action, civic or not.[59]

Public Events

Any compelling theory of the public sphere should be able to give us an adequate account of public events. How does the conventional perspective fare? Consider scandal, the quintessential public event – quintessential because one would be hard-pressed to imagine a public event that draws us more, and because we do so much to avoid it. Scandal is an episodic event that is created with the publicization of an actual, apparent, or alleged transgression to an audience.[60] It lasts so long as there is significant spectatorship. It is experienced, both by its participants and spectators, as the disruptive publicity of transgression. For there to be public interest in it, the transgression typically needs to be linked to a high-status person or entity. A scandal can be about diverse things: abuse of power, heretical ideas, adultery, financial skullduggery, aesthetic novelties, organizational intrigues, celebrity fandangos. Sometimes, scandals seem trivial; other times, grave. Watergate was a scandal; as was the revelation of Paris Hilton's sex tape. So is a great deal of what crams newspapers as well as private conversations. And as journalists and activists know instinctively, seemingly impersonal, structural issues in political and public life usually only become interesting and attention-worthy to regular people if they are presented as scandals – that is, if they appear as the result of transgressions committed by or linkable to elites. This principle applies not only to obviously scandalous transgressions like corruption but also to all sorts of public issues. Consider how the American right and the left recently treated, respectively, the healthcare reform and the war in Iraq as quasi-scandals.

Scandals entertain us; they at once let us peek into the fascinating lives of elites and sooth our resentment against them by offering a spectacle of their comeuppance; they furnish us with an opportunity to wax indignant at the violations of the norms we (pretend to) cherish. Scandals – of others – are frequently appealing. They are ubiquitous in public life too: elite competition in politics and art is frequently conducted through scandal, by public denunciations or commissions of transgressions. And it is through scandals – as a result of the reactions they elicit – that many norms are solidified, problematized, and transformed.

Yet scandals, as other consequential public events registering significant interest, don't hew to the moral and formal strictures of the conventional perspective. Whatever their content, scandals rarely entail civic or civil debate, but rather vile public wrangles among the accusers, the accused, and their allies and associates. These episodes mix strategic cogitation with heightened affect, opportunism with prejudice. People participate in them or observe their unfolding with umpteen tangled motives, quite a few not civic. Those who take part in them are often self-interested or can be reasonably perceived that way. They feature all-out personal attacks, the publicity of things intimate and especially sexual, along with voyeurism on the part of the audiences. They tend to be partisan affairs contaminating all those they touch, sometimes unfairly with substandard evidence. Should they last a long time, they can even contaminate the public. Seldom related to citizenship, they can discredit institutions, depress general morale. When they give rise to social causes – and big ones occasionally do – scandals divide societies. Since they draw forth moralizing attitudes, scandals can look like episodes where a society debates its values. But this is not quite true. Scandals involve a sharp discrepancy between participation and spectatorship: it is the elite who partake in them, often strategically as they compete with one another.[61]

Take one of the most outstanding and momentous public events in French history, the Dreyfus affair. The scandal broke in late 1894 with the trial and conviction of a Jewish captain, Alfred Dreyfus, in a court-martial for espionage and metastasized as it looked like that the officer could have in fact been framed by higher-ups in the French military. The French elite was soon riven into two camps: the traditionalists and the Republicans. The scandal formally ended with the pardon of Dreyfus in 1899 and his reinstatement seven years later, but its repercussions reached well into the twentieth century. Vichy was, in part, the revanche of the anti-Dreyfussard animus. Hardly civil, the Dreyfus affair was a frenzied chapter in French history marked by calumny, distrust, deception, and violence.[62] Even the famous "J'accuse" of Émile Zola, as it was denouncing the genuine miscarriage of justice that the conviction of the Jewish officer was, did not desist from engaging in sexual innuendos or concocting unfounded conspiracy theories; it was indeed a provocation poised to get the famous novelist arrested so that he could defend Dreyfus with fanfare in a court of law.[63] The parties accused each other of willfully, selfishly ruining the country; accusations of grandstanding were common within the camps too. The Dreyfussards and anti-Dreyfussards were not parties in a civic or civil dialogue, but factions in a ferocious fight. Yet the fight did not involve everybody; the vociferous ones were the members of the elite, many with political ambitions. Like in all important public events, most of the French were the spectators of the scandal, not its participants.

If we abide consistently with the assumptions of the conventional perspective, we would have to leave out of the public sphere not only the Dreyfus affair but also the Watergate and Lewinsky episodes, the revolt of the Impressionists, and the sexual abuse scandals that recently roiled the Catholic Church – indeed any public event that is a little more biting than sedate, seemly discussion à la *The Charlie Rose Show*. Or rather we would have to classify all scandals (given the moral distemper and contamination they breed, given the vitriol and prurience they release, and given the apparent opportunism that frequently characterizes their protagonists) critically as symptomatic of a degraded public sphere.[64]

Far from being a fringe occurrence, scandal throws into full relief the logic of the public sphere. And most moral conflict mimics, even approximates scandal the moment it involves high-status personalities – and it is rare for an interesting moral conflict in the open not to devolve into attacks on persons. What make scandal in compatible with the conventional perspective are the very things that make it riveting and consequential. And an account of the public sphere that cannot deal with riveting and consequential events is a deficient one; it needs to be replaced.

2

A Realistic Perspective

The late sociologist and historian Charles Tilly complained, "The concept of public sphere is morally admirable but analytically useless."[1] There is a bigger problem, however. The conventional perspective is not only normative and idealistic; it fails empirically too. The public sphere is not just a concept. It is a phenomenon, more specifically a space: a town square, a radio program, the World Wide Web, a coffeehouse, or a newspaper. And whether real or virtual, the public sphere contains something. Yet this space – whose content is visual or acoustic and not just discourse – is a black box for the conventional perspective; it is ignored, when not misunderstood. The attention is not on the public sphere, but on the civic or civil dialogue to be undertaken in an egalitarian fashion by a collectivity in it. Dialogue is indeed, erroneously, viewed as the raison d'être of the public sphere – accompanied by the equally erroneous assumption that communication can be properly understood without considering where it happens.

Types of Access

General access is what makes a space public. Yet the notion is not self-evident. There are three possible forms of access to a public space: physical, representational, and sensory. Access is physical when one enters a street in person. By contrast, representational access refers to one's name, sounds, words, or proxies becoming visible or audible in public. Finally, we have sensory access when we can access the contents of a public space with our eyes or ears.

Physical access requires a physical public space, such as a street; representational access, often a virtual one – such as a newspaper. But it is possible to have representational access to a physical public space as well. Consider a statement by a president delivered through a spokesperson to journalists: access here is accomplished by a proxy. Representational access can take three additional forms, following the triadic taxonomy of signs proposed by Charles Peirce[2]: one's image on the television screen is an iconic representation; an artwork in a gallery or the voice of a person on the radio is an indexical representation; and words in a newspaper constitute symbolic representations.

For some, urbanists especially, the defining characteristic of the public sphere is corporeal co-presence – its moral telos being civic interaction among strangers. Access that matters is then the physical one.[3] Accordingly, virtual spaces created by technology, the content of which consists of images and words (and not people per se), are excluded. There can obviously be no physical access to these spaces, yet they are denoted as the public sphere both in ordinary language and by most commentators. It is certainly possible to come up with a framework that considers solely physical public spaces – but only at the expense of ignoring what they share with virtual ones. The result would be a poor picture of public life that omits the contribution of media.

As we will see, representational access is paramount to understanding the public sphere. We would, nevertheless, equally err by defining the phenomenon with this type. First, while access implies will, those who appear in the public sphere through their representations may not have desired to do so. Take a hitherto obscure citizen whose foibles are being trumpeted on national television. It would be uncontroversial to say that the details of this person's life have been shoved onto the public sphere. Or consider a hanging at the town square where a convict is exposed before dying to the sight of a crowd so that he* can be better abased. Second, and more

---

* In this book, there will be many situations when I will need to use a gender-neutral third-person singular pronoun to refer to a generic person (for example, "the spectator," "the citizen," the "*flâneur*," etc.) for whom no gender identity is intended or relevant. In these cases, following traditional grammar, I will be using the generic "he." I realize the obvious limitations of this choice, and I am only doing it because the alternatives seem worse. The epicene "they," useful in everyday conversation for simple sentences like "Someone left their umbrella in the office," creates a lot of confusion in writing, especially in complex sentences and when the gender is irrelevant rather than simply unknown. Resorting to "he or she" is fine for a few times, but soon becomes clunky and distracting. Alternating "he" and "she" may seem like an egalitarian solution, but it is also problematic because it has the unintended effect of reinforcing the gender-specific senses of both "he" and "she"

important, while the public sphere implies general access, representational access to public spaces is scarcely general: there are indeed plenty of public spaces that allow for severely constricted opportunities for being seen or heard – particularly if they obtain a lot of attention, conferring fame to those who are featured in them. The op-ed page of the *New York Times* is one. Here, physical access is impossible. Representational access is precious: anyone who speaks English can send an opinion piece, but few will be fortunate enough to see their names printed in that hallowed intellectual forum, entry to which is strictly controlled by finicky gatekeepers. Nevertheless, few would deny that the *New York Times* op-ed page is the public sphere. It is a print space that does admit of general access, but this access is visual access by readers – and not representational access by writers. A street is both sensorily and physically accessible to citizens, so long as they are decently attired and not too unruly, but many other public spaces – typically those whose contents receive focused attention from multitudes – are accessible to us only as spectators. And even on the street most of what we do is simply spectating and subjecting ourselves to visibility.

The general access that characterizes a real or virtual public space is therefore not physical or representational; it is sensory. The public sphere is a space that is generally visible. Its main contents are people and their doings – or images and words that represent people and their doings in some way.[4] People are more interesting than objects. They are less predictable. They act and cause events; to them we owe most of our suffering and salvation. They are thus more likely to command spectatorship. Nature is ordinarily outside the public sphere, unless one can expect some human presence there as well. People avoid sitting in parks where there is no one to see, regardless of the quality of the greenery around. The reason is not just safety considerations. "Nobody enjoys sitting on a stoop or looking out of a window at an empty street. Almost nobody does such a thing," observed Jane Jacobs.[5] The more people there are in a public space, in their bodies or representations, the more central it is.

whenever they are used: since "she" is used in other parts of the text, it is impossible for the reader not to attribute a very strong gender-specific sense to "he" and vice versa. This strategy thus yields a much less gender-neutral effect than the exclusive use of the generic "he" could. Finally, pluralization, which works well in many situations, creates a serious problem here because it turns singular individuals into collectivities, often with the sense that they are acting together, while it is a central point of this book that "the spectator," "the citizen," "the *flâneur*," are each solitary actors.

The public sphere is simply where we are visible. To be more precise, in this book, by "visible," I mean open to general sensory access, open to the sight of spectators, in one's body or representation. Now, as the contents of the public sphere can be visual or auditory, "perceptible" would be technically more correct. But I will be using the terms "visible," "visibility," and consequently "spectatorship" – for several reasons. First, "perceptible" and "perceptibility" are uncommon, clunky words. Second, "visibility" is used in everyday language to include audibility as well: when we say that a person has high visibility, we often mean that he is publicly vocal. Third, as I will argue later, the essence of the public sphere is spectatorship; the visual is more integral to it than the auditory. It is customary to use the terms "audience" and "spectators" interchangeably to refer to a public; for practical purposes, I will do the same. It is, nevertheless, worth noting a difference: an audience is a public who listens, while spectators watch. So, technically, "spectators," is more appropriate for our purposes.

The public sphere is a semiotic universe: the moment they are public, even flesh-and-blood people can become representations – to a much larger extent than in the private world, where such reductionism is both difficult and frowned upon. The public is not a civically oriented, civil, egalitarian, vocal collectivity. It consists of spectators, each knowing that what he sees is seen, or can be seen, by other spectators. But a spectator does not need to be in the public sphere: one can look at the television, gaze out of the window, or search governmental records on the internet in the privacy of one's house.

My account of the public sphere is in line with the usual use of the term "public space," which is, according to Webster's Dictionary, "any place that is accessible or visible to all members of the community." It corresponds to the notion of being in public. When we divulge a piece of information in the open, to the possible scrutiny of others, we say that we have made it public. It is the same thing when governments declassify or release records. When feminists denounce the exclusion of women from the public sphere, they are not only targeting patriarchy and sexism; they are, in a broader sense, endeavoring to expand feminine visibility.

According to legal scholars, when information is available for the consideration of all, when it is not subject to copyright, it is in the public domain. As such, this term is not synonymous with the public sphere, though. The contents of the public domain, especially in its legal use, include only information or cultural artifacts and exclude people and their actions. But the visibility of people and their actions has all kinds of consequences. And information or other cultural artifacts usually become visible as the result of intentional human behavior. Further, the words and images in the public domain are never just simple cognitive phenomena that can be treated completely independently of the people they represent in various ways. Finally, the distinction between the private and public domain has a strong property dimension, which is missing from the private and public sphere dichotomy: the words in a Philip Roth novel are not in the public domain, but they are in the public sphere.

Just like for Habermas and many other commentators, I am including both physical and virtual public spaces in the public sphere, as they both involve general visibility. To be on the street is above all to be visible, and maybe audible – if one shouts or uses a loudspeaker. This is the case even when the motivation is political: hence the slogan "to take to the streets." We don't only do things in physical spaces; print and media are sites of action too. One is in public not only on the street. One can go public in print as well: "publish" means "make public." From the lived experience of the spectator also, there is a commonality. Both big cities and modern media are often blamed for bombarding us inexorably with images and sounds.[6] As unfair as the accusation is, urban and media spectatorships share many characteristics. The public sphere is not a philosophical construct. Those who are all of a sudden the focus of a physical or virtual crowd find themselves in a very real and very distinct emotional and cognitive state. The same holds for those who are in that crowd. As lived experience, being in public – in one's person, image, or words – and attending to things in public are markedly different from life and attention in private.

Two very different criteria are often used to distinguish the private from the public. Something is private if it is hidden or withdrawn, and public if it is open or revealed. Or something is private if it pertains to an individual, and public if it pertains to a collectivity.[7] Let us call these the sensory access and collectivity criteria, respectively. There are several reasons to prefer the former over the latter when we are dealing with the public sphere. First, when we use the collectivity criterion, it is never clear if the public refers to the government or to the people, entities that are identical only under the most utopian – or rather the most dystopian – democratic conditions. Which one is then a public space: a street or Congress? Second, the private sphere is not necessarily always personal. It can be shared: a home, for instance. And what make personal data nonpublic are, above all, restrictions on sensory access rights to them. Finally, even though collective ownership may allow visibility, clearly the public sphere includes spaces that are privately owned as well: a coffeehouse or the *New York Times*. While the US government represents the American people, many of its documents, which in principle belong to the American people since they don't belong to any particular citizen, are not available for public scrutiny – at least not right away. Presidents have numerous times in history claimed executive privilege and refused to release information.[8] Much of economic action by private individuals pursuing their private interests happens in the open, in the marketplace. In fact, the publicness of economic activity is often defended normatively: Adam Smith had a horror of secrecy in economic life, for it permitted collusions by sellers against buyers, by employers against employees. He believed that private interests could harmonize only if commercial activity were open to general observation.[9] Nevertheless, organizational privacy, confidentiality of certain contracts, and copyright considerations, among myriad other things including discretion and guile, keep swaths of economic life under wraps, outside the public sphere. On the other hand, a good deal of consumption – whether seemingly altruistic, such as a lavish potlatch, or egregiously self-regarding, such as a new red Ferrari – is quite visible, if not conspicuous, and undertaken to signal one's worth, identity, or freedom from need, or to simply make others feel inferior. Social norms can, of course, set breaks on such visibility, if deemed to have overly demoralizing externalities – which are sometimes jeered as "obscene" – on spectators.

Habermas argued that the public sphere is where public opinion is created. But, in many instances, it is in private – and at times through clandestine networks – that we arrive at a consensus about the world.[10] In any case, spaces designed explicitly to create public opinion can only do so to the extent that their contents are generally visible. A public debate is not a debate that the public participates in; it is a debate carried out in front of a public. Words will often need to be heard or read by a public to be consequential; widespread public participation in their production is, however, tangential to their consequentiality. In fact, the more a communication matters, the more skewed the ratio between participation and spectatorship: the moment a debate has a chance of being consequential, a plethora of people will want to watch it. This principle holds for all public events. Revolutions are made with few people – few relative to the whole society in which they erupt. The Jacobins, Bolsheviks, and the throngs in Tahrir Square during the Arab Spring comprised only a sliver of the population in the name of which they claimed to speak. In protests attended by hundreds of thousands, most don't do anything other than watch those who give speeches, those who clash with the authorities: they watch those who really act.[11] At any rate, the modern crowds who spill out on the streets are typically outnumbered by those who view them on television or the internet. In fact, the superior number of potential spectators is often the very reason why the event is happening in the first place.[12] It is not an accident that such occurrences are called demonstrations – or *manifestations* in French: their main objective is to show, to make visible.

Hannah Arendt, who was more of a realist than Habermas, maintained that it was the agora of the Greek Antiquity, rather than the Enlightenment coffeehouses, that formed the matrix of the public sphere – which she often, but not always, referred to as the "public realm."[13] For her, the latter is an exposed area where one is seen and heard by unspecified others and submitted to their judgment.[14] All talk and action in public – however putatively civic or rational – are transformed into appearance by the gaze of the spectators. And since the public realm is the space of appearances, competition for distinction, if not for sheer fame, is at its very core. Here are her words in *The Human Condition* about the Greek ethos:

The public realm itself, the polis, was pervaded by a fiercely agonal spirit, where everybody had to constantly distinguish himself from all others, to show through unique deeds or achievements that he was the best of all.[15]

This vainglorious bent, which is incidentally also axiomatic to the Hobbesian state of nature, cannot but make public participation an elite activity – an activity that only an elite excel in, as well as an activity that will beget its own elite. Here, we have a fundamental inequality, curiously overlooked by Arendt, that is intrinsic to the public sphere. In Ancient Athens, the citizens constituted a mere minority; just as it was a minority of the citizens who spoke publicly in the agora or before the Assembly. While democracy is now more inclusive, that the majority of citizens don't participate significantly in it still seems to hold everywhere.

Further, Arendt's account of the public realm is not free of the problems that I discussed in the first chapter. Arendt works simultaneously with two models.[16] The first is a topographic one that conceptualizes the public realm as an agonal space where greatness is achieved and displayed. True enough. Still, we need to keep in mind that political competition was merely one activity among many that could be carried out in the agora: there, Athenians traded, banked, sued, gossiped, danced, prayed, begged, hung out with friends, and watched jugglers and sword swallowers – in addition to engaging in down-and-dirty political intriguing.[17] Aristotle, like countless high-minded intellectuals after him, detested that commerce and politics mingled promiscuously in the same space.[18] And, in his estimation, it was not enough that the political agora be sundered from the commercial agora; the metic noncitizens, who took on the role of merchants in Athens, had to be banned, even as spectators, from the civic arena.

For regular Greeks, however, public life was much more – and much less – than citizenship: it was the hustle and bustle, the hurly-burly of the agora, whose most direct descendants include the plaza, campo, piazza, and grande place – the open places that are the very veins of Latin urbanism.[19] It was the same with the Roman forum, which bristled with a cornucopia of public activity from whoring to worshiping to bartering to sauntering to watching spectacles. The medieval city centers were equally mixed-use spaces, good for everyday sociability as well as for sporting competitions, military exhibitions, and knightly tournaments. Contemporary town squares, along with virtual spaces like the internet, are also very heterogeneous in their functions. Not only is the public sphere, in all its historical and contemporary forms, a stage for sundry doings; it is equally what people watch. And the best thing to watch is a contest, which is *agon* in Ancient Greek. Jacob Burkhardt, who first came up with the term "agonal" to describe Greek culture in general,[20] underlined that this competitive spirit stretched well beyond politics. Greeks organized contests about anything: beauty, singing, drinking, riddle solving, even keeping awake.

Arendt's second model is an associational space – any place where free and equal citizens act in concert. We have here a cognate of the Habermasian public sphere with all its attendant problems. Further, in both of her models, Arendt papers over the insidious aspects of publicity. There was intense pressure for conformity among the Athenians, for whom the verdict of ostracism, voted in the agora by the Assembly of all citizens, was a potential fate – a fact that does not comport easily with Arendt's rosy assertion that the public world is a world of diversity. The Greeks were acutely cognizant of how the agonal organization of politics could nurture temporizing and demagoguery.[21] Part and parcel of politics, the punishment of exile could be inflicted not only on those who were so powerful that they could become tyrants, but equally on the ones who had the nerve to struggle from the majority opinion. A famous denizen of Athens, Aristophanes, was much less impressed with its civic pretensions than Arendt. He satirized in *The Clouds* its youth, "wittering on in the agora about some thorny obscurity."[22]

On the other hand, the Greeks – at least many of them – were also appreciative of the ludic element in public discourse. The Sophists, whose mind games were referred to as *epideixeis*, which means "exhibitions," were lionized like the heroes of athletics. They acquired much fame – not because their spectators believed all they said, but rather due to the playful nature of their delivery.[23] Modern pundits take themselves far more seriously, as did many Greek philosophers who looked down on the Sophists. But when he is as lucky as to find himself on television, no intellectual talking head is better – or worse – than the sophist in his exhibitionism and agonist pursuit of glory.

The Romans were charier still of public discourse. Yet this in no way dulled their admiration for well-crafted speeches at the podium and the bar. This admiration was nevertheless an aesthetic, and not a civic, one.[24] It is not for nothing that the Romans used the same word – actor – for designating criminal prosecutors and stage performers.[25] In the *contio*, too, where citizens could applaud or shout down state officials, what mattered were rhetorics.[26] But it was the Greeks, according to Nietzsche, who, more than anyone else, prized appearances for their own sake. Effusively he lauded them in *Gay Science*:

Oh, those Greeks! They knew how to live: for that purpose it is necessary to keep bravely to the surface, the fold and the skin; to worship appearance, to believe in forms, tones, and words, in the whole Olympus of appearance! Those Greeks were superficial – from profundity![27]

Private and Public

The private sphere, in everyday language as in scholarly discourse, refers to a space whose contents are protected from general scrutiny. It is only meaningful in its opposition to where there is no such protection: the public sphere.[28] The private sphere can be physical: a home. It can equally be virtual: a correspondence, a conversation.[29] Sensory barriers such as walls, clothes, doors, email passwords, and envelopes all protect from exposure. But the private sphere tends to be protected normatively too – by laws or social norms upholding the barriers. Especially when barriers and laws are lacking or weak, dispositions like modesty, discretion, and tact will be crucial in establishing the private-public boundary. For example, third parties are not to eavesdrop on private conversations in coffee shops; when they can hear what is being said, they should – and they usually do – pretend as if they don't.³⁰ One can look at a street through a window; it is not okay to peer into a window from a street.

Still, what is normatively private and what is factually private do not converge fully. The private sphere includes secrets that are justifiable as well as unjustifiable, legal as well as illegal. Further, what is normatively private can be made public: this is a common occurrence in scandals big and small, with or without serious consequences on the publicizer. Technology can be used to expose no matter what. Nevertheless, a lot remains out of the public sphere. Individuals, groups, and organizations struggle with all their might, legitimately or not, to keep documents, communications, bodies, and intentions from becoming visible. Moreover, only a fraction of what is in public can be attended to at any given moment. Much of it is boring anyway. And many things stay in public only briefly. Besides, the activity that reveals us the most, talking, seldom breaks out of the private sphere – in part due to the physical limitations of sound. Maybe a stranger passing by will catch bits of our conversation on the street; still, we are rarely audible to a public.

Those who have access to a private space are usually also directly involved with the content of that space; so they have an incentive to protect it from outsiders. This may or may not be honored by outsiders and authorities. Still, the general principle is that access and involvement go together in the private sphere. Access can be held singly or jointly. An individual can have a private world that no one knows about. But it bears stressing: privacy is not always strictly individual. Indeed, a great deal of personal or even secret information is shared with at least one other person. Even though our sharers can betray us, such sharing is private as long as we have significant control over what and with whom we share, and as long as others are to observe confidentiality – and actually do so. Our Social Security number, however assigned to us by the government, is mostly in the private sphere: while we are not the only ones who know it, we exercise considerable liberty in choosing our sharers. And even when these are strangers like bureaucrats or sales personnel, they are not supposed to transmit the information to others. If we are betrayed, the betrayal is typically private, not public: for the most part, our betrayer simply shares our secret with someone else, rather than hollering it on the street or putting it up on the internet.

Groups, and even organizations, can have some privacy too. Members of small groups – especially but not only families – are intimately connected; they need and desire confidentiality for their communications and dealings. Dyadic conversations between intimates obviously take place in private; so do interactions in a family, even if such interactions involve more than two people. There is such strong intimacy and a real sense of common fate that confidentiality is taken for granted. Outsiders typically uphold the privacy rights of families to a large extent. This, naturally, does not mean there are no secrets that a member may want to keep from others. But many personal secrets are at once family secrets. And simply by being in a family, one automatically takes on the obligation to keep a great deal of what happens in it safely from public view.

The protections that other, larger social groups – say, a religious group – have from visibility are, of course, much weaker. This is because the desire and capability to protect – as well as the normative justifications for protection – are all weaker. Still, many activities remain largely invisible to the outside, and leaders may even be able to bar outsiders from interfering in their affairs or commenting on them. Social groups operate partly in private and partly in public. So do organizations. Board meetings are often held in camera, sometimes with punishments for leaks. Companies possess all kinds of data that they do not (have to) share with the public. On the other hand, the privacy that organizations demand does not and cannot cover everything within their walls. The lived experience inside these entities can also have a private side, especially in the case of institutions that limit visibility. If you die on the street, you die in public. If you die in a hospital room, you probably die in private – all alone or in the presence of a select few. There was a time when people were punished in the open; now, they are sent to prison, and what happens in a prison is largely invisible to outsiders – naturally not because the inmates desire this. On the other hand, there is a great deal of internal visibility in physical spaces like classrooms and prison cafeterias, as well as in a virtual space like a company wiki where employees can post suggestions. The result is that employees, students, inmates, and even patients can lead private and public lives in organizations. Thus, just like social groups, organizations – such as schools, churches, armies, prisons, and companies – operate in both the private and public spheres. Even governments don't completely operate in the public sphere; many of their activities are secret or simply nonpublic. Naturally, organizations don't all enjoy the same amounts of privacy, and there will be quite a bit of variation across time and space in how transparent they are to the outside.

The public sphere proper – a street, the media, open governmental archives, a courtroom, etc. – is unprotected in a general sense from sensory access, again physically and normatively. Now, public spaces can have specific content restrictions. Anyone can go out on the street, but with clothes: streaking is illegal. Rules of evidence stipulate what can be communicated in a court of law. One cannot watch porn on public library computers. There can be sensory access restrictions too. The movie rating system in the United States differentiates legitimate publics from illegitimate ones on the basis of age. An online university directory may require institutional affiliation for access. Similarly, one may need to produce an authorization, which may itself be contingent on citizenship, to retrieve unclassified documents from the governmental archives. Restrictions can be nonnormative as well. You need to be on or close to a street to see what is happening on it. Electronic media can dispense with this condition for virtual public spaces, but only to bring about other ones: we need a connection and rudimentary computer skills to cruise the internet or check out tweets. The *Wall Street Journal* is part of the public sphere; you cannot browse it, though, without a purchase.

Such restrictions, however, don't make the spaces just mentioned nonpublic. They are unambiguously in the public sphere – for several reasons. In all these cases, restrictions are trivial compared to the protections enjoyed by individuals in their private lives and to those enjoyed by groups and organizations. They lack a strong normative element. Sensory access and involvement are divorced from one another. There is not a palpable sense of inside and outside, insiders and outsiders. Further, those who are allowed sensory access are strangers to one another, as well as to whom they are allowed sensory access – even though not all strangers are always given spectatorship rights. Those who are visible in a public space are also, for the most part, strangers to one another.

The public sphere is a world observed by strangers; the private sphere, a world lived by intimates. Spectatorship in public assumes openness; interaction in private, confidentiality. Intimates are highly specified beings; strangers an empty, default category – simply "everybody else." What about acquaintances? An acquaintance is basically an imperfect stranger. He is not anonymous; but he is still someone who can assume – and who will usually assume – with perfect legitimacy the position of an uninvolved spectator to us, to our worries and misfortunes. He may in fact be a more dangerous spectator: he knows who we are. Nevertheless, we could say that the more perfect strangers dominate a space, the more it is perfectly public. Cities are therefore more perfect than suburbs in this regard – and not only because there are very few people on the street in the latter. It is also because the few people who may see us, say while we are walking on our driveway to our car, are more likely to be our neighbors, who are typically acquaintances. By contrast, we are mostly surrounded by anonymous strangers in urban life; this is the very definition of a city.

Strangers can sometimes infiltrate into the private sphere, legitimately as well as illegitimately. Home is the quintessential private sphere, but this does not mean that strangers can never have sensory access to it. The bourgeois living room – the salon – is where the family occasionally displays itself to guests; as such, it can become, when there is a visit, relatively less protected than the bedroom. No matter; we are still in the private sphere: the family has discretion over whom to invite and under which conditions the display is going to take place. Conversations between a patient and his doctor are confidential. Even though the doctor is typically a stranger, he is a nonanonymous one with whom the patient has chosen to share deeply personal information. In view of the nature of the information, law imposes some level of confidentiality on it. And the doctor is professionally obligated to be involved in what he hears from the patient. A collectivity whose communications obtain some privacy can consist of members who are not intimates: a corporate meeting where sensitive material is being discussed or grand jury proceedings that are closed to the public.[31] But in these cases protections cover very specific things, and there is a high common purpose – pecuniary interest in the former and justice in the latter – that justifies confidentiality. And, usually but not always, the higher the protections against the outside, the closer the ties among the insiders.

There are situations where friends and even intimates can constitute a quasi-public. Consider a personal page on Facebook. Is it in the private or public sphere? The answer, in part, rests on our privacy options, which can be so restrictive that one's page is visible only to a few number of very close friends, or so expansive that any stranger with internet capability can have access to it. In most cases, our friends on Facebook are merely our acquaintances. And our personal page is hardly perfectly private. But that is less because we are not that close to our friends in this social medium and more because of the standard communication style on it. A personal status update on Facebook tends to be addressed to all one's friends – that is, to nobody. This alone is enough to transform the recipients – some of whom may even be intimate with the author of the update – into a kind of public, into a collection of spectators who realize one another as such. The recipients become spectators simply because they are to solely read – indeed to observe – a message that does not call, in real terms, for an answer, for any personal involvement; further, each knows that he is only one spectator among many. The page is protected to some degree, but those who access it are for the most part spectating strangers, so they have little concern, much less duty, to keep its contents confidential.

The fact that something is visible – that is, viewable by strangers – makes spectators of us. And a spectator is someone who is not involved – or at least someone who has the right and ability to be not involved – in what he sees. Such is also the condition of all judgment, which "presupposes a definitely 'unnatural' and deliberate withdrawal from involvement."[32] Noninvolvement does not mean an absence of emotions: the spectator may be deeply moved or scared by what he sees – and what can move or scare us will be more salient in the public sphere. But even when the spectator reacts with his words to what he sees, as when he expresses indignation to a wrongdoing, he acts as an outsider, from a distance, facing an object. He knows that what he is seeing is or can be seen by others. And the more a spectator knows that his focus is equally the focus of others, the more the focus will be objectified – and further distanced. Bad as this may sound, objectification is the condition – albeit not the sufficient condition – of objectivity, which is therefore, for better or worse, an impossibility in the private sphere.

Even Adam Smith's impartial spectator in *The Theory of Moral Sentiments* who reaches out in public to someone in distress does this as a distant bystander: his sympathy is momentary and does not stem from or create a long-lasting tie.[33] He sets a number of conditions that would be inconceivable, even cruel, in the private sphere. He will only sympathize with grief if the sufferer exercises considerable restraint. It is indecent to strongly express passions that originate from a bodily experience, such as hunger, sexual desire, and physical pain; these being too private, the spectator cannot be expected to summon up sympathy for them. Not all adversities are fit to be displayed in public:

> It is often more mortifying to appear in public under small disasters, than under great misfortunes. The first excite no sympathy; but the second, though they may excite none that approaches to the anguish of the sufferer, call forth, however, a very lively compassion. Before a gay assembly, a gentleman would be more mortified to appear covered with filth and rags than with blood and wounds. This last situation would interest their pity; the other would provoke their laughter. The judge who orders a criminal to be set in the pillory dishonours him more than if he had condemned him to the scaffold.[34]

Many well-meaning intellectuals and commentators are enamored of public dialogue. There is no such thing. A dialogue is inherently a private phenomenon. It entails reciprocity and involvement: words in a dialogue are addressed to a specific person, produced either as a response or with the anticipation of one. Both parties take turns in speaking and listening. By contrast, spectatorship, that is, sheer looking – and sometimes listening – is all that most of us do, most of the time, in the public sphere. Those we look at usually don't look back at us, and those who speak in public are usually not answered by those whom they address. This would not do in the private sphere: in our dealings with intimates, symmetry is imperative and voice accompanies sight. Keeping silent, adopting a position of spectatorship is cold – if not downright hostile. The other is never an audience in a dialogue; he is an interlocutor. We cannot even be really objective in a dialogue, for that would imply treating our interlocutor as a distant object. Only a distant object can be judged objectively – and objective judgment always requires an impersonal view from nowhere.

The reciprocity and involvement inherent in a dialogue assume and indeed require confidentiality. Any conversation between two people will transmute into a spectacle should, for whatever reasons, third parties visibly turn their attention to it – on television or on the street. And spectacle is, as Guy Debord justly, though with needless despair, defined, "the opposite of dialogue."[35] Dialogue is antipodal to rhetoric as well. Plato, in *Gorgias*, argued that the demagogue persuades the multitude using rhetoric, while dialogue is solely appropriate for philosophical truth.[36] The distinction is apt, but may have less to do with content. Even philosophical debates that get public attention will fall back heavily on the rhetorical. A dialogue is not a debate; nor is it oriented to discovering any objective truths. The term is only truly suitable for a dyadic interaction with no spectators, and the activity is often its own reason. The moment that spectators materialize, words will now be uttered to move them, as well as one's interlocutor. An event in the public sphere is never a dialogue; it is the publication of a book, a revelation about a famous person, a street fight, a riot, the passing of an important bill, a high-profile trial. It is usually a spectacle – or something that becomes a spectacle the moment it is made public.

The private sphere operates on the assumption and the reality of intersubjectivity. Geertz identified the public with the intersubjective.[37] The contrary is true: the public is always a third party, and we can truly treat the other as a subject and expected to be treated in the same fashion only if our interaction is protected from the objectifying gaze of third parties. The moment a private conversation is made public, what one says becomes a reified, alien entity – not only for the spectators but also for the speakers, as it will be now impossible for the latter not to adopt the perspective of the former. By contrast, strictly speaking, there are no third parties in the private sphere.

An audience will then denature a dialogue. But what about three conversing friends? To be sure, to the extent that the members of a triad talk among themselves in confidence, and to the extent that there are strong ties among them, their conversation may have a private quality. But the normative protection that their conversation will enjoy is still rather limited, compared to talk within a family. Further, we reveal ourselves more freely in a dyad, with less of a risk of objectification and awkwardness. A triad is always on the verge of producing a public of two watching the third or a public of one watching a dyad. It always runs the risk of producing third parties. But this is much less likely *en famille*, where the very notion of spectatorship is anathema.[38]

Wittgenstein thought – and Geertz said the same for culture in general – that all language is public, that there could be no private language.[39] He wrote that the experiential concepts making up a language require outward criteria. Yet this can only apply to *langue* in the Saussurian sense of the term: language as an abstract system of rules independent of use. And even then, we have a half-truth: children don't quite learn a language by public exposure to its rules. As for language as *parole*, as actual utterances, especially in a dialogue, the criteria that Wittgenstein wrote about cannot but be partially internal to the speaking context, which is typically an interpersonal, private situation.[40]

It is obvious that domination, even extreme domination such as the master-servant relationship, can occur in private. And domination is naturally shot through with objectification. Note, however, that the practice is, to a significant degree, publicly created and sustained: I (can) objectify my slave only to the extent that he is an instance of the legal category of slave, only to the extent that he is already objectified openly by the state. And the more the relationship between the master and the slave is private, protected from general observation, the more something that is at odds with the legal relationship of property, some sort of intersubjectivity, maybe even some humanity, might creep into it – but naturally without replacing the brutal inequality involved. This, in part, explains why house slaves tend to be treated less terribly than field slaves. It is only in private that intersubjectivity is possible, but that does not mean abuse and exploitation are peculiar to the public sphere. In fact, precisely because they are inflected by a distorted intersubjectivity, the abuses and the exploitations of the private sphere can often be more insidious. But when one publicizes them to liberate oneself from their hold, to denounce them to the whole world, and to seek the universal standards of justice that prevail there, one is acting more as a member of a category than as an individual.

Objectification is ordinarily considered as treating others as means rather than ends – which can certainly happen both in private and in public, explicitly or implicitly, legitimately or illegitimately. Yet objectification is equally the process through which the other becomes a distant spectacle we don't, we can't interact with. This kind is not only specific to the public sphere; it is one of its structural elements: exposed to the real, imagined, or potential sight of a multitude one cannot but feel objectified. This is not always bad for the one being objectified: objectification as such can glorify as well as degrade. And it is, in significant measure, unintentional.

Still, there is a heartlessness about objectification, so people typically reveal intimate parts of their lives only to persons in contexts where some reciprocity, some concern is strongly anticipated.[41] Of course, there are exceptions – for example, the proverbial stranger sitting next to us on the plane, the captive audience of the interminable story of our horrid divorce. We engage in such disclosures, however, usually because we know we will not see the person again. And this sort of thing is a fairly rare occurrence; people are, on the whole, discrete in these situations – despite our confessional culture and the facile exhibitionism through technologies like Facebook. One-sided disclosure, where one person speaks while the other listens, resembles publicity: mutually recognized collective attention on a focus. So it is not surprising that the few who are too habituated to the glories of publicity can behave the same in the private sphere as well: they often deny their interlocutors intersubjectivity and treat them as if they were generic spectators to whom they routinely display themselves. Such an attitude is not particular to the superstars of Hollywood. Here is Edmund White on Susan Sontag:

Years later, after I'd broken with Susan, Marina Warner told me that during a visit to New York she'd met Susan and that I was wrong about her, she was a delight, no one could be warmer or kinder. I was quick to agree with Marina but I astonished her when I said, "But I'll tell you exactly how you spent your time with her. She invited you to a good Chinese restaurant and ordered for you and paid for it. Then she accompanied you to several bookshops and expressed her scandalised amazement that you'd never read Trelawney's Adventures of a Younger Son or Aksakov's Family Chronicle. She bought those books for you and gave them to you in a nice little ceremonious moment. During the unrushed afternoon she talked to you about her struggle with cancer and her love affairs – five women and four men." Marina's jaw dropped and I said, "It's perfectly sincere, but that's the day with Susan. Always the same."[42]

The contents of the private sphere can be secrets. They can be "unknown unknowns," as opposed to "known unknowns," following Donald Rumsfeld's serviceable epistemological differentiation. Matters and objects personal are more apt to be kept in the private sphere. But a great deal of what needs to be protected from the public gaze is common to us all; and we may hide these, to the extent that they reveal our vulnerabilities, even – at times particularly – from our intimates. As a husband writes about the secrets of his wife in Milan Kundera's novel *Identity*,

> Anyhow, he asked himself, what is an intimate secret? Is that where we hide what's most mysterious, most singular, most original about a human being? Are her intimate secrets what make Chantal the unique being he loves? No. What people keep secret is the most common, the most ordinary, the most prevalent thing, the same thing everybody has: the body and its needs, it maladies, its manias – constipation, for instance, or menstruation. We ashamedly conceal these intimate matters not because they are so personal but because, on the contrary, they are so lamentably impersonal.[43]

All biological activities can engender shame in public – especially when they are the focus of a multitude. Even eating. In a famous scene from Luis Buñuel's surrealist film *The Discrete Charm of the Bourgeoisie*, the invitees to a reception sit on toilet seats around a dinner table and retire occasionally to a secret room to eat. But the association between eating and shame may not be so outlandish. Geertz mentioned in *Interpretation of Cultures* that the Balinese, a people who are apparently bashful and subdued to an unusual degree unless they are engaged in violent cock fighting, are embarrassed to eat in public.[44] Even in contemporary America, a surefire way to make a stranger uncomfortable in public is to stare at him while he eats. A core component of the civilizing process was the adoption of table manners: once the higher classes started to use utensils, the common people who continued to eat with their hands came to be regarded as barbaric.

At the heart of the private sphere is sexuality. And the more sexual things are, the harder it is to display them in public. But this is also obviously true: what is deemed sexual can show cultural variations. In middle and late imperial China, there was a taboo against showing the bound feet of upper class women in paintings. Even paintings that were otherwise erotic could not reveal this highly private limb.[45]

Contemporary Americans are fairly comfortable with many representational forms of sexuality, but actual physical intercourse still takes place in private, even in the most emancipated communities.[46] As Randall Collins points out, there is certain disruptiveness to the visual contagion that sexual arousal is likely to set off. Sexual desire – highly irrational, totalistic, sometimes extremely consequential – can also shake up groups, hierarchies, and norms. Restricting its visibility, especially in physical public spaces, serves to stanch the potential ravages of this basic force.

On the other hand, what is kept in the private sphere due to its disruptiveness, maybe even by tacit collective consent, is, once publicized, often immediately interesting. The contradiction, if we can call it so, does not only hold, as it does obviously, for sexuality. Notably when it produces visible suffering, violence is disturbing. It is not any less attention grabbing: however horrified, we cannot look away that easily. It was with both awe and relish that Romans watched gladiator combats; squeamish as we have become about blood, street scuffles still draw crowds – provided that people are assured that they are standing back far enough. Violence, no matter how egregiously immoral, can even glorify the violent in the eyes of the public; there is an elective affinity between the spectacular and the mighty, and there is nothing more spectacular than violence. Hobbes wrote,

> The ancient heathen did not think they dishonoured, but greatly honoured, the gods when they introduced them in their poems committing rapes, thefts, and other great but unjust or unclean acts.[47]

The visibility of real sex and real violence has always been subject to some – but, naturally, wildly varying – restrictions in all cultures. Yet without representations of sex and violence, little would be left in the Old Testament, Shakespeare, and trash television. It is for good reason that Burke placed terror at the center of his aesthetics as "the ruling principle of the sublime,"[48] and nothing beats violence, actual or anticipated, in generating terror.

It is important to not equate the private sphere with the personal and the public with the collective. People sound off about social ills in the privacy of their homes; politicians decide the fates of nations behind the scenes. On the other hand, many personal things – such as the love lives of celebrities or biographical facts about politicians – are already public. The high-toned insist that only what obviously concerns the welfare of citizens should be widely visible. This is a noble position with little traction. In any case, we cannot really know if a given matter is worthy of being a public issue; all we can do is to note whether it has been publicized and whether people, for whatever reason, accord their attention to it. It is of small consequence should some people, especially those who stand to lose from all the talk and display, call the matter a frivolous one that is not worthy of public attention.

We don't leave our private worlds only for the sake of jawing about the common good or fighting for political rights. We often participate in the public sphere or attend to its contents for selfish interests – to amuse ourselves, to escape our worries, among a thousand other reasons. Most of the time action in public spaces is not collective. On the other hand, people are not always centered on themselves when they are at home with their families, where they can do everything from having sex to watching presidential debates to chatting about the causes of genocides and high gas prices. There is no necessary relationship between the publicness or privateness of a space and the kind of action that goes in it. A couple can discuss world peace in bed, but it would be absurd to talk here about a public sphere, unless they are John Lennon and Yoko Ono with a phalanx of cameras glued on their bodies – and at that moment the former Beatle and his wife are in the public sphere, regardless of what they say and regardless of whether their motivation is truly civic or just shameless showboating, the difference being an imponderable one. At any rate, a great deal of discourse in the public sphere – consider mindless American reality television or the historical linguistic classes at the venerable Collège de France in Paris, which are open to anyone – does not even pretend to be about the common good. In fact, people mostly talk about the common good with intimates and in situations where they would legitimately expect auditory privacy for their conversations. This is equally the case with spaces that are visually public such as restaurants, where our conversations take place in an interpersonal, private space, until we start shouting. It was not any different for much of the opinion-building conversations in the eighteenth-century coffeehouses championed by Habermas. In the Athenian agora too, discussion, largely happening within small groups, often involved a degree of confidentiality.[49] One is less likely to say something valuable, the more there are people who can listen in. Most diplomacy would disintegrate in the public sphere, and reference letters for which the students have not waived their access rights are worth little.

Most of our discursive activity is private; we tend to be silent or inaudible in public. In verbal spaces that get high publicity such as newspapers most of us don't appear at all. We may be visible to a certain degree on the web (say on LinkedIn), since its contents are incalculable and ever growing, but typically in a trivial way; only a minority will command any real attention online. It is easy to start a blog; yet most don't blog, and most blogs are not read. The public sphere is saturated with words; most of us consume and do not produce them.

Physical and Virtual Public Spaces

A public space is obviously a site for semiotic activity. A name, a voice, a word, an image are all signs. Yet objects can signify as well: a uniform, the profession of the wearer; marks on a body, an illness. Of course, a person on the street is always a body in his irreducible physicality, which transcends any meaning we can attribute to it. But to the extent that this body can be observed by strangers, meaning can and will be attributed to it by virtue of its coverings, shape, color, etc. A sign is, as Peirce wrote, "something which stands to somebody for something in some respect or capacity."[50] It is anything that represents something else to others. Signification is therefore representation. The gist of a representation is, nevertheless, not necessarily that invisible "something else," about which there may be uncertainty or disagreement. A representation – in art, in politics, as in everyday life – will always have an excess to what it represents. Not a simple derivative, a representation has an ontological independence, stemming in part from the fact that it is represented to anyone and everyone, that it is an appearance, which is, according to Kant, a datum of sense intuition that only exists to the extent that it appears to someone.[51] Better yet: what appears to us is an appearance only to the extent that we know that it can or does appear to others. Appearances are thus specific to the public sphere. Even when one reveals quite a bit of oneself in public, one still cannot but remain an appearance. And to the extent that they are the real or possible objects of the gaze of others, appearances gain a certain facticity. This objectification does not only apply to people proper, but to their visual or verbal representations as well.

Once on a street, we cannot help giving off signs. The semiotic activity in the public sphere is frequently intended, though. Virtual spaces like the internet are constructed with the objective that their contents are going to be displayed to multitudes. Many central urban areas, such as the Roman forum and modern public squares, are stages for the exhibition of political authority as much as they are sites for commerce, debating, and strolling. Physical public spaces involve proximity and co-presence between the spectator and the focus; the possibility of a simultaneity of reception among spectators who are visible to one another; and a mix of visual and acoustic material. By contrast, print and electronic media, constituting the virtual public sphere, entail distance both between the focus and the individual spectator and among the spectators; can produce a lag in reception; and do not necessarily combine the visual with the acoustic. All this translates into a somewhat weaker experience. As much as modern life may depend on them, there is a secondary quality to virtual public spaces. Hence our relative immunity to mayhem on screen – even when it is real – as opposed to the shock that violence that we see without mediation – even when it is simulated – creates. Hence the stark phenomenological disparity between real and representational nudity.

On the other hand, if physical public spaces are more directly experienced, their impact is more ephemeral too. Media, by contrast, can allow things, including the images and words of people, to stay in the public sphere all but indefinitely – even though, in practice, attention is limited. Virtual spaces are less egalitarian than physical ones in terms of opportunities to be seen and especially to be heard. Their public is larger, however. Typology was a significant enabling element in the rise of nationalism, Protestantism, and wide-scale markets.[52]

Levels of Visibility

To be in a public space, in one's person or representation, comprises levels of visibility. First, there is simple visibility: one is, in some capacity, available to general sight, open to the scrutiny of strangers. But this is different from being noticed, which is the second level of visibility. The highest level is publicity, the situation where one is the focus of a multitude whose members think or know they are looking at the same thing.

A public space is an "attention space;"[53] the more attention we get (voluntarily or not), the more we are actors in the public sphere. Nonentities thus sometimes transgress in public with the hope of becoming visible, with the hope of becoming somebodies. What also matters is how much of us is being revealed – which itself depends on the amount of control that we have over our appearance. Most of the time, most of us are anonymous in public. The anonymous are less likely to be noticed; and in public, what is not noticed may well not exist. As any journalist knows, it is the name – but of course not just any name – that makes the news. But the anonymous one cannot always avoid being seen as a member of a category, not as an individual, by the signs he produces – inevitably or by choice, accident, or compulsion. A name will differentiate more; public words, even more. And the more we appear different from others, the more visible we will be. The more the signs we produce interfere with the routine, the more they are different, conspicuous,[54] indeed "obtrusive,"[55] the more we are likely to be noticed. Visibility has its advantages; nevertheless, the more we are visible, the more vulnerable we may become. For example, once a female nude model is no longer anonymous – has a name – her nudity is transformed into nakedness. She loses "the protective mantle of convention"[56] as her own unclad body takes over the abstract female body. It is because the public sphere is dangerous that people try to control their visibility.

The public sphere is a world of appearances: the mere surfaces are all there is the moment one turns one's gaze into the street, to books, to the television, to the internet, to art, to politics. In public, being is appearing. Internal states count for little – even when people are not completely silent. The role of intentions in liability correlates inversely with the distance between someone and those before he appears.[57] The dependence on appearances is, in part, due to lack of information. Further, the opinion of others, if and once coalesced into a consensus, will fast become obdurate. So we discipline our appearances; action or speech in public, on the whole, tends to call for formality and etiquette,[58] along with a continuous effort not to be misunderstood – unless one wants to engage in a deliberate provocation, at one's own peril. In public, one is responsible for the way one appears; the more publicity there is, the more this is the case.

The private world is different. We interact repeatedly with intimates: we usually don't have to – and in any case we are not supposed to – rely on their appearances in our interactions with them. The other is seen and has to be treated as a subject with a unique essence – not as an object that can only offer us its surface. In any case, one can't just appear in the private world. One is never just an instance of a category or a member of a group; one always has a name – and more. We are expected to reveal and be responsible for a face that is exclusive for those with whom we interact, a face that will be hidden from others.

Some sociologists, following Erving Goffman, argue that all interaction is performance, that others are but an audience. Yet this convinces only in the public sphere or in formal situations where we are to be, as a matter of fact, reduced to our social roles and where behavior explicitly follows a script – say, between a doctor and a patient. Regarding the interactions between intimates in the private sphere, however, Goffman's dramaturgical vision does not hold at all: the other is nonfungible, authenticity is required, and reciprocal participation is a central principle. Obviously, we behave differently with different people in the private sphere. But this does not turn our behavior into performance – at least, normatively speaking. We may not reveal all to our interlocutor, we may even deceive him; he does not remain any less a subject who cannot be legitimately addressed or treated as an audience. Performance is the norm in public, a transgression in private.

That the public sphere consists of appearances means that what emerges there will be subject not only to moral but also to aesthetic judgment. It is the more beautiful that dominates on the street, on the television, in the art gallery, and in the courts. It is not a coincidence that performance – any action or speech in public that gets attention – is primarily an aesthetic category.[59] Appearances are not merely important to the aesthetic sensibility; they constitute its very nature, its very purpose. And it is because no appearance – overtly artistic or not – can avoid an aesthetic verdict that whatever is displayed in the public sphere runs the risk of vulgarity. Aesthetics will reign supreme in professions that require publicity. Looks obviously matter very much in the entertainment world, as in contemporary politics with its heavy reliance on mass media. Academia is no less superficial: professors who are better looking are rewarded with dramatically higher scores in their course evaluations.[60] Yet we should bear in mind that the beautiful does not exhaust the domain of aesthetics, and thus the privileged contents of the public sphere. Alexander Baumgarten wrote in *Reflections on Poetry* that any entity generating a strong sensual experience is already a part of aesthetics, a discipline that he founded.[61] Following the same logic, the beautiful is interesting for the public, but it is not the only interesting thing.

People who appear in the public sphere are largely reducible to their most outstanding appearance. They instantiate types for the spectators – the synecdochic propensity being the stronger, the more distance there is between those who appear and those who watch. In the private sphere, at home or in a personal letter, per contra, we delve – and are expected to delve – deeply into each other's souls. We relate to intimates in singular terms: they are not interchangeable; it is cognitively and morally hard to think of, or relate to, them as tokens.[62] By contrast, publicness encourages fungibility. The tendency to generalize using public cues is, in part, a rational reaction to imperfect information. It is also a type of mental shortcut based on what is available to observation. The practice is common in police surveillance.[63] Yet profiling, however lamentable, is not any less rampant in the interactions among strangers and in their assessments of one another. It is indeed structural to any appearance in public. According to Jack Katz, frustrated drivers caught in Los Angeles traffic cannot but surrender to a visceral compulsion to engage in ethnic stereotypes – and this naturally includes cursing.[64] Similarly, individuals who find themselves entangled in events like scandals are seen as – but they themselves also often act as – instances of their groups. The corrupt politician will then represent the corrupt political class. And the more a transgression is publicized, the more it will contaminate those associated with the alleged offenders. If the transgression is a salient one, the contamination will be wide-ranging and potent. So will the impulse to parry it: Hollywood studios once blacklisted screenwriters denounced for being communist; high-tech companies now fire employees who tweeted sexist remarks.

The same logic, which we can call synecdochic because it makes the part stand for the whole, also explains how individual victims can become symbols of causes as their stories are made public. Similarly, we are often impelled to conceive of and interpret characters in novels or movies as representatives of collectivities. The main reason is the public nature of literature and film; the impulse just described is much less strong when we exchange gossip. Admittedly, this attitude is apt to create bad art and bad criticism. In any case, the synecdochic logic is never realized in full; one always has some autonomy from what one is supposed to represent, especially if the representation and its interpretations are complex.

Public discourse – spoken or written words that can be heard or read in public – yields a high level of visibility. It creates more of a focus for the audience; as such, it is more of an act. Another important point is that without words, images – and a fortiori objects – are semantically ambiguous. Meaning conveyed by visual arts is inchoate, indeterminate: a painting will typically need words (a title, a gloss by the painter or a critic, a moral condemnation by detractors, etc.) for its sense to be fixed. This principle does not only apply to abstraction but even to "realist" arts. A good example is a photograph by Andrew Serrano, which is that of a crucifix immersed in a hazy, glowing, translucent liquid. The image is aesthetically pleasing; its meaning, at first sight, nebulous. It is only after one reads its title – *Piss Christ* – that the artwork starts to signify something more specific.[65] Similarly, images of combat on television, however bloody they may be, don't automatically ignite a strong moral sentiment. Only commentary will make them tolerable or intolerable by stabilizing their meaning.[66] World War II reporting, while at times very graphic, did not turn Americans against the military effort. For an image of war to make us feel guilty, we must already feel guilty about war or we must be made guilty about it by words. The semantic ambiguity of an image paradoxically stems from its proximate, parasitical relationship to reality; meaning, by contrast, is always an organization, indeed a reduction, a repression of the real. Images – just as the physical reality that they represent – can overpower us.[67] Even then, however, their effect does not surpass what T. S. Eliot referred to as a "general mess of imprecision of feeling."⁶⁸ Hence the irreplaceability of words:

> Today, at the level of mass communications, it appears that the linguistic message is indeed present in every image: as title, caption, accompanying press article, film dialogue, comic strip balloon.⁶⁹

This observation of Roland Barthes, made in the 1960s, is as valid as ever. Much of media is commentary. Significant public events come with words. Nevertheless, the public sphere is essentially a visual phenomenon – for several reasons.

First, most public sensory content is only visual. There are many public spaces, such as print, that admit only of visual access; the only one with exclusively auditory content is the radio. Otherwise, one rarely just hears a person in public; one also sees him. And we are more visible than audible in physical public spaces: we are audible only when we speak, whereas we are visible when we just are. Visual appearance is constant; voice, sporadic. Television is auditory as well as visual; yet we watch, and not listen to, television. Further, we rarely speak publicly in the public sphere – a tiny minority does that, and even this tiny minority does most of its speaking in private. Our words are usually not loud enough to be heard by many, unless we are shouting or using sound technology; while conversing with a friend in a park we are visually, but not verbally, in the public sphere. As Georg Simmel remarked, the city, the quintessential public sphere, is characterized by the preponderance of visual over auditory stimuli.⁷⁰ The urban dweller, forced – on the street, in the subway, etc. – to be proximate to strangers that he will not interact with, needs his eyes far more than his ears. Modernity has then only accentuated the visual experience of the public sphere.⁷¹

Second, when one's voice is heard widely in a public space – as in the agora or on television – it is usually accompanied by the physical appearance of the speaker. In fact, a voice in public cannot but clinch attention to the person, to the body uttering it, even when the utterer is making a sober, impersonal statement. When one is heard, one is never just heard; one is equally noticed. Children are to be seen and not heard only because the child who is heard will now have to be noticed – and no longer cursorily surveilled. There can be no disembodied voice in the public sphere: voice is always foremost an invisible synecdoche, an index of the physical being that is its source. It has less autonomy than a text from what it represents. In cases where there is no discernible body from which the voice is emanating, it is this very absence that the discourse will have to represent in a negative fashion. The lower the status of the speaker, the less his speech will enjoy autonomy from his physical appearance. This is why, as Marc Breviglieri shows, the words of a homeless person addressed to pedestrians simply make them focus – only briefly of course – exclusively on his miserable physical appearance.[72]

Third, even when words are spoken in public, our relationship to them strongly resembles, even approximates sight. Public utterances, unlike private utterances, are not part of a dialogue. An utterance that is addressed to everyone is addressed to no one. It is to be heard and not responded to; few may respond, most won't. For the hearer in this asymmetrical relationship to the speaker, such words partake of the distance and objectivity of an image – the more numerous the audience of the utterance, the bigger the distance and objectivity.

Fourth, most public words are written words, they are texts; as such, they are "part of the visual world."[73] Not heard, they are seen – which endows them with a static quality, the very opposite of the dynamism of spoken words, of utterances.[74] An utterance is an integral part of an ongoing conversation, an organic part of its ephemeral interactional context. Indissociable from its source, it is always directed at a specific being. Not evanescent and invisible like an utterance, a text, on the contrary, is almost as concrete and fixed as an image. Severed from its source, yet equally distant to its addressee (if it has a specific addressee, which is seldom the case), a text enjoys a significant autonomy from its physical and temporal context, an autonomy that will be further magnified to the degree that it is made public to large audiences. A text is language objectified, as is any utterance that is later written down. The distance, fixity, and concreteness of the written word enable – indeed compel – us to be more objective, less personally concerned with it. Print also allows for anonymity on the part of the addresser – which is harder to achieve through the spoken word. For instance, reviews and articles published in much of nineteenth-century British periodicals and newspapers were anonymous. One proponent of the practice wrote approvingly that the writer in such a situation is "merged in the court which he represents, and he speaks out not in his own name, but ex cathedra."[75]

Things appear to us visually without this already constituting some sort of contact. The spoken word, per contra, is itself intercourse the moment it is spoken: it "intrudes upon a passive subject," as Hans Jonas put it.[76] Shutting one's ears is harder and less effective than looking away. There is an immediacy to sound that things or their visual representations are bereft of. This is so even when sounds are not words. Watching a horror movie with the sound off, without the predictably dissonant soundtrack, drains most of the scare element; it is the lesser film directors who rely on music for emotional effect. When something visually appears to us, we can very well do nothing; when something is said to us, we need to answer. In the former, objectivity is possible, indeed expected, for what we see remains stolidly an object; in the latter, objectivity is neither easy nor acceptable: the one who talks to us is always a subject. We can therefore say that, following Martin Buber's terminology, the visual, dealing with objects as well as objectifying all others including people, creates an I-It situation; whereas when we are speaking, interacting with another subject, we cannot but be in an I-Thou relationship.[77] Helen Keller grasped the distinction pithily, albeit negatively: "Blindness separates us from things, but deafness separates us from people."[78] At the same time, the strong ties created by spoken words require constant reaffirmation. Objects, hence texts, on the other hand, can produce weaker, albeit longer-lasting, ties. Texts are nevertheless not integral to the private sphere: face-to-face groups can do without writing.[79]

Many thinkers, from Aristotle to Rousseau to Saussure, have comprehended the written word as a poor copy of the spoken word, itself simply an imperfect reflection of richer mental states. A text is then a second-order linguistic act, the derivative of a derivative in this logocentric tradition[80] which disregards the creativity of representation. This is not, however, because texts, as Jacques Derrida and his deconstructionist disciples have insisted, unceasingly multiply meaning through an endless play of shifting signifiers. Some texts are indeed polysemic, open to multiple interpretations, all the more if the readers are so inclined; others are very straightforward. But all text, regardless of its semantic depth, is objectified language, especially when widely publicized; and objectification through writing always generates a surplus. As long as we are talking in private, what we are saying can be modified, improved, taken back. What we mean is securely anchored in an interactional context, over which we have significant control. When textualized, however, words are exonerated of their subordination to us; they now determine us more than we can determine them, in the eyes of a real or possible public as well as in our own. As they are objectified, they become alien. This is why Socrates never wrote – even though he could not escape Plato's posthumous betrayal. And objectification has fateful effects in large contexts too. For instance, the ideological positions of the conflicting parties were notably hardened in the Protestant Reformation, in comparison with earlier intra-religious conflicts, because fixity created by print rendered public discourse irrevocable.[81]

3

Publicity

Not all public spaces are created alike. The more a public space is apt to receive general attention, the more central it is. An urban street is more central than a suburban one, more of a public sphere. Further, central public spaces are where publicity – the highest level of visibility – is more likely and more strongly to happen.

By publicity, I mean attention on a focus by a public: spectators, each of whom thinking or knowing that there are others watching the same thing.[1] Consider a crowd watching an accident on the street or readers who read about a controversy in the newspaper. Making something public and publicity are not quite the same. Making something public is simply making it available for general scrutiny; publicity entails an audience. In the same vein, to be in public is not necessarily to be in front of an already constituted public; it is to be available to the sight of those who can turn into a public. There are things that can stay indefinitely in the public sphere; publicity entails, not always but very often, a short episode. It is possible to get quasi-constant publicity, though: consider the modern American presidency.

Publicity is what allows the public sphere to achieve its full potential. It is not only that consequential events in public tend to obtain publicity; publicity affects the events themselves both in their production and reception. Naturally, unless we are famous, outstanding, beautiful, or simply eye-catching, or unless we do something unignorably disruptive, we will receive no or little publicity. Technically, the contents of all libraries are in the public sphere. Google Street View stores recordings of almost all American streets in perpetuity. The government archives are bursting with data; it takes a second to find almost anyone's address online in America.

The regulations and executive orders of the US government are published in the Federal Register. Yet very little of all this is effectively publicized. Likewise, the quasi-infinite content of the World Wide Web is disjointed, strewn helter-skelter, an overwhelming majority of it not attention grabbing. Moreover, most of us abide with norms that discourage looking too conspicuous to strangers in public; those who notice untoward attire or comportment are wont to exercise civil inattention.[2] Still, any public space and its contents can ipso facto be subjected to publicity. In spaces that are explicitly designed with publicity in mind – such as a town square, a popular newspaper, or Congress – things appear as a matter of course to an already constituted audience. One can also organize a rally in a forest – not much of a public space in itself – and broadcast it to the entire world. Publicity is often generated in a speech act that orients the attention of spectators to a focus. But an event can equally create publicity by itself. An accident will transform pedestrians into a public, however fugacious. Publicity in some areas is in posse, difficult to attain due to coordination problems. Suburban streets are typically deserted. Yet even then, timorous of publicity – always a possibility in the public sphere – we strive to control our appearances as much as we can.

Publicity in physical spaces, such as a court of law, is direct; in virtual spaces, such as newspapers, it is mediated. The effects of publicity vary also by audience size, composition, and interest, and by duration. More important, the essence of publicity, the source of its distinctive power, is not the relationship between the individual spectator and the focus, but rather the relationship among the spectators. It is the mutual knowledge of or belief in one another's attention that transforms their relationship to the focus. The cognition at hand is usually a matter of degree, directly affecting the strength of publicity. The reader of a newspaper will not know the exact number of others who read the same newspaper, or their names, or whether they are reading the same article at the same time. What he knows about the other members of the audience may not involve certainty at all; it may simply be a belief. At a religious ritual, I may not know for a fact that everybody else is paying attention to what I am paying attention; in fact, it is highly likely that some people's minds are elsewhere. There is still publicity. It is the reality, the significant possibility, or the assumption that there are many others who are focused on what I am focusing on that creates publicity.

Whether the spectators are visible to one another or not and the distance among them matter a lot in determining how strong publicity will be. Physical and virtual spaces differ considerably in this respect, as the

French statesman Malesherbes underlined in 1775: "What the orators of Rome and Athens were in the midst of a people assembled, men of letters are in the midst of a dispersed people."[3] The less the spectator can maintain his privacy, the wider yet less intense the publicity will be. On the other hand, the less visible an author is to his readers, the more he can reveal more of himself. Montaigne was able to display, if not flaunt, his most private thoughts only because he was not physically visible to his readers; and his readers could read his risqué introspections without discomfiture only because they were not physically visible in the public sphere.[4] It is again thanks to the same principle that Rousseau could with impunity prattle about his penchant for getting spanked in his *Confessions* – not unlike how first video and then the internet normalized the consumption of visual porn. It is the atomistic organization of an audience in the private sphere, where the spectators are not visible to the focus or to one another, that allows for audacious content. The downside is that as the spectators are less visible, each will emote with or imitate others at a lower intensity. Regardless, even though we now take it for granted, the capacity to access the public sphere from a private space was one of the most momentous developments in human history, which not only extended the domain of communication but also enhanced the liberty of all.

Publicity is deeply consequential, but the public sphere can still be consequential without it. Here is an extreme example. Megan's Law in the United States places the names, pictures, addresses, and specific offenses of all sex offenders in the public sphere. And owing to the internet, this information is forever and very easily accessible by anyone with a Google search on the public sex-offender registry. Obviously, for such information to have consequences for the offenders – for juvenile offenders the consequences are lifelong – publicity is not strictly necessary. Many Americans will shun a person on such a list irrespective of whether they think others have seen his name. But the more someone thinks that it is likely that others may have seen it, the stronger the shunning should be.

Publicity and Common Knowledge

The dynamics of the public sphere that I discussed in the last chapter become all the more robust in situations of publicity. Yet publicity has particular effects too. To understand them, however, we should not confuse publicity with communication tout court – as the conventional perspective is wont to do.[5] Most communication usually takes place in the private sphere. Gossip and rumor, for example, are interpersonal and serial; such word-of-mouth processes tend to keep information within restricted circles.[6] While publicity can extend communication across social boundaries, it is not just any wide transmission or dissemination of information.

Publicity is also different from common knowledge, which is the situation where everyone knows that everyone knows that everyone knows, so on.[7] Common knowledge is typically differentiated from "pluralistic ignorance," a term that Allport coined to describe the state where everyone knows the same thing but does not know that others know the same thing.[8] That situation can create a serious problem since people often want to be in agreement with others before they act. Madison formulated the concern best in the *Federalist Papers*: "The reason of man, like man himself, is timid and cautious when left alone, and acquires firmness and confidence in proportion to the number with which it is associated."[9] Common knowledge is thus superior to pluralistic ignorance in that it makes coordination easier. It can also solve other collective action problems such as the assurance game, a situation where someone will only act if he knows that others will do the same.[10]

There are many who see a very close association between common knowledge and publicity. Michael Chwe, for example, defines publicity as "common knowledge generation."[11] Now, under very specific conditions, publicity can generate common knowledge. Yet this hardly exhausts all that publicity does; in fact, it does not capture the essence of the phenomenon at all. What is publicized is often not knowledge in the usual sense of the term. It may simply be an assumption or even a suspicion. In the case of public rituals, such as a royal procession, it may simply be the attention of others. Also, those who are exposed to the publicity of something cannot always know for sure what others know. They cannot even know for sure if everybody else has focused on what they have focused on themselves; they may simply only have a belief that some others must have lent their attention to it in some capacity.[12]

Further, common knowledge very frequently does not need any publicization at all. Open secrets, which we pretend don't exist, can be common knowledge. Or they can be quasi-common knowledge: I may not be completely sure that others know and that others know that I know, but I am almost sure. Further, many hard facts about human nature ("we all lie")[13] and life ("we will all die one day") are common knowledge. But they don't necessarily require or result from publicity. On the contrary. No politician, no public figure, actually no one at all – other than depressed people if they ever get the chance – will say in public that we all lie. Similarly, in some cultures there are strong taboos about talking about death, especially in public. In fact, we all mostly live our lives as if we did not all lie and as if we would not all die one day; these are truths that paralyze. And common knowledge without publicity may be easy to ignore – not all the time, but often. Embarrassing things in closely knit groups, especially families, are common knowledge, but they are simply ignored. People collude, tacitly, to not talk about open secrets; they show tact. This basic fact is overlooked by philosophers and economists, who typically approach common knowledge through functionalist lenses, who even argue that its raison d'être is to simply solve coordination problems.

And common knowledge – not to mention common belief – is strategically ignored in large groups too. Let us consider the famous Hans Christian Andersen fairy tale, where two swindlers pretending to be weavers promised a vain, sartorially obsessed emperor a new suit. They claimed that the cloth that they were going to use would be so exquisite that it would be invisible to any man "unfit for his office or unpardonably stupid." The emperor accepted. He wanted a new suit and took to the idea of being able to identify the unfit and the stupid in his realm. He soon dispatched his ministers to the swindlers to check on their progress; although they naturally did not see anything, as the looms were empty, they still said the cloth was exquisite indeed. When the emperor eventually paraded before his subjects in his new suit, no one dared say that he did not see any clothes. All exclaimed that the emperor's suit was incomparable, until a little child exploded finally, "But he has nothing at all." This is how Andersen ends the fairy tale:

"Good heavens! Listen to the voice of an innocent child," said the father, and one whispered to the other what the child had said. "But he has nothing on at all," cried at the last the whole people. That made a deep impression upon the emperor, for it seemed to him that they were right; but he thought to himself, "Now I must bear up to the end." And the chamberlains walked with still greater dignity as if they carried the train which did not exist.[14]

A common interpretation of the fairy tale is that, before the child's intervention, we are in a situation of pluralistic ignorance about the emperor's suit. I see that the emperor is naked but I assume that others may actually be seeing a suit, so I don't dare say what I see lest I be treated as stupid or unfit for my position. And since everybody has the same incentives I have, we all behave the same way. But it is not obvious from the story that there was no common knowledge – much less common belief – about the nakedness of the emperor: at any rate, from the perspective of a powerless subject, it matters little if he knows that others equally know that the emperor has no clothes. Whether there is pluralistic ignorance or common knowledge, he is better off keeping quiet. While common knowledge is superior to pluralistic ignorance, it may still not make a difference: each can still pretend ignorance to others, especially if the open broaching of the issue is somehow risky or would create a general contretemps. The matter is not restricted to oppressive regimes. Civilized life is inconceivable without tact. Hence the dictates against publicizing discreditable information that can nevertheless be legitimately gossiped about. It is acceptable to chatter in private about the adultery of a colleague, but not so to bring it up in a gathering, thereby making the issue a public matter[15] – even if the adulterer is absent and even if each attendee is aware of other attendees' knowledge of the transgression.

Once a child says that the emperor has no clothes, however, the situation suddenly changes. Imperial nakedness, once publicly uttered, is now impossible to ignore – or at least much harder to ignore than before. Once in the open, both visible to and attended to by a multiplicity, thereby highly objectified, this truth will now impose itself on me: not only did I hear it, but my hearing was also seen by others, who not only heard it too, but also saw everybody else hear it. True, I can still act as if there is nothing wrong; but it is not as easy. People will have different thresholds; but the more others join in, the progressively harder ignoring will be for me. To be sure, Andersen is not clear whether the child cried out the truth in a way that all could hear it. Still, judging from what the father says immediately after, it seems that it must have been audible at least to some.

A standard way that publicity is created is through a denunciation – of the "J'accuse" type. Publicity usually requires words: the presence of an elephant in the room[16] may not suffice. Yet these words are very often texts, and texts are visual material. In any case, publicity through words – spoken or written – is only powerful to the extent that it draws our attention to something physical, whose truest, most natural representation will be visual. And public speech establishes an asymmetry between the speaker and the hearers that is structurally similar to what happens in sight.

We see then that publicity – mutually recognized common focus by a collectivity – has a distinct superiority over other communicational forms. It makes it harder for us to ignore or avoid things that we already knew. Unless effectively publicized, a lot of what is already in the public sphere will not get much attention.[17] But publicity – and the truth that it imposes on us – is not always a good thing. Hence Frank Knight's ending of the Andersen fairy tale:

That evening the people awoke to the realization that they had no emperor and the wise men were anxiously discussing what to do. You can't imagine a man as emperor after he had solemnly paraded the streets as his bare self, can you? The wise men couldn't agree of course, and the next day there was war. And in a year, a prosperous, happy nation had been destroyed and a civilization reduced to barbarism. All because a child made an innocent remark about plain matter of fact. And back of that, because an emperor was fool enough to let people see the human being inside an emperor's togs – which certainly everyone knew was there. Truth in society is like strychnine in the individual body, medicinal in special conditions and minute doses; otherwise and in general, a deadly poison.[18]

Here is a real situation with similar dynamics. One of the staunchest myths of American political history is that Watergate was the ultimate triumph of truth over cover-up: the people found out that their president was crooked, and he had to go. Yet from very early on in the scandal, most Americans already seriously doubted their president's veracity. According to a poll conducted in August 1973, after the testimony of White House Counsel John Dean against Nixon in the Senate hearings, 76 percent of the public believed that the president was guilty in one way or another – either for the burglary itself or for its cover-up. This is all the more remarkable in that it seems that 76 percent actually thought that Nixon was guiltier than he really was – after all, no evidence has ever been established for his involvement in the burglary. However, only 17 percent of Americans – overwhelmingly liberal Democrats – wanted him to resign at that point.[19] Republicans were partisans in their assessment of Nixon, but, more strikingly, the Independents – and some Democrats as well – also thought that the president's ouster would be too costly for the country. Belief in Nixon's corruptness, even if this belief was to some extent common – after all these polls were made public – was not enough for people to want Nixon out. Further, these very Americans did not want the White House communications between the president and aides – which could shed light on the matter – to be made public. The same August survey found that Americans were more likely to agree than disagree with Nixon as he refused to release the White House tapes. According to 49 percent of those polled, the confidentiality between the president and his aides was an absolute one; only 33 percent of Americans did not think so. More important, 46 percent of Americans were of the opinion that forcing Nixon to release the tapes might damage the office of the presidency and the country, against

39 percent who disagreed.[20] So it seems that almost half of Americans, while thinking that Nixon was guilty, did not want him to resign; nor did they want his guilt or innocence to be publicly ascertained through the release of the tapes. Much less than half of the population opposed this position.

And poll evidence shows that the Independents and large swaths of Republicans bolted the president only after the Supreme Court forced the release of the White House transcripts, something these groups had largely not been in favor of.[21] The divulged material did not reveal any specific crimes. In any case, most people were already convinced long ago that Nixon was guilty. Yet the widespread, impossible-to-ignore publicity of the informal, unrestrained conversations between Nixon and his staff, overflowing with gangland language – punctuated in the transcripts by the ubiquitous editorial note "expletive deleted" – imposed on Americans all the details of how politics is really done in the Oval Office and prevented many from keeping subscribing to the otherwise useful myth of a quasi-sacred presidency. Tacit collusion was no longer possible. It was only after this public humiliation that irrevocably, unsalvageably contaminated his office that the majority of Independents and moderate Republicans started to regard Nixon as an undesirable. It was only then that the polls found, for the first time, a plurality of Americans supporting impeachment and removal.[22]

People tend to report that they are personally immune to the influence of media while overestimating the latter's influence on others. And if everybody overestimates everybody else's vulnerability to them, media will indeed determine some behavior by making people falsify their opinions against an imagined brainwashed majority.[23] Yet media can be powerful even if there is no overestimation. The primary – or at least a very important – effect of media is not the simple communication of new facts or ideological inculcation. Nor is it eliminating pluralistic ignorance, which can generate the overestimation problem that I just mentioned. Reading about an event in the paper, with the knowledge that others are doing the same, turns the event into a fact, into something as real, distant, and finished as an object. And, to that extent, the event is now something harder to ignore. In fact, even the assumption or reasonable speculation that others may also be reading about the event is enough. This is why politicians often treat media as indicative of public opinion, which can rarely be objectified independent of media.

Publicity may be ephemeral, requiring repetition for effectiveness. But this is not because – or primarily because – repetition makes something true. It is rather because repeated publicity strongly objectifies something that could otherwise remain just a fuzzy notion. George Stephanopoulos, Bill Clinton's chief of staff in his first term, realized this well as he was trying to deal with his boss' scandals and media image: "Stopping CNN was key. If they ran the story all day, however briefly, other news organizations could cite them to justify running their own stories."[24] Each channel or newspaper may well think that the story is not obviously worthy of being aired or published; once it is publicized strongly, repeatedly, especially by a central player like CNN, the question is no longer relevant. The story has acquired a facticity, even if it is nothing but allegations, thanks to its difficult-to-ignore visibility.

Public events[25] become transformative, in part, due to publicity. Take norms. Now, many norms are never explicitly made public. Consequently, we may not be able to articulate the norms that we nevertheless adhere to. Consider the amount of physical distance that should lie between two strangers so that neither is uncomfortable – an amount that varies from culture to culture, though the principle that physical distance should be calibrated as a function of social distance is universal.[26] Most Americans cannot specify the number of inches they want between them, but they know viscerally when someone is standing too close or too far. Or consider language: very young children follow with great ease very intricate grammatical norms that they would not be able to formulate. Still, publicity is at times so essential to normative systems that a norm that is publicized, but is not privately believed in, can be valid as well as one that we privately believe in, but is not public. The same holds for all cultural codes. Here is an example that Ann Swidler offers from everyday life:

When I was in college, an enterprising reporter for the campus newspaper wrote an article about the "three flavors" categorizing campus women – as I remember them, vanilla, chocolate, and lime – describing middle class public schoolers, arty bohemian types, and upper-class socialites. The morning the article appeared, my friends and I faced a crisis: what to wear. As we stood half-paralyzed before our mirrors, we were responding to the fact that a new code had been unleashed in our community. What one wore would now convey something new, and perhaps something one never intended.[27]

It is publicity that creates the cultural code here. And the code is only powerful – impervious to subjective disagreement – to the extent that it has been objectified through publicity. If a female student wears lime, she risks being seen as a real or wannabe upper-class socialite. But this is not because all the students have read the article or agree with the code that is proclaimed in it. Rather, because – and only because – the code is effectively asserted in a space that ordinarily gets high publicity for the community in question, a person who has read the piece, regardless of his own opinions, will be inclined to assume that all or many others have read it as well and assume also one or more of the following: (i) this is how others think, (ii) this is how others will think after the publication of the piece, (iii) this is how others will think that others think after the publication of the piece. It does not matter which of these three is assumed; the short-term result is the same. A code will thus be established only because of publicity, which will set a new equilibrium that will be hard to contest or replace by a single person – independent of whether people privately think that the code is a good one. The equilibrium will remain in place until a novel code is publicized in a similar fashion or until oblivion kicks in.

Some scholars – such as Claude Lévi-Strauss[28] and to a certain degree Pierre Bourdieu, who maintained in *Distinction* that all taste is distaste, that all social symbolism is negative[29] – closely follow Saussurian linguistics: they consider culture to be structured like language – that is, as a system of difference – and argue that the meaning of a sign is derived solely from its relationship to other signs. Others like Geertz[30] are less rigid: culture is a text, a multilayered web of symbols themselves always subject to interpretation by social actors so that they can only be comprehended through a second-order hermeneutics. And there are pragmatists who insist that the meaning of a sign is contextual and determined by use. According to Wittgenstein, an utterance can only be explained within the specific language game it functions.[31] For John Searle, it is intentionality that accounts for all meaning.[32] There is some truth to each approach; meaning is complex, overdetermined. Yet they all miss a crucial element: how general visibility, and especially publicity, can also affect signification.[33]

This can be best seen in the case of transgressions. When it is publicized, a transgression – whether real, apparent, or alleged – acquires a novel meaning and consequently elicits novel reactions. Certain acts – such as many biological and sexual ones as well as a lot of informal language talk among friends and family – become transgressive only if they are made public. And when the same transgression – for example, drinking during the Prohibition – is committed in public as opposed to in private, it molts into a defiance, hence into a considerably bigger deal for the authorities or society.[34]

Further, we treat a transgression differently, more harshly, after it has been publicized, even inadvertently, even if we already knew about it. Before publicization, we may prefer to ignore a transgression – for various reasons. First, the transgression may be one of those things that we, and maybe also those in our immediate circle, commit now and then without too much fuss, either because the norm itself is unreasonable or because enforcement is lax. Professional groups, for instance, have in practice lower standards than what they profess publicly. In any case, justifying a dubious act or actor is, on the whole, easier in private than in public. People tend to be categorical in their public moral discourse, centering impersonally on the transgression. By contrast, private moral assessment is attuned to the particularities of the context, and the transgressor takes prominence over his transgression. This style often becomes unjustifiable – and makes us look bad – once the transgression becomes public. Our words can get very nasty in the private sphere; mercy is more likely there, too. Second, it may be that the transgression is committed by a powerful person, by someone feared or depended on. This should naturally lead to underenforcement as long as the transgression remains private. Third, publicity can hurt various third parties. Elites represent groups and institutions, with the consequence that the publicity of their transgressions can affect the reputations and life chances of those associated with them. There might also be something about the transgression – as it is the case with most taboos, particularly sexual ones – so that its publicity would contaminate audiences. Finally, enforcing a norm is usually unpleasant business; many would rather not confront offenders if they can help it. There is the risk of self-contamination for the public accuser. Even legal officials take enforcement costs into account, usually euphemized as exercising discretion.

"Fiat justitia ruat coelom" is often the only defensible public position; in practice, if people fear that heavens may indeed fall in the pursuit of justice as a result of publicity, they may well, singly or collaboratively, look for a more quiet way to deal with the problem or not deal with it at all – unless, of course, the cat is already out of the bag. There is a double truth to Disraeli's aphorism, "What is crime among the multitude is only vice among the few."[35] The elite, especially natural or artificial aristocracies, are indeed usually more tolerant of moral transgressions. An open scorn for the hidebound ways of the middle class, along with a taste for villainy, has always been a part of the aristocratic ethos. More important, however, is the fact that what is tolerated in any group, lowly or not (and a lot is tolerated in all groups), will come across as intolerable once exposed to the masses.

Take Oscar Wilde, whose homosexuality was a widely bruited open secret in London during the late 1880s and early 1890s.[36] Rumors ran rife; in some circles, the writer's carnal predilections were quasi-common knowledge.[37] Homosexuality was implied in one of Wilde's short stories, "The Portrait of Mr. W. H.," and in his novella *The Picture of Dorian Gray*. His effeminate public persona was an exact specimen of the Victorian stereotype of the homosexual. Wilde paraded about town with a green carnation boutonnière (at the time the emblem of French gays), lectured young men about Socratic love in chic restaurants, caroused with prostitutes in luxurious hotels, and took up houses with paramours. His affair with Lord Alfred Douglas was a society item. Books such as Henry James's *Tragic Muse* parodied him and his entourage with innuendos, albeit without naming names. The police were cognizant as well about Wilde's goings-on.[38]

People would not, however, make the scuttlebutt public. Spoofs remained spoofs. No one openly questioned Wilde's sexuality. There was malevolent private talk in spades in various social milieux – yet no public denunciation or legal action. This was hardly because Victorians were tolerant of homosexuality; capital punishment for sodomy in Britain was only repealed in 1861 – to be replaced by life imprisonment. Rather, being monomaniacally prudish about sexuality in general, the Victorian higher classes and authorities thought that the publicity of homosexuality would deeply contaminate public life in general, as well as the families of the accused in particular. They were therefore averse to denouncing or prosecuting homosexuals, especially elite ones, as long as their sin remained private.[39] Further, those with the best evidence about Wilde's affairs – relatives of his lovers – were also the ones with the strongest reputational disincentives to speak out, lest their own families be besmirched by scandal. Many elites, knowing or suspecting that homosexuals were among their kin, had no interest in having illicit networks revealed in court. In addition to the desire to avert all these third-party effects, there was equally the fact that it would be a risky proposition to fight in court a fixture of the English bon ton. Tough English libel laws with a very high burden of proof made a public attack harder still: defendants had to both prove the veracity of their assertions and show that the public would be served by their publication. Consequently, the dramatist – just like many other Victorian gays – could do more or less as he pleased in London society a long time after his homosexuality became well known.

As I said earlier, there are very good reasons to not do anything about a transgression, even when it is common belief or common knowledge, so as to avoid the negative consequences of its publicity. Yet blinking at it will be difficult when a transgression is already effectively publicized in the form of a revelation or, worse yet, a vigorous denunciation; everyone will now risk looking bad in the eyes of everyone else. We will then display zeal toward the offender only to signal resolve or rectitude to one another – reactions ratcheting up through a self-feeding process. The wider and more intense the publicity, the more homogeneous the public, the more visible its members are one another, the more vigorous this propensity will be. Before the publicity of the transgression, the high status of the transgressor and anticipated third-party effects will encourage inaction by society and authorities. After the transgression is already publicized, however, these elements will yield overenforcement.

We see these dynamics clearly in the case of Oscar Wilde. Once already widely publicized, homosexuality, for Victorians, had to be punished vehemently, no matter how substandard the evidence could be. And, alas, Wilde's sexual activities came unavoidably into the open in 1895 in a libel suit he opened in response to a public attack by the Marquees of Queensberry, the father of his lover, Lord Douglas. Queensberry was an iconoclastic peer: a notorious atheist, he had abnegated his seat in the House of Lords because he would not take the religious oath of allegiance to the queen. Queensberry, a black sheep of his class, also had a habit of hounding prominent people in public, sometimes even through litigation. Given his eccentric nature and outsider position in society, he cared neither about his family's reputation nor about his own. And he was hell-bent on withering Wilde – who had not desisted from seeing his son despite Queensberry's menaces – by exposing his homosexuality. The peer began to pursue Wilde in public places – posh restaurants, theater halls, and finally the Albermarle Club, where he left a calling card with an insulting, in part illegible, and misspelled message on it: "To Oscar Wilde, ponce and sondomite." Wilde was in a quandary. The situation had changed. He was now attacked "no longer in a private letter and as [Lord Douglas's] private friend, but in public as a public man."[40] Certain that a scandal was inevitable anyway, Wilde decided to preempt his nemesis by suing him. In his favor was the fact that evidentiary standards were especially high in libel cases. Further, the Queensberry witnesses were all self-confessed prostitute accomplices with records of blackmailing.

The dramatist lost the libel trial – in part because he unwisely played in court the provocateur who placed himself beyond good and evil, even as he denied his homosexuality. He had acted similarly in the past without a problem; but now, facing open allegations, his provocations looked beyond the pale. What is worse, all sorts of stories – some apocryphal, others not – started to swirl about London regarding other homosexuals linked to Wilde. While the rumors were not new, they were aired in the press. Not only that, but the name of the prime minister, Lord Rosebery, was enunciated in court in letters written by Queensberry, who nurtured a lifelong rancor against him. The peer believed that Rosebery had seduced his other son, who had then committed suicide, when threatened with exposure over their affair.[41] One of the letters could be read to imply that Wilde was like the prime minister: in it, Queensberry called him a "damned cur and coward of the Rosebery type."[42] Some were saying, naturally in private, that the prime minister was pressuring the prosecution to drop charges against Wilde, who was his friend. Others falsely suggested that the dramatist was blackmailing the government.

Victorians had underenforced the homosexuality laws, in part, to prevent the exposure of the dirty linen of their elites. Such an exposure is, of course, exactly what happened with the trials of Oscar Wilde, and once it happened, authorities had to manage the ensuing contamination; they felt, after Rosebery's name was uttered in court, particularly pressed to avoid the appearance that they were trying to cover up.[43] As a result, the unfortunate dramatist was, after the libel trial, prosecuted and condemned to the fullest extent of the law, although the evidence against him was circumstantial, uncorroborated, and tainted. Legal officials demonstrated unusual fervor in securing a conviction – with a two-year prison-with-hard-labor sentence for gross indecency – in a second trial, when the first one terminated with a hung jury. Wilde used to be the beloved of the upper crust. After his already well-known homosexuality became unavoidably public during his trials, he morphed into an outcast as those who were long privy to what he was up to were now compelled to outdo one another in shunning, when not vilifying, him – so as to distance themselves from him and to appear righteous to one another.[44]

Publicity will therefore exacerbate attitudes toward a transgression. But if a transgression is publicized widely and repeatedly, without vigorous but ideally with some mild condemnation or punishment, so that the transgressor can come across as courageous and even receive kudos, then the outcome can be quite the opposite. If there are no serious sanctions, the threshold for making others imitate the transgressor will be lowered. The public can eventually get inured, if not jaded, and the transgression normalized.

Here is an example – maybe the very example – from the artistic world. The Impressionists were at first met with derision and disdain. Their paintings' apparent sketchiness, deliberately fashioned by unrestrained and ostensible brushwork to foster an impression of vibrancy, was read as carelessness and clumsiness. The shallowness of their composition could only be incontrovertible evidence of ineptitude. Yet the reaction to the Impressionists was hardly limited to their technique. To the critics, the natural feminine figures that they kept painting, especially the nudes, looked brazenly hideous, bespeaking an obsession with vulgarity. Their subject matter – everyday life on the boulevards as well as in the boudoir – and their amoral gaze made them common pornographers peddling their perversions as art. But consider the speed with which these painters ultimately revolutionized painting through a string of provocative artistic transgressions.[45] Manet had stirred big scandals with his *Déjeuner sur l'herbe* and *Olympia*, in 1863 and 1865, respectively, when the paintings were displayed in the Salon, the annual exhibition of work approved by the Royal Academy. Yet only a decade later, both the Impressionists and their critics were already grumbling that the painters had imitators everywhere, including in the Salon. Scandalous art, as any other scandalous deed, loses its bite with time and repetition, paving the way to still more daring material, which then undergoes a similar process.

Collective Effects

Publicity can create groups by making isolated individuals focus on the same thing. Reading the morning paper makes citizens out of individuals not only because it is, in the celebrated formulation given by Hegel, "the realist's morning prayer," but equally because each individual imagines that others are doing it as well. Hence the historical relationship between the printing revolution and nationalism.[46] Technology does not have a straightforward relationship with publicity, though. Obviously, with cable television, internet, and social media, it is now easier to publicize no matter what. Technology should generate ever larger publics. On the other hand, the general public has been fragmented as spectators have acquired more and more a say in what they want to be exposed to. Once in America everybody read *LIFE* magazine and watched Walter Cronkite. Nowadays fewer people read or watch the same thing at the same time. Two of the most bewailed consequences of the digital revolution are that we only get information from sources we agree with[47] and that the audience for news has itself shrunk – since many would rather watch entertainment.[48] But another consequence may be a weakening of large-scale solidarities.

Publicity can equally strengthen solidarity in existing groups. Realizing that others are experiencing simultaneously the same emotion intensifies our own experience. The same joke sounds funnier to us when we are in a crowd; the same person elicits deeper wrath in a lynching, be it a real one on the street or a digital one on the internet. Consider also the patriotic effects of national media events.[49] Publicity is a core ingredient of rituals, secular or not. Durkheim asserted in *The Elementary Forms of Religious Life* that sacred symbols, being the materialization of collective ideals, draw the members of a society together. The causality may be converse, though. It is, in part, the mutually recognized attention from individual spectators that sacralizes the focus in religious contexts.

Publicity can produce similarity within a group as well. When an opinion is somehow publicized as public opinion, when it is made the mutually recognized focus of a collectivity, diverging private views will be less likely to be openly voiced. One will mimic others who are deemed representative of public opinion. Those who lack information about their peers, who may or may not privately subscribe to the official position, will be all the more likely to do this, especially if they think there are costs to dissenting from the majority position.[50] If the public is dispersed, if the ties within it are weak, then the upshot could be high similarity.[51] These mechanisms, already operative in mediated publicity, will be all the more marked in face-to-face contexts. The mimetic tendencies will be stronger the more similar are the spectators, the less social distance there is among them, the more visible they are to one another, the more simultaneous is their exposure to the focus, and the more emotional their attitude is.

It must not be assumed, though, that publicity will always strengthen or homogenize groups. If the focus is something that the group had suppressed before – for example, something that would reveal internal tensions – publicity can undermine the group, at least in the short run. Collective action spurred by publicity is not necessarily beneficial to the group either. Take the publicity of alarming information about imminent danger that actuates a panic – a situation where publicity incentivizes individual actions whose sum makes the collectivity worse off. Publicity can equally bare, and thereby aggravate, private fears in a group, the process culminating in a self-defeating collective stance. An illustration is provided by Ivan Ermakoff, who contends that the parliamentarians of the French Third Republic endorsed the transfer of full executive, legislative, and constitutional authority to Marshal Pétain in July 1940 – whereupon a political regime essentially committed suicide – only when they arrived at the conclusion that no one would oppose it. While opinions had vacillated at the onset whether to oppose the Nazis or not, statements that publicized hitherto private fears eventually compelled the deputies of the French National Assembly to mimetically align on the surrender option.[52]

In many situations, we only do what we do because we think that the others are doing it too. But sometimes we don't know what the others are doing, yet we think we do. And ironically, such erroneous thinking may be due to the publicity of the mimicked act, which creates the impression that it is more common than it is the case. The consequences can be momentous. Catherine Turco and Ezra Zuckerman show this mechanism in an ingenious analysis of the private equity market bubble of the mid-2000s.[53] Here was a situation where there was common knowledge of the existence of a bubble: everybody knew that the emperor was naked, and everybody knew that everybody else knew, and so forth. Yet the two sociologists found that only 25 percent of the private equity firms curtailed speculation. The majority of firms danced: that is, they knowingly speculated with inflated prices with the expectation that they would be able sell at even higher prices and get out before the others could, which naturally only inflated the prices further. One danced for various reasons. First, while it would have been smarter in the long run, sitting out did not generate revenue. Second, not doing anything did not feel good. Third, those who speculated immediately collected transaction and management fees, which translated to compensation and bonuses for themselves. Fourth – and most important – the dancers incorrectly thought that everybody else was dancing. And if everybody else was dancing, the prices would surely climb still higher; there was no reason to sit out just now.

The dancers were wrong. Not everybody was dancing; some warily sat out the bubble. Yet investors who danced could only see other dancers. Why? By the mid-2000s, investment banks, wanting to serve as advisors to target companies, started to run formalized and blind public auctions in which firms bid against one another. Now, these auctions publicized the identity of the firms that participated as well as the final winning bid. Visibility was not complete, though: the firms could not see one another's bids. But even sitters participated in these blind auctions to obtain information about the market. While they naturally lost bids because they refused to pay the inflated prices, their publicized participation – along with the high final prices – made the dancers think that everybody else was dancing as well. For this, the dancers would pay dearly shortly after.

Social Status Effects

Publicity aggrandizes the focus – an individual or his representation – by establishing equivalence with a spectating multitude. The bigger one's audience, the bigger one's importance – all the more so when the attention is positive. It is, in effect, only through positive and widespread publicity that individuals will be glorified and sometimes even attain mythical, sacred heights. Hence the expression that the Greeks used to call their heroes: *andres epiphaneis*, "men who are fully manifest, who are highly conspicuous."[54] Public attention is enhancing in itself, a signal asset in life, no less weighty than economic, political, cultural, or social capital.[55] Scholars want to be cited, presidents are preoccupied about their legacy, athletes seek fame, marginal groups desire media representation. And recognition feeds on itself. Daniel Boorstin's quip that a celebrity is "a person well-known for his well-knownness"[56] does not exclusively apply to the likes of the Kardashians. Any celebrity, including Einstein and Mozart, will equally be known for being known, as many laypeople will be hard-pressed to ascertain for themselves whether the famous really deserve the attention they get. Their being known will always provide us with an adequate rationale to take note of people. Celebrity worship can have a strategic use too: it is a little cheap to say, but one often focuses on what others focus on so that one has something to talk about. There is more usually, though. Desire is mimetic,[57] and it is rare for the members of a public to mimic one another's desire without the object of desire turning talismanic along the way.

Simply being known – amidst scores of anonymous competitors – confers great advantages. Any publicity, however obtained, can be a boon – all the more if there are no objective or at least widely agreed-on ranking measures. Contemporary art in the United States is a case in point. High modernism of the 1940s and 1950s, especially to the extent that abstract expressionism was its epitome, seemed recondite to the uninitiated. Critics, such as Clement Greenberg and Harold Rosenberg whose exegeses were indispensable to artists and buyers, functioned as arbiters of quality. But the 1960s saw the rise of pop and conceptual art; both, the former with its democratic outlook and the latter with its minimalist anti-aesthetics, proved impervious to critical authority. "Who needs criticism if anything can be art," wrote the prominent critic Barbara Rose in 1964 in desperation. The situation has not changed much since then. Here is a more recent groan from Jerry Saltz of the *Village Voice*:

At no time in the last fifty years has what an art critic writes had less of an effect on the market than now. I can write that work is bad and it has little-to-no effect, and I can write it is good and the same thing will happen. Ditto if I don't write it at all.[58]

With the 1960s and 1970s, dealers, collectors, and galleries started to have an increasing say in determining what deserved public attention as works of art; and their assessments, with the decline of critical authority, were directly affected by marketing, in which they had more than a hand.[59] Being a celebrity became less a consequence and more a reason as to why one acquired the status of an important artist – especially in the 1980s. Jeffrey Koons – but consider Julian Schnabel or Ross Bleckner too – owed his meteoric ascent during the late eighties and early nineties in large part to his self-advertisements in art magazines, as well as to photographs of him having sex with his porn-star wife.

Also consider how in the contemporary era, publicity has been shaping prices. A museum exhibition, publication of the work in a catalogue raisonné, mention in books and magazines, and representation by a famous dealer all make a painting more expensive.[60] What matters equally is prior ownership by someone famous, and this has become more important recently. For instance, Rothko's "Untitled," which belonged to David and Peggy Rockefeller, sold for more than $72 million at a Sotheby auction in May 2007. A week later, another Rothko, comparable in size and date but with a much less illustrious provenance, could only fetch $29 million.[61] As the power of famous collectors rose, so did the ability of their names to raise prices. It seems that when Charles Saatchi buys the works of a new artist through a dealer, he only pays half of the gallery price; the value that the famous collector's well-publicized purchase adds to the other works of the same artist will more than make up for the discount.

A central way in which publicity has been driving up prices is through open auctions. In the sixties, auction houses did not customarily sell works by living artists represented by major galleries. But in the 1970s, collectors like the Sculls took to putting their acquisitions on auction. Now almost half (48 percent) of the art market takes place in auctions – the rest is still invisible. Auctions pique more attention than museum shows; they are more exciting. Their publicity gives people the assurance that they are paying market price and not getting swindled – as it will also, after the big purchase, reassure them that they did the right thing. Finally, there is the element of challenge, as well as the prospect of fame in participating in an auction.[62]

What grants a lot of publicity to a work of art, especially in the contemporary era, is its price. And owing to the rising popularity of auctions, prices are increasingly public and high prices generate more and more attention – which, as other criteria of worth decline, only hikes the prices further up. High prices in auctions will raise the prices of all the other works by the same artist. Maybe more important, once an artist's work starts appearing in auctions, all discussion of it centers on the price it did or did not achieve.[63] The more public pricing becomes, the more price functions as almost the only signal of quality. Philistine billionaires avid to fill huge wall spaces are no worse than curators in this regard. Fancy museums are much more predisposed to show works if they paid exorbitantly for them, as the Tremaines, renowned collectors, discovered when their donations ended up right away in storage:

With good reason, Emily [Tremaine] thought the museums appreciated works most if they had to pay for them. When the Metropolitan paid a great price for a work, people came to see it, and even if tainted by commercialism at the moment, it was displayed as a major work of art with the full prestige of the museum behind it.[64]

The growing role of auctions in the contemporary art world – and, more fundamentally, publicity becoming the source and standard of all value – creates a winner-take-all market. Of the 80,000 established artists who live in London and New York, only 75 are stars; 300 show with major galleries; and 5,000 have some kind representation but need to do something else on the side to make a living.[65] The rest are not established in any sense of the term. Only one artist in 200 will ever have his work offered at a Christie's or Sotheby's auction – which is necessary, but hardly enough, to be a star. Very few make it. Those who make it, often make it big. Still, those who make it big are forgotten fast: high publicity creates rapid turnover in auction stars.

The growing importance of publicity in contemporary art is not the simple outcome of the increasing difficulty of differentiating the good from the bad. Publicity is now part and parcel of the artistic enterprise itself. This is so also because art took on an explicitly theatrical pose in the contemporary era, especially with minimalism.[66] Works of art – in their making as well as interpretation – became more and more mere objects placed in a public setting for observation, bereft of any subjective meaning or value transcending the specific context of their consumption. As the critic Robert Hughes derided a sculpture of Carl André's that simply consists of 120 cream-colored bricks that are placed on the floor in two layers of 60, "A Rodin in a parking lot is still a misplaced Rodin; *Equivalent VIII* in the same lot is just bricks."[67] It is a cynical position, but nowadays publicity, for the most part, is what turns objects into art.

In all realms of life, publicity is, in part, a question of preference. For whatever reason, some actively seek publicity, even when it takes the form of notoriety; others avoid it like the plague. Ability counts. Some, by dint of natural gift or acquired skill, have a knack for publicity; others, suffering from too much or too little self-consciousness, are bad at it. Social processes matter also. Fame begets fame. Elites find it relatively easier to obtain access to channels of publicity and to impress others. Not all activities generate equal amounts of publicity: acting, art, teaching, and politics involve performances in front of audiences; tax law requires privacy. In politics and art, general fame is a precious, invaluable asset; by contrast, most top scholars are only known by insiders in academia, unless these are public intellectuals. Finally, societies differ in their accommodation and encouragement of publicity seeking.

While most don't have a penchant for widespread publicity, there is a pleasure in being seen, a pleasure that many, now and then, like to indulge in. The figure best associated with this tendency is the dandy, "a man who lives to dress," in the definition that Carlyle gave him. The dandy wants to be recognized as someone different; there is no easier way to seize attention. But he impresses people who notice him only to the extent that he does not seem to want to impress. He must therefore appear indifferent, indeed a bit contemptuous, to his audiences. And the dandy is not only putting on a show; he is typically a *flâneur* as well, always on the prowl for new sights. Here, too, there is a catch, though: the dandy should not seem to be moved by what he sees.[68] Few of us are dandies. We may, however, occasionally seek some attention in the public sphere – usually without giving up our anonymity. And cities and all their assorted spaces constitute the only public sphere in which most of us can ever hope to be really visible. So we spruce up to go downtown, if only to take a stroll. Couples will dress up for each other usually only when they are going out, only when they will be visible to third parties, to complete strangers.

But the public sphere remains inegalitarian. We saw that Habermas's critics from the left denounce the inequalities that restrict the public participation of certain groups. Significant as they may be, these inequalities are socially and historically contingent. There is a more profound, intrinsic asymmetry at the heart of the public sphere: a world where attention would be equally allotted would be the most utopian of all utopias. Any public sphere, attention being its sole yardstick, cannot help being inegalitarian, invidious. This is inherently bad for some: the two dyspeptic detractors of mass media, Adorno and Horkheimer, writing before the advent of talk radio, thought that radio was just like Hitler: one could talk back to neither.⁶⁹ Yet, no matter its real dangers, the inegalitarianism of publicity can be neither wished nor denounced away. Not everybody is equally good to look at, and people's rhetorical skills greatly vary. Even in public rituals where there is considerable participation – say the Protestant liturgy as opposed to the Catholic mass – there is a leader serving as a focus of attention, the asymmetry crucial to the affective effectiveness of what is going on.

Needless to say, public attention is not all good. If it is malicious, the gaze of the multitudes can degrade, even demonize. Nietzsche commented cavalierly in the preface to his *The Birth of Tragedy* that the strength of the public "lies solely in numbers."⁷⁰ But numbers matter greatly. Reputations can be immediately, irreversibly crushed by widespread negative publicity – a catastrophe for the members of professions whose authority is fiduciary. The discreditable evidence may well be scant, but the spectators can still assume that the focus is guilty; they can even fake outrage, especially if they are visible, to signal rectitude to one another – or at least to ward off any semblance of moral apathy. Assuming guilt is often less risky than assuming innocence. Moreover, in many instances, due to the semiotics of general visibility, which are amplified with publicity, the accused party will represent a negatively stereotyped group – this further lowering evidentiary standards and magnifying moral fury.

It is by virtue of its degrading potential that publicity has had an elective affinity with punishment. When the two are combined, one is objectified in one's most vulnerable state. Today we are nicer; yet publicity was an essential part of punishment in medieval and early modern Europe. The widely visible suffering and execution of the offender were dire deterrents to third parties; they equally served to degrade him as much as possible. Even the corpse of the offender could be visited by further public violence.⁷¹ The sole punishment meted out would sometimes be simple exposure, which ranked eminently higher than confinement in the severity scale. Such a sentence could be executed on the scaffold – frequently with rods hanging over the shoulders of the offender so as to redound to his discomfort. Exposure could be aggravated by extra mortification, as when the offender was made to stand under the gallows with the rope tied around his neck, which meant that he had barely escaped death.

The pillory, a staple of public punishment, allowed some participation from the spectators, who could express their scorn by hurling rotten food, mud, or dung at the ill-starred offender. But being set to it was itself already a calamitous humiliation: according to Adam Smith, the pilloried offender can receive sympathy only because he is objectively in a situation that cannot generate sympathy. That publicity was a major concern for the authorities is also revealed by the fact that certain crimes had to be punished out of the public sphere. In some countries, sodomy offenses warranted indoor executions: the authorities were loath to unintentionally publicize the transgression while they punished it. In prerevolutionary France, sodomy and bestiality convicts were executed without their verdict published, lest the young learned about such abominations.[72]

The effects of publicity on social status are complex, even in the case of public punishment: while being damned, the focus is still getting attention. And as all children, along with artists and criminals, know, attention – whatever the reason – bestows some grandeur. In the public sphere, and only there, to be is to be perceived. If the focus has been hitherto an unknown entity; if the consensus regarding his wrongdoing is mostly the result of people being scared of voicing their real sentiments; if his act seems courageous; or if he is shameless or has the gumption to make hay of his notoriety, then the pros of attention can trump the cons of disapproval.

Publicity tends to transform interpersonal disputes into matters of honor. The existence of an audience increases the likelihood of a verbal spar spiraling into a barroom brawl.[73] Collective attention can grant the focus opportunities to perform and acquire honor by displaying rectitude or courage. Appearing righteous often requires observing a norm in public at a visibly high cost. We can also morally upgrade ourselves by successfully tearing into a higher-status person, for publicity here would make us look courageous to those who are watching. Naturally, our opponent would rather not recognize the challenge we present him with and could in effect ignore us if we are not his equal. Still, if the challenge is particularly potent or cunningly crafty and if there is already strong public interest, ignoring it may not work. And insomuch as our public challenge is recognized, the attention that spectators accord us lets us effectively establish equivalence with our opponent – in addition to batten on his fame, if he has any.

Public performance can promise high status for all, including the most downtrodden. There is no better illustration for this than the gladiator fights in Rome. To us moderns, as it was to the legion of coeval Christian critics who never ceased to denounce it, the cirque seems to be little more than a sanguinary cesspool where idle spectators went to take sadistic delight in watching senseless violence and unstinted suffering. Huizinga wrote that there was something ludic, even joyful about the gladiator fights.⁷⁴ Yet they were equally about the exhibition of courage, the chief antique virtue. In a nontrivial fashion, the bloody episodes served to publicly ascertain the moral superiority of the fighters, most of whom were slaves who died "erect and invincible," over those who merely watched. "Many spectators and few men" was a popular saying about the Roman amphitheater.⁷⁵

Performance can only raise social status because it is risky. Publicity will degrade the focus if he acts in a way that betrays cowardice or a lack of control. Engendering a high level of vulnerability for the focus, publicity can confound without any attribution of wrongdoing, all the more if his moral or physical integrity is compromised. To be forced to undress in front of others, to be accused of a misdeed at an office meeting, or to be given a dusting on the street, fairly or unfairly, will all abase. And publicity is a risk for the focus even in front of adulating spectators. For those of us not used to general attention, there is always something embarrassing about receiving praise in public, and not only because we would be privately compelled to ask ourselves if we are worth all the limelight, but also because the collective gaze, however positive, cannot but transform us into an object. A revered object is still an object. And the gaze is not unambiguous. Apropos the revering rabble around his carriage, Cromwell is said to have dryly noted, "There would be as many, and as glad, to attend me at the gallows."⁷⁶ Clark Gable reportedly conveyed the same conviction – but in a matter with lower stakes – to David Niven after he heard about the death of the actress Thelma Todd:

> We all have a contract with the public – in us they see themselves or what they would like to be... They love to put us on a pedestal and worship us and form fan clubs and write thousands of letters telling us how great we are. But they've read the small print, and most of us haven't – they expect us to pay the price for it all... we have to get it in the end! So, when we get knocked off by gangsters, like Thelma did, or get hooked on booze or dope or get ourselves thrown out of business because of scandals or because we just get old, that's the payoff and public feels satisfied. Yeah, it's a good idea to read that small print.⁷⁷

Glory – and especially the ersatz glory of our celebrities – created by publicity is precarious. Pure fascination with public personalities without some dormant resentment – especially in egalitarian cultures – probably never exists, which often gives rise to abrupt and unforeseeable vacillations between complete veneration and complete demonization. There is a steep asymmetry between us and celebrities, one based on false intimacy.⁷⁸ They are either below or above us. We follow their every move; they don't know we exist. They supposedly talk to us; we listen, but cannot respond.

The asymmetry glorifies celebrities. But there is no glorification without objectification; hence the indispensability of the visual element to fame. This is why the genesis of the celebrity culture in the West owed much to the printing revolution, especially to the widely publicized portraits of writers such as Erasmus and Luther.[79]

Those who appear strongly in the public sphere, those who obtain a lot of publicity become ipso facto actors. Arendt points out in *Life of the Mind* that it is *doxa* – which means both "fame" and "opinion" in Ancient Greek[80] – that at once motivates and legitimates the actor in the public sphere.[81] It is thanks to *doxa* that the actor can become a hero. *Doxa*, however, can only be bestowed by inactive spectators, whose gaze cannot but objectify the actor.[82] It is one of the aporiae of the public sphere that it creates objectified actors. Objectification ensures that he who is glorified loses at least some of his autonomy too: he is but the appearance that he makes on others. And his appearance – given unquenchable public curiosity – can expand to any part of his life, including the most personal. He will thus lose the one thing that all losers have, to a far from negligible degree, thanks to the neglect they suffer from: privacy. Further, his behavior, if not his self-worth, is now dependent on public perceptions and expectations. There is more: wide publicity can turn a hitherto glorified focus into a clear, easy-to-attack target later.

The public sphere is then replete with perils, all the more for those who appear in it with their names. It is not surprising that many don't post their names when they make public political comments in chat rooms. That it allows anonymous participation – as well as anonymous spectatorship – is a major advantage of the internet. Even if authorities can deploy technology to track down the identity of a user, one typically still enjoys privacy vis-à-vis the other users, which makes people not only crass but also free and honest about their opinions. Still, the fact remains that the genuine actor – someone who takes a risk and seeks to be recognized for it – needs a name, if only a nom de plume, or at least a sobriquet.

The riskier an act, the more spectacular it is. And spectacularity has significant consequences on the spectators. Take the Balinese cockfight, a bloody national obsession that Geertz famously analyzed. According to the anthropologist, the beloved cockfight is no mere pastime; it is culture. But it is not culture, somewhat blandly, as the norms and values of a people, or the way they do things, or as meaning making in general. Rather, it is culture with a "C", culture as stylized, aesthetic expression. Insofar as it cultivates the sensibilities of the Balinese people by providing them with a "sentimental education" about manhood, the cockfight is culture as *King Lear* is culture.[83] Yet the cockfight can do what it does only because it is high drama – not unlike the Roman gladiator fights. And it is high drama because it is violent and because it entails a conflict in public with enormous risks. For the owners of the animals – and to some extent for their associates – the cockfight is "deep play:" a gambling situation described and condemned by Bentham where the marginal utility of winning is dwarfed by the marginal disutility of losing. The bids are irrationally high, but the stakes are not only financial. The fight is about honor, and one universal way to earn honor is courage – by putting oneself in a risky situation in front of others and, à la Hemingway, by exercising grace under the pressure of their gaze. Naturally, it is the cocks that do the actual fighting and the dying, but one can fight and die spiritually too. The Balinese men associate the animals with their sexual organs to such a degree that their whole masculinity is tied up in the event; losing cannot but be an oversized blow to their honor. The highly violent and risky nature of the fight, which is indeed the very source of its dramatic élan, also renders it emotionally absorbing – as well as simply exciting, something that Geertz neglects in his account[84] – for the spectators. This is why it is worth watching. And the more gripping the spectacle, the more it, as a piece of culture, enables the Balinese to make sense of themselves, to realize what it means to be a human being in their society. Hence the imperative to make the fight as violent, as unforeseeable, as chancy as possible.

These dynamics are common to many, especially consequential, public events. No wonder then that many rituals across time and space take the contest form – and that honor, more often than not, requires competition. Anything can serve as fodder: not only bravado and insults but even politeness, as in the Chinese courtesy rituals where it is with kind words that one humiliates one's interlocutor. Public attention can turn any activity into a competitive one that hinges on losing or gaining honor.[85]

4

Politics in Public

Many major practices in society – including art, politics, and law – are carried out partially in public, with varying levels of publicity. These naturally retain their proper logics. And they are not completely public: artists paint in their studios, politicians cut deals clandestinely, prosecutors are not to leak information during their investigations. Yet artists appear – in the strongest sense of the term – in the public sphere when they exhibit, politicians when they appeal on the stump to their constituencies, prosecutors when they plead in court. To that extent, the words and deeds of such actors, in their production as in their interpretation, will be shaped by publicity – unlike those of simple citizens, who are usually anonymous and voiceless in public, out of choice or by necessity.

Political action is ventured in public by all kinds of people, from whistleblowers to presidents. This is why the public sphere and civil society should not be conflated – as they commonly are. A few scholars make a differentiation: Craig Calhoun, for one, conceptualizes in a sophisticated analysis the public sphere as the "operationalization of civil society's capacity for self-organization."[1] But even then, the public sphere is subsumed within the parameters of civil society: visibility and especially publicity – things that affect and concern all political phenomena – are thereby glossed over. Congress, a municipal park, national archives, and a court of law, which are obviously not civil society, are all public spaces. Most important public events often happen in spaces dominated by noncivil society actors like prosecutors or politicians. Consider high-profile cases or Senate hearings where national controversies are played out to wide spectatorship.[2] At the same time, putatively civic discourse in the public sphere – including nongovernmental spaces like town squares, newspaper columns, and television programs – is hardly under the monopoly of civil society actors. On the contrary, such activity is usually the specialty, the forte of career politicians. There is no necessary relationship, not even an elective affinity, between civil society actors and the political use of public spaces. Hence the need to differentiate between two types of conflict: those among groups in civil society and those about visibility in public spaces.

All political actors – i.e., all those who pursue decision-making power in society, opportunistically or for the common good – need to publicize themselves and their causes. Publicity is not only a basic component of politics; it can equally be a priceless resource or a redoubtable constraint for political actors, who, more than anyone else, rise and fall as a function of its vicissitudes.

Use of Publicity

A good deal of politics takes place behind closed doors, through confidential communications; all political actors, nevertheless, also pursue publicity in assorted arenas, from streets to courts to rostrums to blogs. They want to be noticed and heard. Publicity is not only good for disseminating one's ideas. Political actors try to achieve recognition for those they claim to represent, especially if the latter are invisible – a key issue in identity politics. In effect, some see recognition in itself – the pursuit of which was for Hegel the engine of history – as a basic right in contemporary democracies. Political actors scramble for attention, chase after fame and glory, here or posthumously. They seek to form groups around themselves. They strive for altruistic reputations by concocting civic narratives that will hopefully resonate with the public. They endeavor to seem courageous by lacing into mighty opponents – or opponents they paint as mighty: political actors are forever fabricating appearances through performances that they are solitary Davids representing the common weal against Goliaths who, hiding behind high-flown façades, plot selfish schemes that they do not dare acknowledge in public. All presidential candidates in the United States, for example, frame their campaigns as righteous uphill battles against Washington special interests.

Machiavelli asserted notoriously in *The Prince* that a concern with appearances should trump reality in political conduct:

It is not essential, then, that a Prince should have all the good qualities which I have enumerated above, but it is most essential that he should seem to have them;

I will even venture to affirm that if he has and invariably practises them all, they are hurtful, whereas the appearance of having them is useful. Thus, it is well to seem merciful, faithful, humane, religious, and upright, and also to be so; but the mind should remain so balanced that were it needful not to be so, you should be able and know how to change to the contrary.[3]

This is because, the Florentine philosopher added, "The vulgar are always taken by appearances and by results, and the world is made up of the vulgar, the few only finding room when the many have no longer ground to stand on."[4] But political actors are not only interested in appearing a certain way and suppressing discordant facts about themselves; they are also assiduously struggling to smash the appearances of their rivals. Yet even when they are successful, what remains are other appearances. Inauthenticity pervades politics – to the extent that it is public. By the same token, as appearances are its stock-in-trade, politics cannot but have an aesthetic aspect, as Diego von Vacano points out.[5] Contrary to Arendt, not all appearances are political. On the other hand, all appearances, however produced by those without an explicit political ambition, have the potential to become so. It is due to the protected nature of the private sphere that its contents – so long as they stay there – are spared this destiny.

Publicity in political life is a scarce resource. Access to channels of publicity is unequally distributed, correlated with status. And these channels vary greatly in the amount of publicity they get. The more effective a channel, the less carrying capacity it will have. Modern information technology may have decreased publicity costs: Twitter enables anyone to potentially have some audience for almost anything one can say, and Donald Trump successfully used this technology to bypass the hostile media in his 2016 presidential campaign. But we should underline that it is the high-status people who get attention on Twitter. And all political actors must still contend with two scarcities – the scarcity of public spaces that get a lot attention and the scarcity of the attention of citizens themselves. The latter scarcity is often a more formidable challenge.

In democracies, the public to whom things are made visible and to whom politicians appear is the body from which political power is in principle to originate from. Yet whether political power truly represents the people – a fictive category especially when so many don't vote – is constantly contested. The incontestable fact, however, is that citizens are almost always spectators, and politics the spectacle that they are faced with. Rather than abstractly representing the people, elected officials simply represent power in various ways to the public for legitimacy. As we saw, what matters in representation – in politics as in other public semiotic loci – is as much, if not more, the fact that something is represented to somebody as what is being represented. Representation is never a derivation.

Politics in representative democracies is, above all, elite competition in front of an intermittently interested citizenry, a body whose knowledge usually consists of smatterings and who is, by and large, looking for distractions. Decades of political science research have found that most citizens lack clear political preferences and well-articulated views. In Schumpeter's words, they have "a reduced sense of reality" when thinking about public matters – and an "absence of effective volition," for good measure.[6] Politics can be engrossing at times; it is usually only indirectly, if at all, connected to our immediate life concerns.[7] No wonder genuine interest in it is sporadic, transitory.

And when the citizen votes, he does it in secret, outside of the public sphere: his principal, and usually sole, political act is also one of his most private acts. Interests and values do obviously affect his vote. But mere spectatorship may matter too: politicians who perform well, who offer a gripping spectacle often have an advantage. On the other hand, the gaze of the citizenry objectifies, and objectification, as we saw in the previous chapter, can undermine. Particularly when negatively and collectively focused on the same thing, and insofar as it is visible to the focus, the gaze will be all the more objectifying. Nevertheless, despite what many postmodern and feminist thinkers say, the gaze of a single individual is little more the stance of someone who remains, either by choice or necessity, passive. The individual gaze can be an act, Merleau-Ponty wrote.[8] It is true that a disapproving stare from a stranger on the street as we litter can make us think twice about what we are doing. Yet this is not much: the individual gaze is action, in the strong sense of the term, only in the private sphere, where it is hard not to recognize and where it is typically accompanied by speech. In any case, what matters in politics is the collective gaze, which is different from the sum of individual gazes, in a situation of publicity.

To be sure, publicity is not specific to democracies. Kings and dictators obviously use publicity copiously – not just to communicate their actions, but equally to legitimate and glorify themselves, to build groups around them, to humiliate opponents. Michel Foucault argued in *Discipline and Punish* that power became more invisible and impersonal in modern times. He was not quite right: regardless of the type of regime, all authority needs some, and often high, levels of visibility and personalization – but, as we saw, not without objectification. And visibility and personalization go hand in glove: power cannot escape embodiment in an actual person who publicly represents it to others. This is so even for rational-legal authority à la Weber, which never quite dispenses of a leader with significant visibility – consider the CEOs of top companies or the president of the United States. Leaders, claiming to represent institutions or people, are always more and less than their claim. They are less, because their claim is relentlessly challenged by their rivals; they are more, because they cannot but appear and be treated in public as real individuals, never only as disembodied incumbents performing a role. The more a political actor is subject to publicity and the more he reveals of himself – through his words and image – the more irreducible will he be to the office that he represents.

For all political actors, including the institutional and noninstitutional ones, displaying courage or civic-mindedness – not unlike what happens in the Balinese cockfight – is often vital to attaining power. Power is, however, usually somewhat of a theoretical matter. Even when someone indisputably already has some, holding onto it may require him to signal to others that he is indeed powerful by performances – demonstrations by activists, royal progresses, perp walks of policemen and district attorneys, Roman triumphs, gay pride parades, etc. – in spaces liable to draw maximum publicity. These performances do not necessitate the presence of the actor; it suffices that his power is represented in some way to the public. Such representations are not always refulgent. Take the public executions of early modern Europe, at times preceded by gruesome tortures inflicted on the condemned criminals. These were indeed spectacles marked by an elaborate semiotics inscribing, through the hand of the executioner, the might of the avenging king – who was himself physically absent from the ceremony – on the body of the gibbeted convict. And it was through the mutilation of the body of the condemned that the immortal spiritual body of the king – a body that, for Ernst Kantorowicz, was the basis of political sovereignty in regimes legitimated by divine law[9] – was reaffirmed. "In the darkest region of the political field the condemned man represents the symmetrical, inverted figure of the king," wrote Foucault.[10] There is some truth to this poetic reckoning; but, more prosaically, the public executions also served to play up the brawn of the central authority against peripheral rivals during the late medieval and early modern periods – as Leviathans parceled Europe among themselves and monopolized the use of violence within their borders.[11] Publicizing violence to effectively communicate strength, especially in the market for protection, is a common strategy for criminal elements too.[12] But when a political entity grows adequately confident of its control within its jurisdiction – as was the case with the sovereigns of the eighteenth and nineteenth centuries – less necessary will the public displays of violence be. In any case, any performance carries some risk, even for the seemingly almighty potentates.

The use of spectacle to affirm power abounds in history, from Antiquity to the seventeenth-century baroque court in Catholic Europe to contemporary nationalism.[13] And spectacles need not be violent or all that extraordinary. The royal absolutism of Louis XIV was erected upon publicity. To reestablish central authority after the Fronde rebellion, the Sun King gathered the entire Gallic nobility to inhabit the court of his lavish Palace of Versailles, thereby reconfigured into a tightly regulated public sphere – a world where all watched all, all the time, an enclosed system where one rose and fell by one's appearances. Life under such high visibility consisted of an incessant string of excruciatingly ostentatious rituals featuring the king as their focus. The attending nobles were to wait constantly on Louis XIV as he got up in the morning, changed his clothes, went to bed, in the course of quotidian royal walks and hunts, in moments both most lofty and most profane, including during his bowel movements. "A king lacks nothing except the sweetness of a private life," observed the contemporaneous moralist La Bruyère.[14] Every moment of royal life was turned into a spectacle. But the nobles did not just look at the king, thereby boosting his magnificence; they also looked at one another looking at him, which enabled each, using royal attention as a touchstone, to assess everybody else's social standing in Versailles.

The main intention of Louis XIV was to pacify the nobility, many of whom hailed from families who had previously taken arms against the Crown during his minority. He distributed favors based on attendance – already a reward itself. Courtly rituals formed a hierarchy, nobles hoping, striving to take part in the more prestigious ones. The system naturally generated severe competition and atomized the nobility while the constant publicity of the king glorified him. Norbert Elias, in his celebrated analysis of the court, noted, "In power that may exist but is not visible in the appearance of the rule the people do not believe. They must see in order to believe."[15] There is more, though: the king only became glorious to the extent that his being watched was watched by all.[16]

Discontents for Political Actors

The public sphere, and more specifically publicity, can prove stumbling blocks for political actors, however. First, the more their activities are transparent to wide publics, the more they will be judged by their appearances – over which they may have limited control. Because of their fiduciary pretensions, political actors need to appear uncorrupt. Their audiences lack full information or expertise to confirm whether they have committed an offense. And appearing to do wrong can corrupt others: one's appearances, especially in high-publicity practices like politics, should not "give scandal" – defined in Thomist ethics not simply as perpetrating a sin but as providing occasion "for another's spiritual fall."[17] Political actors may be stumped, and not always fairly, by how their appearances are interpreted. The number and heterogeneity of those that they face will call for extra gingerliness: the larger and the more diverse their public, the harder will it be for them to stabilize the meaning of their words or actions. Predictably, their discourse – particularly in democracies – will be often vague, prosy, if not claptrap. The powerless are also prone to talk in an empty, obsequious fashion in public, thereby contradicting what they customarily say in private: either fearful of the wrath of the powerful or to wangle advantages from them, they may well conspire to "to reinforce hegemonic appearances."[18]

The burden of appearances, particularly onerous for professional politicians, will bear down on anyone who enters the public arena with political objectives. Electronic media will further destabilize political actors by rendering it difficult to segregate audiences and say different things to different groups.[19] Due to innovations such as YouTube, political actors cannot know for sure whether the performance they give to a certain collectivity, with an expectation of confidentiality, will not be transmitted to a different, larger one. Here are some recent examples. In his 2008 presidential campaign, Barack Obama, at a San Francisco fundraiser, groused about a Middle America, bitter about unemployment and, in response, "clinging to guns or religion or antipathy toward people who aren't like them or anti-immigrant sentiment or anti-trade sentiment as a way to explain their frustrations." Four years later, Mitt Romney, similarly campaigning for the White House and speaking at a fundraiser in Florida, complained about the "47 percent" of non-tax-paying Americans who are "dependent upon government," who "believe that they are victims," and who "will vote for the president no matter what." The same thing happened in 2016 when Hillary Clinton, at a fundraiser attended by wealthy liberal donors like Barbra Streisand, stated, "You could put half of Trump's supporters into what I call the basket of deplorables. Right?" After waiting for the laughter and applause to subside, she added, "The racist, sexist, homophobic, xenophobic, Islamophobic – you name it." In all these instances, the presidential candidate addressed the liberal or conservative elite in a protected setting with a speech that was decidedly derogatory to a specific section of the American lower classes. All presidential candidates in the United States are confronted with the same conundrum. They need the monies of the elite (unless they are Donald Trump, who could spend his own money) and the votes of the masses. Yet flattering or scaring the elite, so that they finance campaigns, is usually predicated on belittling the masses or depicting them as dangerous. So what one says to a select few should not be heard by the multitudes: a task that is getting harder and harder to achieve as many sensory spaces in society are shedding their hitherto thick boundaries, relaxing their access restrictions. In all these cases, the speeches of the candidates were surreptitiously taped and publicized to the American population; uproar ensued.

Publicity is a double-edged sword. It can enhance as well as degrade. It can backfire, spawn unintended consequences. The powerful can lose control over how they look, and those who are exposed to the masses can overturn the tables. One reason why European authorities discontinued public executions is that the attending rabble could turn rampageous, sometimes riotous, and root for the offender. In effect, the event offered the offender, who was at times subjected to public torture before the execution, the possibility, if he exhibited mettle on the scaffold, to reclaim his honor, to maybe upgrade to a martyr glamorized in broadsheets. While the spectacle was designed to underscore royal omnipotence by debasing the offender, the ordeal could equally make an unbowed hero of him. The executions permitted prestige-enhancing performances by the offenders especially when they were, as the religious custom dictated, accorded the right to offer public amends.

No less thorny is the matter for the authorities when the status of the offender is high. The Bolsheviks acted sagaciously when they slayed the Romanoffs stealthily, in contrast to the French revolutionaries, whose open regicide would eventually bolster opposition to the new regime. The Jacobins were not as imprudent as to let the condemned king speak publicly before going under the blade of the guillotine. Louis XVI was not even clearly discernible on the gallows; the soldiers besieged the stunned crowd. But the execution, receiving huge, albeit eerily silent, attention, was a major public event nonetheless and could not fail to have ramifications throughout France. In a similar vein, the widely disseminated images of Saddam Hussein's execution in December 2006 worsened the sectarian fissures that were already deepening in Iraq.

The fact that a good deal of politics involves public performances means that much of political power is inherently tenuous. Such is notably the case with charismatic leaders who, in the absence of institutional moorings, need to resort constantly to public performances to assert themselves. Max Weber wrote about how ancient Hebrew prophets had to do exceptional deeds in front of others for legitimacy: Zachariah inflicted wounds on himself and Ezekiel consumed dung.[20] Moreover, the publicity that a political actor enjoys, while potentially glorifying and maybe even immunizing in the short run, can ultimately saddle him with unrealistically high expectations from his audience. Dissatisfaction and distrust will follow. And the less the public trusts a political actor, the more transparency will be imposed on him, the more limited his license will be, the less control he will have over the way he appears, and the more some will demand authenticity.

Public authenticity is an oxymoron, though – a delusion that can sway any of us now and then, but never for too long. Yet authenticity is routinely claimed by public figures in today's world. This is partly because of distrust in political institutions and partly because of the intense personalization of political leaders through mass media. These factors tend to further accentuate the relative independence of the person from what he is representing. Search for and pretensions to authenticity are also closely linked to an anti-institutionalist ethos. It is a rare political movement whose leaders don't brag that it is an artless, spontaneous grassroots occurrence. In the same vein, one would be hard-pressed to find a presidential candidate who does not play the undesigning, idealistic outsider against the cynical, malevolent Washington operatives. Even Hillary Clinton said in a 2015 interview to CBS, "I cannot imagine anyone being more of an outsider than the first woman president."[21] Few buy the outsider narrative; those who buy it do so briefly. The same applies to authenticity.

Trump had more success than Clinton playing the outsider in 2016. After all, here was a man who had never held office, someone who campaigned not only against the Democrats but also against almost all American media and the establishment in his own party, a candidate transgressive not only in his demeanor but also in his populist discourse. Yet, notwithstanding his outsider posture, Trump won not because he seemed more authentic. He won simply because he convinced – in the most old-fashioned way – many working- and middle-class voters in the swing states of the Midwest that their interests would be better served with his economic policies. Many of those he did not convince, including those who had voted for Obama four years ago, were not convinced by Clinton either: disastrously for the former Secretary of State, they stayed home on Election Day.

Authenticity is in any case elusive for politicians. Intensified, extensive, and imposed publicity can discombobulate them, making it difficult to appear authentic. Appearing authentic requires much effort, which, when uncovered, vitiates the appearance itself.[22] And all political actors – whatever their professed sentiments and rhetorical acuity – can always be suspected of grandstanding and harboring selfish agendas under virtuous veneers. Since politics, due to its highly public nature, selects for and fosters narcissism among its practitioners at any level, from local community advocates to presidents, audiences will frequently find their worst misgivings vindicated.

Its agonal aspect turns democratic politics into a spectator sport. Media swamis – as well as regular citizens – regularly, explicitly approach it as if it were simply horseracing and judge politicians on how they perform, often independent of the substance of what they say. Consider any watercooler or cable news pundit evaluations of candidates in the aftermath of a presidential debate. At the same time, many look for authenticity in politicians. Despite the evident contradiction here, people oscillate nonchalantly between these two attitudes.

American Presidents

The public sphere is inherently ridden with paradoxes for political actors. Publicity is essential to power; it can also be a stumbling block. An example is the American presidency. Except during extraordinary circumstances such as the Civil War, until the early decades of the 1900s the presidency was a much weaker office than what it would become later.[23] Presidents could claim little independence from the party machines. Federal government was indistinguishable from patronage politics; in any case, most governance was state governance. So the White House had to make do with a meager staff, and executive departments reported to Congress. Relative isolationism from the world further trimmed the role of the presidents in the general polity.

These factors bore on the visibility of the office. Only 20 percent of the political reporting in Washington was allotted to the presidency in the nineteenth century.[24] Equally important, presidents were barred from bypassing the Washington elite to directly appeal to the people for backing in their scrimmages with Capitol Hill: when he barnstormed across the country during his impeachment trial to glean support against his congressional deprecators, Andrew Johnson was widely slated as a demagogue overstepping his authority.[25]

The idea that presidents have a popular mandate is nowhere be found in the Framers' design of the American political system.[26] After all, the Constitution stipulates that the president is to be elected not directly, but indirectly, through the Electoral College. Moreover, it is technically the Constitution that gives the president powers – not the people. So even when Lincoln temporarily stretched the scope of his office during the Civil War and unilaterally suspended habeas corpus, he justified himself on constitutional, and not democratic, grounds. Be that as it may, the danger that the president could present himself as the highest representative of the people remained. Despite the mediation of the Electoral College, American presidents are still the only officials in the realm who can link their legitimacy to the nationwide vote. And, if it comes off, a claim of popular mandate – the highest democratic legitimacy, which could always be potentially parlayed into dictatorial powers – could be destructive of the system. This is why nineteenth-century Americans thought it was necessary to ensure that presidents would not dare turn into dangerous demagogues. They were therefore not to address the people on important issues in normal times. The few popular addresses they gave – save those given in time of war – were ceremonial; they did not touch on domestic policy. Of course, presidents did address Congress publicly, but not with words fashioned for the general public. At any rate, nearly all presidential communications in the nineteenth century were written. Until the twentieth century, presidents, on the whole, consented to such reins on their discursive prerogatives. The main concern of George Washington, for instance, in his visits throughout the land was not public speaking; it was "seeing and being seen." Lincoln, like many others, would explicitly decline to talk in a public speech about an issue that was being discussed in Congress.

Yet the American presidency eclipsed political parties and Congress during the first half of the twentieth century, notably with the New Deal and the Cold War. Economic and administrative modernization, coupled with the government's progressive engagement in the world, increased the public's dependence – real or imaginary – on the presidency. More and more the myth of the presidential mandate turned into a reality. In the critical summing up of Robert Dahl,

> Thus the presidency has developed into an office that is the very embodiment of the kind of executive the Framers, so far as we can discern their intentions, strove to avoid. They did not wish an executive who would be a tribune of the people, a champion of popular majorities; who would gain office by popular election; who as a consequence of his popular election would claim a mandate for his policies; who in order to mobilize popular support for his policies would appeal directly to the people; who would shape the language, style, and delivery of his appeals so as best to create a public opinion favorable to his ambitions; and who whenever it seemed expedient would bypass the members of the deliberative body in order to mobilize public opinion and thereby induce a reluctant Congress to enact his policies.[27]

Armed with vastly expanded powers, the White House became the fulcrum of the government, with the incumbent emerging as the unifying figure of the nation and the center of public attention.[28] Accordingly, in the course of the twentieth century, most reporting on the government shifted to the presidency.[29] Thanks to the radio, the voice of the president ingressed into the intimacy of the American household. Television only added to presidential visibility. As they attained far-flung, constant, and intense publicity, presidents from Theodore Roosevelt onward could circumvent the Washington elites and appeal straightway to the American people. Deeming it too monarchical, Jefferson had discontinued the custom of delivering the State of the Union address each year in person in Congress. Wilson reestablished it. Franklin D. Roosevelt, more than anyone else before him, forged a direct link to the American people with his radio talks and tried to present himself as a leader super partes – notwithstanding, or rather to counter, the enmity of the moneyed interests during his four terms. Presidential news conferences grew ever more frequent in the twentieth century, the use of polls by the White House routine.[30] The office of the presidency now thoroughly plebiscitary, the incumbents' positive public image – measured and publicized continuously by polls – increasingly served as the chief justification of executive action. The high level of publicity obtained by presidents added to their clout in their dealings with the Washington elite.

The twentieth century then gave rise to a highly autonomous, highly personalized presidency perpetually at the center of the American public sphere. Despite heightened attention, however, presidents could largely control the way they appeared. The press was by and large deferential until the late 1960s. The private lives of presidents were either only portrayed in a flattering light or not touched at all:[31] for example, journalists kept mum about the mistresses of Wilson, Harding, Franklin D. Roosevelt, and Kennedy. The identification of the moral integrity of the presidency as a public good required that information compromising the office be kept under wraps as much as possible.[32] It was in the twentieth century – and especially after World War II – that the presidential withholding of information, in the form of executive privilege, became unexceptional.[33] Since the Constitution does not make unambiguous stipulations regarding the confidentiality of executive documents, the issue is political through and through,[34] one that is closely tied to the general standing of the office of the presidency. From June 1955 to June 1960, Congress was denied information forty-four times by executive branch officials. The entire nineteenth century had witnessed fewer such cases than those five years. The presidency ascendant, propped up by strong public confidence in the office, allowed the presidents to keep information from Congress and citizenry as they saw fit. Both Truman and Eisenhower could, without any fuss, assert privilege against the House on Un-American Activities Committee, the infamous anti-communist juggernaut, on the matter of congressional access to executive information regarding the security files of government employees. In 1948, Nixon pressed Truman to release an FBI letter impugning a prominent scientist of disloyalty. White House disobliged; the jeremiads of the California congressman were futile. Even when a president grew unpopular, as in the case of Truman whose approval ratings tobogganed at the end of his last term, the institution of presidency still commanded much awe[35] and retained its confidentiality prerogatives. In 1952, Truman could successfully claim privilege even for executive officials considered security risks by his own administration.[36] So could Eisenhower – with the blessings of the editorial page of the *New York Times*, which proclaimed that internal deliberations of the executive branch were confidential and that their disclosure would impede "candid exchanges within the administration."[37]

While the presidents obtained high levels of publicity until the late 1960s, many of their activities were ensconced safely outside the public sphere. But what served presidents before undercut them later. High publicity personalized the presidency, which turned presidents into glorified, sometimes even quasi-totemic beings. By the same token, visibility also eventually led to ever-rising expectations from presidents, who more and more commenced their terms with high approval ratings and left office with low ones.[38] The personalization of the office sapped the institutional protections of presidents when they were distrusted.[39] An asset in a time of strong confidence, high publicity could constitute a liability with the burgeoning anti-authority ethos of the 1960s, which only radicalized with Vietnam and Watergate. The percentage of those who reported to be trusting the federal government "all or most of the time" dropped from 76 percent in 1964 to 53 percent in 1972. In 1958, 24 percent of American believed that the government was "run by crooks" – a figure that rose to 32 percent in 1970, 36 percent in 1972, and 45 percent in 1974.[40]

As a result of declining trust and rising suspicion of wrongdoing, an expanding portion of the operations of the presidency was thrusted onto the central regions of the American public sphere. The White House was stunned by subpoenas from independent counsels,[41] while congressional oversight activity escalated.[42] The Supreme Court waxed disrespectful of White House's privacy claims. The presidential competence to assert executive privilege was crimped. All such assertions were regarded by a leery Congress as duplicitous maneuvers. Some presidents felt compelled to disclose even personal documents: Reagan voluntarily turned in his diaries during the Iran-Contra investigation. Clinton found himself forced to testify about his sex life. The exigency of transparency was extended to all executive branch officials. Passed in 1976, the Government in the Sunshine Act opened federal agency deliberations to public scrutiny. The 1978 ethics legislation required cabinet members to make full public financial disclosures.

Presidents found it ever more difficult to master their appearances. Transparency, which was a reaction to distrust, led to still more distrust, as American presidents were impelled to invest ever more in public relations.[43] The only job of more than 30 percent of the White House staff during the Carter administration was tackling the media.[44] Constant polling to monitor the image of the president became part and parcel of executive governance.[45] All this, however, not only deprives presidents of resources that could otherwise be expended to run the country. Visible engagement in public relations also renders presidents prey to inauthenticity accusations.[46]

These processes further chipped away at public confidence. The percentage of those who had "a great deal of confidence in the White House" fluctuated between the low teens and mid-thirties from 1972 to today, with the exception of 2002 and 2003 (50 and 40 percent, respectively) – years marked by a rallying-around-the flag patriotism in the wake of the terror attacks on the Twin Towers on September 11, 2001.[47] By contrast, until the mid-sixties the media had been very respectful. A study of the

New York Times coverage of the presidents found that 12 percent of the stories were negative in the 1950s, 17.5 percent in the 1960s, 32 percent in the 1970s (or 26 percent if Watergate is omitted), and 28 percent in the 1980s.[48] Reporters turned pugilistic in White House press conferences.[49] Coverage of presidential campaigns moved from substance to strategy.[50] But also note that the negativity of such news coverage is not always correlated with the approval ratings of their specific target,[51] the reason being that trust in media is itself very low.[52]

Some commentators have argued that the declining trust in political actors is due to increasing scrutiny by modern mass media.[53] But there has to be more. Increasing scrutiny is itself in significant part a reaction to distrust. And, at least in the American context, distrust in politics, which started with Vietnam, preceded the rise of media hostility toward politicians. And presidential scandal, which was quite frequent in nineteenth-century United States, preceded modern mass media. Even the ways in which contemporary presidents deal with the media, their rhetorical techniques, have a long pedigree.[54] Incidentally, while it is second nature for presidents to go public over the heads of the Washington elite, the strategy does not always work. It seems that the radio appeals of Franklin D. Roosevelt could not add one percentage point to his approval ratings. "Reagan would go out on stump, draw huge crowds, and convert no one at all," observed ruefully his press secretary, Marlin Fitzwater.[55] In the majority of cases, presidents lose on their major legislative initiatives, especially in times of divided government.[56]

Scandal and Politics

Politics being inevitably about appearances, no wonder scandal is integral to it. Political actors spend a significant amount of time attacking – openly or, ideally, on the sly – one another's appearances through scandal. That is, they publicize – or help publicize – things that clash with their opponents' public status: secret money, selfish interests, corporal appetites, etc. Leaking or releasing discreditable documents and making moral denunciations in public are unremarkable in the struggles among political actors. Much of political competition – to the extent that it involves moral attacks – adopts the form of scandal, even when it is not explicitly denoted as such.

We cannot make sense of the strategic use of scandal independent of the semiotics of the public sphere. First, actors gain or suffer in scandals simply because of the way they appear. Evidentiary standards are low in the public sphere. Scandal obeys the principle of guilt by suspicion – a logical extension of the being is appearing principle, the modus operandi of the public sphere. Second, apparent offenders, as an extension of their publicness, stand for collectivities. They can be discriminated based on their associations, or their disgrace can be extended to their groups through a contagion, as scandal obeys the principle of guilt by association – a principle that flows from the synecdochic logic of the public sphere. Political actors, institutional ones as well as those in civil society, who have recourse to scandal exploit these characteristics: they publicize – or leak so as to elude the self-contamination hazards intrinsic in a public denunciation – legally substandard evidence; they tarnish their rivals with the guilt of their associates; and they attack groups through their high-status members.

Further, the logic of publicity is central to the dynamics of political scandal. Reactions to offenders are governed by how publicity affects the meaning of their acts and the incentives of the spectators. Widely known and tolerated things often pique harsh reactions only after they are made unavoidable through publicity. For example, most financing of political campaigns in France during the twentieth century was illegal.[57] It consisted of donations from businesses and affluent financiers, assistance from the Soviet Union (to the Communist Party), kickbacks from procurement contracts, sub rosa payments from publicly funded voluntary associations, transfers from state-owned corporations, and the use of secret funds of the Matignon (the prime minister's office). While these practices were common knowledge in the political world, they were also mostly accommodated, and even privately justified – after all, the French people were not too keen on financing campaigns with their taxes. Enforcement was haphazard, perfunctory. It was only when their financial skullduggeries were successfully publicized in judiciary probes during the 1990s, as a result of which it became hard to ignore them, that the French politicians suffered opprobrium.

Scandals, laying bare the power of publicity, can boost the status of those who create them – for example, through denunciations. If the denouncee is of high status, the scandal will more likely register attention. It can even aggrandize the denouncer, if the denunciation is successful and seems courageous. The French investigating magistrates specifically and the French judiciary in general acquired greater autonomy from the executive branch as a result of the corruption probes, which gave rise to scandals through leaks to the media, in the 1990s and 2000s. But the higher the status of the denouncee, the riskier the denunciation – as Joseph McCarthy discovered to his chagrin in 1954 when he shifted his attacks to the American military in his hunt for secret communists in the government. The French judiciary could go after the political elite through leaked investigations only because the political elite had already undergone a decline in prestige, which contrasted with their high institutional status, and had thus become vulnerable to moral attack.

A public denunciation comes with risks, though. It may upset powerful people, instigate retaliation, elicit general disapproval. It always expresses anger, and, as Adam Smith says, the impartial spectator finds it harder to sympathize with this moral sentiment.[58] If what the denouncer exposes is contaminating (as in sexual transgressions), if he is personally close to the denouncee, or if he is unable to signal impartiality then the scandal can degrade him as well. A public denunciation is indeed a performance that can misfire. Any whistleblower or member of Congress who denounces an evildoer risks a comedown if he unwittingly reveals ill intentions or if the denouncee can retaliate in kind.

Many scandals break when a wrongdoing is publicly denounced. But one can cause a scandal through transgressing provocatively in public too. Outsiders or lower-ranking political actors are more likely to do so: they have less to lose, and they are hungrier for recognition. Naturally, their provocations are less likely to be noticed. Yet such acts, when they are well publicized, can yield courageous reputations, even if the spectators don't agree with the transgressor. And they can be quite consequential. Consider civil disobedience, whose power often lies in provoking the authorities into exposing their real, violent, illegitimate nature. Transgressions in public, especially insofar as they generated motivational cascades encouraging further such transgressions, did facilitate the fall of communism.[59] Repeated public drinking seems to have hastened the repeal of Prohibition – and in the regions where drinking remained private afterward, the anti-alcohol norms subsided for some time.[60] If we can safely transgress an unpopular or too exacting norm in private, so that we don't have to challenge it in public, it will be easy to keep paying lip service to it. By contrast, if a norm cannot be easily transgressed in private so that the transgressions will have to be visible to others, sustaining public support for it could be harder. This is why an anthropological study has found that the more permeable the materials used in wall construction, the weaker are the norms against female premarital sexual activity in preindustrial societies.[61]

Liberal Democracy and Publicity

Visibility has a bearing not only on the life chances of political actors but equally on liberal democracy and collective welfare. Let us begin with its positive impact. A national public sphere where state operations are transparent to the citizenry and are consequently open to critique has long been considered a requisite for liberal democracy. Publicity makes political actors and institutions accountable. It can disinfect and deter. While the notion of *arcana imperii* still holds in matters of national security and during emergencies, a secular decrease in governmental secrecy has stamped the course of Western modernity. Parliamentary deliberations and trial procedures became public during the eighteenth and nineteenth centuries. The mysteries of the state treasury were divulged for the first time for all to see on the eve of the French Revolution, in 1781 when Necker, the finance minister, published his *Compte rendu au roi*, a record of royal finances – although the figures he provided later turned out to be fudged. Publicizing discreditable information about opponents has always been unexceptional among the political elite;[62] yet it was with liberal democracy – which both imposed universal norms on the business of governing and created open venues for the airing of transgressions – that scandalmongering became a big part of jostling for power.

There are many philosophical justifications of publicity. The utilitarian tradition's view is even a lofty one. "Without publicity, no good is permanent: under the auspices of publicity, no evil can continue,"[63] Bentham declaimed. John Stuart Mill was also an enemy of concealment, a position that led him to denounce even the secret ballot. A classical liberal justification of publicity in political life was given by Kant in *Perpetual Peace*: "All actions relating to the right of other human beings are wrong if their maxim is incompatible with publicity,"[64] asserted the German philosopher. Publicity is indeed the very test of the Kantian categorical imperative. The principle behind an action is a universal one only if it can be successfully defended in public to strangers. If not, the action is illegitimate. And since universality is for Kant a necessary condition of the categorical imperative, it follows that there can be no morality outside the public sphere. A contemporary philosopher, Jon Elster, has supplied another, a more modest justification of publicity: it can enhance the quality of debates by replacing "the language of interest by the language of reason."[65] Seyla Benhabib goes further:

The very procedure of articulating a view in public imposes a certain reflexivity on individual preferences and opinions. When presenting their point of view and position to others, individuals must support them by articulating good reasons in a public context to their co-deliberators. This process of articulating good reasons in public forces the individual to think of what would count as a good reason for all.[66]

The discursive constraint of the public sphere, the necessity to sound as if one desired the common good, will then, hopefully, create civility and even curb brute selfishness. Maybe, publicly pretending to be civic, simply by going through the motions of civicness, we will indeed ultimately become genuinely civic – not unlike Pascal's skeptic who defeats his own skepticism simply by kneeling and praying. Further, one could add, glory – however always fleeting – is not always without beneficial byproducts: after all, it usually cannot be attained without doing some good for others. It requires courage too: seeking glory, at the higher echelons of government as in other organizations, should urge one to take innovative actions that could eventually benefit everybody, albeit unintentionally.

But the public sphere is not unequivocally conducive to liberal democracy. A state without secrets will find it arduous to protect itself and its citizens. Even the legendary whistleblower Daniel Ellsberg held back the most sensitive documents among the Pentagon Papers, namely those regarding the diplomatic efforts to end the Vietnam War. Less obviously, publicity will hinder political actors when they attempt to strike bargains and achieve compromises.[67] The highfalutin' rhetoric of liberal democracy, with openness as its sacrosanct value, is incongruent with the hole-and-corner wheeling and dealing that no politics can do without. Political discourse – to the extent that it is public – is all about abstract categories and principles regarding the common good. Yet actual politics – that is, the struggle over decision-making power in society – to the extent that it has to involve protected interactions between particular beings, can scarcely skirt the interpersonal element. What is more, politics, even liberal politics, cannot be entirely innocent of the friend/foe opposition,[68] and one needs secrecy to talk with friends and plot against foes. In a state of conflict, particularism will win over universalism. Some political action – not all of it nugatory for the public – can only be successfully executed behind the scenes. Political actors say different things to different groups, and not always out of self-interest. Secrecy permits flexibility, which is vital for consensus building.[69] Here is how James

Madison defended the secrecy under which the Constitutional Convention of Philadelphia of 1787 operated:

> Had the members committed themselves publicly at first, they would have afterwards supposed consistency required them to maintain their ground, whereas by secret discussion no man felt himself obliged to retain his opinions any longer than he was satisfied of their propriety and truth, and was open to the force of argument. For the public may view hesitation and trial and error as signs of a lack of commitment, which may disadvantage those representatives truly taking part in the discussion, hence inhibiting them from adopting a genuinely deliberative posture.[70]

In a comparative analysis, Jon Elster found that the secrecy in the American case produced rational discourse, unlike the overheated discussions in the French *Assemblée Constituante* of 1789, which deliberated in public.[71] Although arguing in terms of the public good seems like a good thing, publicity invites inflexibility. A study has found that legislators are more likely to be respectful of one another and show empathy when they meet in closed sessions as opposed to open ones.[72] And publicity tends to elicit grandstanding from the ambitious. At the same time, exposed to the public gaze, particularly wary politicians may be discouraged from taking any positions altogether. Fear of retribution would have kept many framers from participating in the constitutional debates. It was similarly to avoid the adversities of publicity that James Madison, Alexander Hamilton, and John Jay published the *Federalist Papers* under the pseudonym Publius. Publicity may bring out the courageous individualist in some; it will not fail to make cowardly conformists of countless others. It was no other than John Stuart Mill, who, while on the whole praising the positive effects of publicity on deliberation, nevertheless, warned about "the yoke of public opinion" on public officials.[73] Further, the courageous ones in the public sphere are usually only courageous to the extent that they seek glory, and the good that can come from glory seekers is sporadic, spotty, and to be weighed against the collective costs of their recklessness. "The Court," wrote Pierre D'Ailly (and he could have replaced it with politics) "is the empire of ambition" – a public passion. Yet La Rochefoucauld was skeptical about ambition: "a mere mask for the private sentiment of jealousy," he called it.[74]

Some seek public glory. But being unremittingly visible – all the more if one is second-guessed at every turn – understandably renders many others apprehensive about taking initiatives. Full-blown transparency will then foster formulaic deportment among state officialdom.[75] Democratic legislators who vote in public – by acclamation, roll call, or show of hand – will be accountable to the citizenry. By the same token, they will also be vulnerable to pressure from special interest groups, who tend to be better monitors of what parliamentarians do.[76]

Bentham argued that the distrust that we should naturally experience with regard to our political leaders is a sound justification for the publicity of political life:

> Is it objected against the regime of publicity, that it is a system of distrust? This is true; and every good political institution is founded upon this base. Whom ought we to distrust, if not those to whom is committed great authority, with great temptations to abuse it?[77]

And there is evidence that in times stamped by widespread distrust of authority, the public – or more precisely, those who claim to speak in its name – is given to ballyhoo for more transparency.[78] But increasing transparency, especially with the passing of ever-expansive freedom of information laws,[79] has not improved trust in American political institutions.[80] On the contrary. According to a Gallup poll, in 1975, one year before passage of the Government in the Sunshine Act, which was very soon followed by other transparency measures, 40 percent of Americans had either "a great deal" or "quite a lot of confidence" in Congress. The figure has dropped steadily since then and was only 8 percent in 2015.

In fact, transparency contributes to the discrediting of political institutions by increasing politicians' vulnerability to scandal – instead of dispelling doubts about their probity.[81] The annual number of officials convicted for corruption in federal prosecutions has increased fivefold since the transparency laws of the late 1970s.[82] The proliferation of scandals will, consecutively, weaken public trust in government, which can harm the public itself since some trust in government is a public good in itself. It is not a fluke that the two state institutions that still enjoy higher prestige, the military and to a lesser extent the Supreme Court, both have had relative success in keeping their operations out of the public sphere. The deliberations of the latter are conducted in secret, and cameras are not allowed in the Court proceedings. The American military, naturally, enjoys still more protection from the public gaze. Contrariwise, the most transparent branch of government, Congress, is also the one that is the most despised.[83] In 2015, only 4 percent of Americans, according to the Gallup poll, expressed "a great deal confidence" in the legislative branch.

Some propose a "publicity principle:" the idea is that one should publicly – and democratically – decide "to what extent (if at all) publicity itself should be sacrificed."[84] This sounds good, but it takes a lot of courage to defend secrecy in public: it makes us look like we have something to hide, and even though we all do have something to hide and even though we all know that we all have something to hide, it is still hard to say things in public that implies to others that we may have something to hide.

Visible Citizenship

Visibility has ambivalent effects on citizenship as well. About them, the conventional perspective – curiously since its focus is citizenship – is either silent or too sanguine. It is a truism that circulation of information and access to public venues where we can criticize government officials are vital for liberal democratic governance. At the same time, intensified citizen activity in public is frequently both a symptom and an aggravating factor of dysfunctional polity. Citizens are often overpoliticized when professional political actors and institutions are not seen as meeting expectations – not all of them reasonable. Further, politicization can intensify polarization within society. Public registration of party affiliation, for instance, raises the level of partisanship.[85] And polarization, many argue, wears away liberal democracies.[86] Weimar is a limit case;[87] but commentators of contemporary American politics equally worry about polarization, despite the fact that the evidence shows that it is mostly an elite and not a mass phenomenon.[88] Even public discussion is not always very good: usually pivoting around fundamental values – and not facts, which, in any case, rarely speak for themselves – it is unlikely to change anyone's mind or narrow ideological differences.[89] On the contrary, publicity compels us to make our stances as logically coherent and morally pure as possible, which then renders compromise elusive. The more Americans discuss abortion in public, an issue in which there has been significant polarization in the recent decades,[90] the more they are split and unbending. By the same token, the more a group or an organization is able to sweep under the rug its fundamental ideological divisions on major issues, even pretend as if they don't exist, the more solidary it will remain, and the better its members will get along in everyday life – at least in the short run. This state of affairs would not be advantageous to everybody, or to the same level, and there is always a chance that such divisions would eventually become public one way or another. But an aversion to publicly talk about, even allude to such things will enable us to form unofficial, unacknowledged practical compromises – which are both publicly indefensible and existentially indispensable – in private. All this holds for smaller collectivities as well. The moment a variance in a couple is advertently or inadvertently made public, the more serious and insoluble it will loom to everybody, including to the disagreeing parties, and the more unyielding their positions will grow. Only already very tight, homogeneous groups whose members are highly interdependent can survive unscathed the publicity of their internal disagreements.

While the politicization of civil society through open discussion can breed polarization in liberal democracies, the mandatory publicness of civic activities will smother all dissent in repressive settings. It is the authoritarian governments that require their citizens to vote in public; it is, in part, because the public sphere can make the voter knuckle under social pressure that we have the secret ballot. The more public the political life of the citizen is – regardless of regime – the more the minorities will be justifiably fearful of the tyranny of the majorities and cowed into silence, acquiescence, or mendacity. Indeed, a world of highly visible civic activism is a world where not participating is equally visible – and scarcely tolerated. And in such a world, a lot of participation will involve falsifying in public what one really thinks in private. As the French Revolution radicalized, secret voting was supplanted by show of hand, which yielded more radical results.[91] The high visibility of citizenship went beyond the form of voting: quasi-mandatory participation in ceremonies, along with public confessions and purges in the Jacobin clubs, was an integral part of the Reign of Terror of 1793–4. The overall politicization of civil society, through the imperative of publicness, had as its official objective the cultivation of a republic of virtue; the upshot was chaos and fear.

An obvious illustration of the dangers of the public sphere is provided by the history of the secret ballot. Rules of secrecy in voting were introduced in the United States in the 1890s. Prior to that, voters either deposited a party ticket or called out candidate names.[92] A high premium was placed on openness in the nineteenth-century Western world, even by philosophers. In the words of John Stuart Mill,

> The moral sentiment of mankind, in all periods of tolerably enlightened morality, has condemned concealment, unless when required by some overpowering motive; and if it be one of the paramount objects of national education to foster courage and public spirit, it is high time now that people should be taught the duty of asserting and acting openly on their opinions. Disguise in all its forms is a badge of slavery.[93]

Secret ballot gave free rein to selfishness, according to many of its opponents. Also – but this has been completely forgotten today – limited suffrage provided an additional justification to viva voce voting. One voted on behalf of those who did not have this privilege, and it was only thanks to the visibility of the vote that the nonvoting masses could administer some control over the voting elite.[94] On the other hand, open voting was not bereft of problems. A serious one was corruption. As one historian puts it,

> The American polling place was thus a kind of sorcerer's workshop in which the minions of opposing parties turned money into whiskey and whiskey into votes. This alchemy transformed the great political interests of the nation, commanded by those with money, into the prevailing currency of the democratic masses. Whiskey, it seems, bought as many, and perhaps far more, votes than the planks in party platforms.[95]

And it was not just whiskey. Prices per vote varied in Connecticut from $2 to $20.[96] Secrecy made voting less corrupt; it also did away with a tangible incentive to vote.[97] A historical analysis of gubernatorial elections has found that the secret ballot lowered turnout by as much as 7 percent.[98]

The open ballot can generate radicalism too – especially if there is no market for votes. In the course of the French Revolution, the more voting became public, the more radical the votes were.[99] Caucuses, compared to primaries, in contemporary American politics tend to be more dominated by militants.[100] One explanation is the high costs of participating in the former, but the open ballot is part of the story as well, for caucuses are typically held in small communities. There is also evidence that those with a taste or habit for civic participation are more likely to vote in caucuses – but not necessarily due to political reasons, since these very people may be more vulnerable to social pressure or may be more inclined to distract themselves by voting, rather than by staying home and watching television.[101]

As a general rule, the smaller the number of voters, the more consequential the publicity of voting should be. In legislative committees, just as in university departments, leaders can easily sandbag others if voting is public. Pressures can originate from elsewhere too. The US Congress became more transparent in 1970 with the recording of individual votes in the Committee of the Whole. This raised the incentive to vote in Capitol Hill, which is usually considered good, but the consequences have not all been unequivocally salutary. Special interest groups follow Congress more intently than the regular citizen; the more voting in it is visible, the more they can exert influence or offer inducements for votes in their favor.[102]

Those who are vociferous for more civic involvement are frequently the ones who are the most apprehensive of the formal or informal privacy rights of collectivities such as families and organizations – but also, to a degree, ethnic and religious groups. These entities, to the extent that they are suspected of oppressing or exploiting their members or the rest of society, must then submit their internal standards and operations to public view so that we can ascertain that they don't run athwart of the universal tenets of justice. Yet families – and, in some measure, social groups and organizations – are not only functionally necessary but also provide much of the security and meaning that individuals seek in their lives. And to operate successfully, they require some level of sensory protection, some privacy, and some discrepancy between what they actually do and what they publicly say they do. They cannot maintain their integrity, be of value to their members in any other way. The more what happens in these collectivities is open to general sight, the weaker they are, and the more atomized and exposed we remain. Among them, the family is the most significant; it is no accident that all totalitarian systems, extreme ideologies, and "greedy institutions,"[103] hailing from the left or from the right, have always assaulted its privacy claims.

5

Content Regulation

Political power has a dialectical relationship with the public sphere. It is partially exercised in the open. At the same time, all sorts of political actors control – or rather attempt to control – the contents of public spaces. The public sphere is then not only the container of much of political activity; it is equally an object of state regulation. It is, in part, through politics that visibility norms change; in fact, a significant portion of social and political conflict is strictly about what can be seen and heard in public.

Censorship

The rhetoric of free speech in liberal democracies notwithstanding, all governance entails some censorship. Its pejorative connotations and the different forms it takes make censorship a concept hard to capture. Despite its technical legal definition, which is "prior restraint of unwanted expression by state officials,"[1] censorship often occurs subsequent to publication in the everyday use of the term. Usually, censorship evokes the legal restriction of expression that criticizes government, attacks religious values, or corrupts public morals. Governmental control of speech, however, greatly exceeds that – even in advanced liberal democracies. Consider the American laws regarding privacy, defamation, fraudulent advertising, broadcasting, blackmail, threats, offering bribes, suggestive material in the workplace, crying fire in a crowded theater, public advocacy of imminent lawless behavior, restriction of speech in airports, or testimony.[2] Consider when a judge institutes gag clauses on a settlement. Obviously, not all governmental control of speech looks like censorship – consider crying fire in a crowded theater. But a great deal does. Instances of many of these restrictions listed above are often decried as censorship by their targets. And much of censorship, again in the everyday sense of the term, is social, not legal. Consider the following situations: an editor demands that a manuscript submitter soften his attacks on a fellow scholar; a book is removed from a library for racist content; a company fires those who criticize its products in public. Again, at least some people will see one or more of these situations as censorship. So there is an intellectual benefit to not limit ourselves to the technical definition when we are dealing with censorship and think of it as an extreme form of speech regulation. Of course, censorship targets not only speech per se but also texts, images, and other semiotic matter. Still, so as to be in line with the legal discourse and everyday language, here I will be using the word "speech" to refer not only to utterances but also to texts – even though, as we saw, there are crucial differences between them. Similarly, "speaker" will denote both the one who talks and the one who writes.

Many social scientists, as well as activists, emphasize how language is integral – or at least connected to – power. What then make language powerful are typically the ideological content of speech and the status of the speaker. In other words, language matters to the extent that it performatively describes the world, and it can only do this to the extent that it is produced by the powerful.[3] Yet, as such, language can only reproduce the existing state of affairs, the powerful authoritatively defining and redefining the world, their hegemony forever perpetuated in the process.[4] This reduction of language to ideology or to the speaker also papers over the autonomous force of speech acts and prevents us from distinguishing situations when words matter from those when they don't. Speech is not always an act. What turn speech into an act are largely its consequences, which are often independent of the status or intention of the speaker – at times even from the content of what he says. And it is usually only when words are somehow consequential – or deemed as such – that they risk being restricted. The royal road, therefore, to study how language matters is to consider how, when, and why it is regulated – especially, but not only, through censorship.

Censorship establishes a strong inequality between those who regulate and those who are regulated. No wonder we associate it with illiberal regimes. Blasphemy – heresy when committed in public – was a crime in premodern times; it still is in many Muslim countries. The Elizabethan Star Chamber deemed scandalous and abrogated all public criticisms of state officials – the veracity of the utterances exacerbating their criminality.[5] By contrast, liberalism is more latitudinarian of critical, even blatantly belligerent discourse on authorities. On the other hand, all regimes restrict speech in one way or another.

A utilitarian – or more precisely consequentialist – logic is frequently proposed to explain, but equally to justify, speech restrictions by governments: certain images or words are harmful either to everybody, or to some audiences (like minors), or to specific individuals (as in defamatory language); and if their harms outstrip their collective benefits, they should and will be subject to regulation. Those who are the most systematic in their utilitarianism, such as Richard Posner, include in their calculus factors such as the immediacy, probability, and gravity of the harm, as well as the cost of its prohibition.[6]

The emphasis on harm is well placed. Some talk is indeed harmful. And accordingly, not all talk is cheap: insofar as talk has harms, regulation may make it so that they are borne on the speaker, in the form of punishment. But what needs to be underlined as well is that it is often through publicity that speech, quite independent of the status or intention of the speaker, takes on a "perlocutionary force"[7] – thereby becoming something that can harm. An example is crying fire in a crowded theater when there is no fire: a speech act that is prohibited by the government for its publicity cannot but generate an acute coordination problem with high collective costs (i.e. a panic).[8] Harm can at times even be quantified – as in libel cases where public falsehood about character is assigned monetary value. Simply telling someone's employer that someone does not pay his debt is allowed by American law; yet one cannot cry aloud the accusation on the street or post it on a window. To be actionable, the disclosure of the compromising facts needs to be a public one.[9] Consider also the difference in the common law treatment of slander and libel, of oral and written defamation. Slander is actionable only if the defamation attributes a criminal act, a loathsome disease, female unchastity, or professional unfitness to the defamed person – or if the latter can provide proof of special damages or monetary loss. Libel tort requires less: the injured party has to prove that he has incurred damages only when his identity is not evident.[10] An important reason for this differential treatment is that libel is usually more of a public act than slander; as a result, its effects are wider and longer lasting. The role of publicity cannot be overstated: this is why even though libel originally referred to words in print, it eventually ended up encompassing highly visible and permanent forms such as pictures, effigies, and movies.[11]

In all these cases, regulation is regarded as justifiable so that the government can reduce or eliminate the harms of publicity. These harms can be collective or individual, tangible or nonmaterial. Some political censorship, including the kind that seems indisputably illegitimate to us now, could be understandable – albeit not necessarily defensible – once we consider the collective harms of public speech. Take Renaissance England. In the sixteenth-century English common law, neither holding nor publishing dissident opinions, other than heresy, automatically constituted a punishable offense. Yet political language became actionable when it involved treason or *scandalum magnatum*: "inventing or spreading false news about the monarch, royal ministers, or chief peers."[12] Such a vehement response to critical discourse about high state officials may seem self-evident given the nonliberal nature of the Elizabethan epoch. But there is more. This was a time when all politics, due to the low institutionalization of the government, was interpersonal and took place in the secret chambers of the aristocratic courts.[13] Personal reputation, something that was more central than it is to us now, called for extra protection – especially given the paucity of means by which one could correct calumnies. There was yet another reason for draconian censorship. We moderns countenance public aspersions of our leaders more easily not only because we have become liberal and egalitarian, but also because political institutions are now more complex and autonomous from officeholders. Where a ruler, à la Louis XIV, could say "the State is I," where he was himself at once the fount and the expression of the entire political system, a defamatory attack on his person in public could significantly undermine governance and thereby hurt everybody – or at least many people. Such a defamation was never simply a personal issue, but the very destroyer of public peace, the dangers of which were deplored by all, even by the libelists who libeled their opponents by accusing them of libel. Such verbal aggression would create a great scandal. In the same vein, we find stricter defamation laws in societies where family reputation is a key concern: in such settings, a bad word about a member traduces the entire unit. It is not a fluke that in early modern English, "scandal" and "slander" were synonymous, meaning "malicious or defamatory gossip" or a "general comment injurious to reputation."[14] And a scandal, for us as well as for the Renaissance mentality, only comes about when a transgression, real or alleged, is publicized with significant audience interest, the publicity inflicting various harms on third parties. In all cultures, it is to prevent scandals and their disruptions that much of speech regulation is put in place.

In the contemporary world, in contrast with Elizabethan times, political rule is relatively more impersonal and institutionally complex; the people representing it are therefore relatively more dispensable, and malicious public talk about them is less scandalous. Modern political systems can afford scandals more because modern scandals are relatively less disruptive. Of course, given the high level of political scandal activity in the West, it is obvious that morality and personality play a role in political competition. Yet the effects of scandals are more checked. The Lewinsky affair, for instance, caused a full-blown constitutional crisis and culminated in the second impeachment of a president in US history. But the consequences of Clinton's ordeal on general governance were remarkably contained: the stock market – a reliable barometer of political stability – kept soaring.

A similar logic also applies to dissident speech, which is, on the whole, less tolerated – if not by law, then by society – during wartime.[15] Military conflict boosts deference to institutional authority and to its representatives because of a need to establish solidarity and morale that could come undone as a result of dissent. It goes without saying that such a need can be real, perceived, or strategically manufactured by those who would profit from it – and often it is unclear which is the case. Regardless, one of the upshots is a heightened accommodation of the privacy claims of governmental institutions – which further increases political leaders' ability to master their appearances. Consider how presidential privacy distended after September 11 in the United States during the "war on terror." The Harris poll recorded that trust in the White House climbed from 21 to 50 percent; shortly after, Bush fils signed an executive order that authorized former and sitting presidents to claim executive privilege over their own papers and those of a past administration. Using signing statements, he was equally able to constrict the inspectors general's reporting to Congress on the Iraq war.[16]

Content in the public sphere is usually calibrated to the specific audience expected to access it. The result is an inverse relationship between access restriction and content regulation: spaces that obtain extensive publicity (such as prime-time television) are, on the whole, relatively more regulated so as to protect vulnerable groups (such as children). Books tend to be less censored than television. One reason is that sexual images, being more visceral, are in more need of regulation than sexual words, even though in most public spaces euphemisms are preferred over more crude expressions of carnality. Another is that the audience of television is larger. But we should equally consider that while a book can generate significant publicity, it does this with less simultaneity. And readers can read the same words in private far away from one another. Very raunchy material can therefore be put in public through books without a stir. Consider the Bible, the most sacred book of the Western world, as well as its top bestseller. There seems to be almost no sexual transgression that is not reported in it, no matter how abominable, including incest and bestiality – and not always with a clear condemnation. The more privately one can access the public sphere, the less censorship we should expect.

Utilitarianism is useful yet limited in accounting for censorship. Judges, scholars, and laypeople commonly weigh the harms created by speech against the expressive rights of the speakers, but then we are already engaging in some kind of deontological morality and dealing with incommensurable things. Moreover, it is often hard to satisfactorily quantify or compare the harms – and benefits – of public speech, even less so of public images. In any case, the harm that is involved may be a symbolic or emotional offense – as in the impact of publicly denying the Holocaust, uttering obscenities on the radio, or insulting the official values of a society. The more effects are nonmaterial, the more uncertain they are, and the more disparities we should expect in the perceived consequences of publicity and in laws regarding speech. And where there is uncertainty, powerful actors can successfully define certain speech as harmful – possibly at the expense of the interests of others. Hence the variations in censorship and other forms of speech restrictions in liberal countries that remain enigmatic from a strictly harm perspective. Its public effects are the main reason why speech is regulated, but these are not assessed uniformly everywhere; further, political actors seek frequently to change these assessments. All this means that censorship will tend to also require cultural or political explanations, those having to do with the general norms of a given society or the power relations in it.

The United States has been long known within the Western world as the beacon of free speech. Again, I am referring here both to written and spoken discourse as well as to nonlinguistic expressions. Other democracies restrict speech more. Yet the First Amendment is mostly a twentieth-century matter: the Supreme Court started issuing major decisions defending free speech only in the 1930s – in part because of the activism of advocacy groups such as the American Civil Liberties Union (ACLU). And although the ACLU is now both extolled and excoriated as a free speech absolutist, the organization balked during that earlier period at defending sexually explicit literature.[17] It was in the course of the twentieth century that "clear and present danger" (which is the constitutional justification for speech restriction) came to be defined more and more restrictively, that legal accommodations for dissident speech – including the advocacy of the violent overthrow of the government unless "such advocacy is directed to inciting or producing imminent lawless action" – were enlarged.

There are significant legal variations among liberal democracies regarding free speech as well, which again often require a cultural or political explanation. The United States and the United Kingdom, both common law countries, treat libel disparately. Public figures can do little against libel in the first country: after the Supreme Court's 1964 decision *New York Times* v. *Sullivan*, plaintiffs have to prove malice on the part of defendants. While racist speech is placed under the aegis of law in the United States, it is not in Germany, obviously due to its Nazi past; those who gainsay publicly the Holocaust in France bear penalties; and according to the 1986 Public Order Act of the United Kingdom, it is a crime to "use threatening, abusive or insulting words or behavior with respect to color, race, nationality or ethnic or national origins." In contemporary America, unlike in many other countries, public figures – who include not just governmental officials but also those in whose conduct the citizens have "a legitimate and substantial interest" – are considered to have somehow relinquished most of their rights to privacy. But it is not always clear who is a public figure. Nor is it obvious when our interest in people who find themselves exposed in the media is legitimate or substantial.[18]

A standard situation where a state resorts to censorship is when someone publishes – or attempts to publish – its secrets. A certain degree of transparency of the legislative, judiciary, and executive operations is mandatory for legitimacy in constitutional regimes; nevertheless, there are significant disparities among liberal democracies regarding the extent to which state operations are in the public sphere. These reflect political and legal traditions, which are again impenetrable from a utilitarian perspective. States with deeper bureaucratic pasts, such as France, tend to be more opaque than their Anglo-Saxon counterparts. There are international differences regarding the classification of official documents: the British Official Secrets Act authorizes more secrecy than what is enjoyed by the US government.[19] To prevent a "prior restraint on speech," the *New York Times* was given imprimatur to publish the Pentagon Papers – the stolen Defense Department documents that disclosed classified and damning information about the conduct of the Vietnam War – in 1971.

Social norms as to what is publishable change from country to country as well. These also usually defy utilitarian logic. For example, the *New York Times* decided not to publish the cartoons of the French satirical magazine *Charlie Hebdo* after most of their staff were massacred in a terrorist attack in 2015. The editors of the US "newspaper of record" found the cartoons to be gratuitous insults to Islam and Muslims – not "news fit to print." Yet they evinced no compunction about streaming the last seconds of the dying police officer on the paper's webpage. The French media did the opposite – published the cartoons and refused to run the video on the basis that it would be indecent to publicly expose a man in his most vulnerable moment. Another – far more obvious – domain of national variation in what can be published is sexual content.

American legal scholars, following the 1942 Chaplinsky decision of the Supreme Court, differentiate between high-value and low-value speech. The former includes political, scientific, and artistic speech and is more legally protected – because of its supposed benefits for all. By contrast, commercial speech, threats, attempted bribes, perjury, criminal conspiracy, price fixing, criminal solicitation, unlicensed medical and legal advice, libel, obscenity, fighting words, verbal sexual harassment all have low value. Some of this speech is prohibited in all situations, whereas the legal status of others may vary by context: commercial advertising may be subject to regulation, for example, if it is false or misleading. While the distinction has been important in the development of First Amendment jurisprudence in the United States, the quality of speech does not always determine whether it will be legally allowed or not. At times, it is all about the space where a particular speech is produced. A lot of political speech that is lawful on the street may not be articulated on private university campuses. Sexual images that are suitable in a gallery would be fulsome in an advertisement on the street. The fora doctrine of the Supreme Court differentiates among public spaces with regard to speech: even though regulation is minimal in "traditional fora," such as streets, the US government can limit speech as it wishes in the concourse of an airport.

Nonutilitarian factors also have a bearing on legitimate content across different public spaces. It is possible to think of a national public sphere as a loose system of public spaces, with internal boundaries of varying clarity, and with a symbolic center and periphery. This topography is not independent of content regulation. The Confederate flag cannot be flown from public buildings in many states, but can be displayed in front of one's home. Profanity is typically banished from the center, which is crowded by spaces like Congress and high-status media. Peripheral, lower-status spaces are, however, not always laxly regulated: a parochial private college will have an easier time restricting "hate speech" than a leading state university. Similarly, libel laws that apply to private citizens are invalid for some politicians: the members of the legislature cannot be prosecuted for telling untruths on the floor of Congress.

Distinguished spaces like museums enjoy high symbolic legitimacy, but it is equally there that content that would be excessively scabrous for lower-status spaces, like subway walls, can be presented. Consider Mark Twain's reaction to a celebrated nude by Titian, *Venus of Urbino* (1538), showcasing a naked woman reclining on a bed staring at the viewer with her left hand clamped on her pudenda. He called the painting "the foulest, the vilest, the obscenest picture the world possesses." Twain added,

> Without any question it was painted for a bagnio and it was probably refused because it was a trifle too strong. In truth it is a trifle too strong for any place but a public art gallery.[20]

He was only half-ironic. Art has customarily been a privileged domain for the public representation of sexuality. Many images that could not be shown elsewhere can be shown in a gallery if the content is pegged as art. That said, the following rule of thumb still holds: when content is not regulated, the gaze usually is. The more apparently lubricious a painting, the purer and higher-minded the gaze of the spectator in the museum should be – or at least should seem that way – unless a distancing irony can be brought in to mollify the contradiction. Something similar goes on in nude beaches, too.

Censorship is not only a key mechanism through which public spaces and their audiences are regulated. It is equally a tool. Much of politics consists of conflicts over visibility: the public sphere is then not only the container but also the very object of political action. And it is frequently through political conflict that the visibility of something is defined authoritatively as a benefit or a harm. Contemporary culture wars in the United States involve not simply clashing views of the common good, but rather what should not appear or be heard in loci such as television and university campuses. Further, Americans routinely fight over what and how much individuals and organizations should be forced to make public: conservatives are skeptical of the privacy rights of persons, and liberals of those of groups and organizations.[21] Many conservatives and feminists denounce pornography, whereas liberals condemn the omnipresence of graphic violence and discriminatory language in the American public sphere. Most crusaders in civil society as well as in institutional politics push for censorship, naturally without owning up to it, in one public space or another – at times with resounding victories.

Sexual censorship tends to be associated with puritanism. But puritanism is not simply an intolerance of nonprocreative sex: it tends to target the publicity of transgressions, rather than the transgressions themselves. A central characteristic of puritanism is that it treats sexuality, and a fortiori sexual transgression, as taboo. Taboo is a dangerous, polluting entity – it can be an object, idea, word, or person – that needs to be avoided.[22] The universe of taboo comprises the sacred along with the profane:[23] the name of God is, for example, unspeakable for Jews. Nevertheless, social scientists have not been sufficiently alert to a signal difference between taboos and other social prohibitions: a single sensory encounter with the visual or verbal representation of a taboo can be hazardous. Equally important, taboo prohibitions can be violated in private. Nudity, acceptable in private, is a taboo in public. The same applies to profanity, albeit to a lesser extent. Brahmins and untouchables can often safely eat together – thereby breaching the pollution norms of the Indian caste system – as long as they do so in a nonpublic setting.[24] Malinowski reported that Trobrianders could brook even incest as long as it was not openly denounced.[25] Taboo is, therefore, intrinsically linked to publicity. It, is after all, the most vital functions routinely discharged in private, such as defecation, that are regulated by the strongest taboos, which severely restrict their actual as well as representational publicization. And their contravention is frequently shameful for audiences too.

Another characteristic of taboo is that, inasmuch as the violation is public, the intention of the violator becomes immaterial. Take, for instance, "nigger," a contemporary taboo word, which demeans African Americans and incites our anti-racist sensibilities. The word, many believe, pollutes public life with such virulence that similar sounding but etymologically or semantically unrelated words such as "niggardly" have come to share its ignominious fate. Unless one is black, one cannot utter the word in public, even in an ironic fashion or to condemn its racist use. Of course, the term is rife in rap music, the underlying idea being that as long as the speaker and the addressee are both black, the parties will know that nothing racist is meant. But "nigger" can pose a moral peril for anybody. Many African Americans who would tolerate the word in private conversations among themselves are offended when one of them utters it in public. And the word is definitely a taboo when it is enunciated in front of whites – that is, in a bigger, more heterogeneous public setting. Randall Kennedy, an African American law professor, who is also the author of a book called *Nigger: The Strange Career of a Troublesome Word*,[26] was asked not to say the word in a radio show while discussing his work. He referred to it as the "n-word." Writing it, with scare quotes, is obviously easier.

As we saw in the sad story of Oscar Wilde, a perfect example of taboo is homosexuality in nineteenth-century England. Precisely because it was so terrible, sodomy was an "unmentionable" crime. Sir William Blackstone, the authoritative reference of Victorian legal ratiocination, called buggery "a crime not to fit to be named" in his *Commentaries on the Laws of England*.[27] Precisely because it was a taboo, the laws against homosexuality were underenforced.[28] The officials were loath to act. The majority of offenses were brought to court by private individuals, a huge majority of whom hailed from the lower classes, who were less mindful of the taboo.[29] And many – according to some researchers, most – of the offenses were committed against minors, obviously something less easy to overlook.[30] Officers who apprehended homosexuals could themselves be tainted; barristers mocked them and juries speculated darkly as to how the evidence must have been obtained.[31] Very often, the arresting officer and not the suspect – especially if the latter had high status – had to prove his probity. It was only in the twentieth century, when homosexuality became less of a taboo but remained a crime, that cops would be more comfortable in having recourse to entrapment as an enforcement technique.

Arrests in Victorian England resulted overwhelmingly from activities in public spaces such as streets, parks, theaters, and urinals. And the police acted only when people were visible: parks were not monitored at nighttime.[32] Attorneys successfully pleaded for acquittal in incidents that took place in private. In the words of one, "Since publicity constituted the very essence of this offence at common law, it should be proved... that the parties had committed those acts in a public place, such that the natural consequence would be that they would be seen by others."[33] When a male brothel frequented by aristocrats was discovered on Cleveland Street in 1889, the lord chancellor urged inaction so as to avoid "very wide publicity."[34] Only two peripheral figures were detained; their sentences were light. Homosexuality involving many teachers and students in prestigious single-sex public schools such as Eton was also, while an open secret, similarly hushed up.[35] The consensus was that the more homosexuality and lesbianism were prosecuted, the more they would become familiar. In effect, lesbianism was never criminalized in England precisely so that innocent women would not learn about the abhorrent act.[36] Judges prohibited the presence of young people in homosexuality trials.[37] Victorians were draconian against homosexuality only when the transgression was committed in public or when the crime had already become public.[38] We encounter the same logic in many others settings. For instance, in Ancien Régime France, sodomites – as well as those suspected of bestiality – were rarely pursued by law.[39]

Comstockery, the American version of Victorian puritanism, is another example.[40] The sensationalistic penny press and underground pornographic market provided enormous salacious content in the antebellum United States. Prostitution grew visible with the urbanization of the post–Civil War era. Social reform groups started to insist on frank discussions of sex for medical purposes. The Comstock Act of 1873 was a reaction to these developments that introduced more and more sex into the American public sphere. It was largely the brainchild of Anthony Comstock, who, with the help of his rich sponsors in the YMCA, had founded the New York Society for the Suppression of Vice in 1872. The act not only prohibited the distribution of "obscene" materials by mail – obscenity here mostly referring to contraceptive and abortive devices and texts about them – but also ushered in widespread, state-enforced censorship of all sexual content. Obscenity as a legal category had not existed in the United States before passage of the act.[41] Comstock, albeit a private citizen, was authorized by Congress to enforce the obscenity statutes as a special agent of the post office. His crusade was launched at a time when the American elite wanted to differentiate itself from the masses, and one way to do that was practicing, and imposing, reserve about sexual matters – even though the excesses of Comstockery, especially in the artistic domain, were ridiculed by many in the upper crust.[42]

The New York anti-vice society, like many others in the country, did not go after prostitution but targeted obscenity, with a view to protect children from the corrupting influences of the publicized sexuality.[43] Willoughby Cyrus Waterman, in one of the earliest sociological treatments of prostitution, pointed out that the proverbial oldest profession was not a crime in common law.[44] About early twentieth-century New York, he wrote that statutes targeted prostitution only when it became "an annoyance to the passerby." The problem was not so much immoral behavior as its visibility.

Nowhere is this as evident as in the Beecher-Tilton affair of 1872.[45] Henry Ward Beecher, a high-flying Brooklyn pastor as well as an inveterate womanizer, was having an affair with Elizabeth Tilton, the wife of Charles Tilton, the editor of a well-known liberal newspaper. The husband finally got wind of the affair – as many had already in the community – yet all maintained silence to avoid a scandal until Victoria Woodhull wrote about it in her weekly magazine. The journalist did not denounce the dalliance; on the contrary, she claimed to be defending the legitimacy of free love. Respectable society, much less open-minded and much more prudish, however, unanimously condemned Woodhull for the exposé. Comstock arranged her to be detained on obscenity charges; the journalist spent a month in Ludlow Street Jail. It was in the aftermath of the Beecher-Tilton affair that the Comstock Act was passed.

Censorship undertaken by the state is an extreme form of public sphere regulation. We witness milder forms – either by laws or nonlegal norms – in some liberal countries too. Things to be regulated vary greatly. Consider, for instance, religion, which has been a redoubtable agent of censorship in history. But its visibility, often deemed as divisive or dangerous, has also been regulated in secular regimes. Secularism tends to be presented as the separation of state and church. This is somewhat misleading. Separation is always a matter of degree. A number of Western countries, which we would not hesitate to call secular – such as Italy, England, Finland, Greece, Denmark, and Spain – have established state religions. In many more, churches are funded by the government.[46] Except for France, optional or obligatory religious instruction in public schools is provided across Europe, where we see openly Christian political parties as well. And even France, the apotheosis of militant secularism, allows for the public funding of private schools, most of which are Catholic. So rather than a strict, clear-cut separation between state and religion, secularism entails the control of the latter by the former. Take the *Conseil français du culte musulman*, an entity under the authority of the French Ministry of Interior, which is responsible for the construction of mosques, training of imams, and certification of halal meat.

An integral part of the secular control of religion touches on the visibility of things religious. It is an obviously limited control. European cities are awash with churches. Nevertheless, if religious speech and symbols are permissible in some public spaces, they are not in others. French law, for instance, bans ostensible religious symbols from public high schools. Moreover, although it is not illegal, political actors who make overtly and particularistic references to religion can be pooh-poohed by mainstream opinion in many countries. In the same spirit, anti-Islam attitudes in Europe are motivated by and centered on Islam's visibility in public spaces. One reason why Islam looms as more of a menace for Europeans than for Americans is that it is more visible in the Old World. In most of the United States, the physical public spaces being sprawling and typically empty, a Muslim is someone whom one sees rarely on the street. In Europe, by contrast, dense urban life imparts a significantly higher visibility to Muslims, already conspicuous as they are dressed not only differently from the majority but also in assertive observance of the precepts of their religion. European Christianity is a presence mostly through beautiful but sparsely attended, indeed deserted, churches. By contrast, Islam generates much more publicity in Europe by dint of new mosques springing up in cities; clothes and bodily markers, such as the veil and the beard, that openly – to some provocatively – identify Muslims as Muslims; and in-your-face rituals like collective praying on the streets. Christianity is visible in Europe through the relics of an age gone by; Islam, by mosques that are no longer backyard and hidden but streetfront and imposing, as well as through vibrant public practices. Their spectacular visibility is partly why the height of minarets – along with the audibility of the *azan* (the public call to prayer) – has been at the forefront in recent European debates on Islam, transforming, for many, the mosque into a public political statement. A Swiss referendum against minarets in 2009 showed that 57.5 percent of the population was in favor of their ban.

Intolerance for the visibility of the religion of the other is not a Western vagary. Consider how Islam has historically treated the *dhimmis*, protected but second-class Jews and Christians living in the Muslim lands. Here are some of the conditions of the Umar Pact, named after the second successor to the prophet Mohammed, many of which are strictly about visibility:

The dhimmis shall wear the ghiyar, a distinctive sign ... yellow for Jews, blue for Christians.

They shall not build any house higher than those of the Moslems

They shall not ring their bells nor read their books aloud, nor what they tell of Ezra and the Messiah Jesus.

They shall not drink wine in public; nor display their crosses or swine.

They shall bury their dead in silence and not allow their lamentations or sounds of mourning to be heard.[47]

Contemporary controversies about the Islamic veil, all too obviously, also have to do with visibility. Ironically, the more Muslim women cover themselves in public, the more Islam becomes visible to larger society: it is often difference that creates salience. Simple visibility – as distinct from speech – is a central object of many political controversies in the public sphere. A recent American example is the brouhaha around the Confederate flag.

Expansion

Much of political action revolves around expanding or restricting the contents of the public sphere. Take the sexual politics of the last fifty years in the United States. Since the seventies, a passel of actors – including feminists, LGBT activists, avant-garde artists, along with mainstream politicians – have been politicizing sexual matters. But sex can only be fully politicized to the extent that it is visible through some form of representation – actual sexual activity, despite liberalization and easy access to pornography, remains for the most part private. Sexual politics has therefore taken the form of attacks on the conventions that had formerly kept sexuality out of public view. At the forefront of the struggle, feminists placed the public expression of sexuality at the heart of women's liberation. Their watchword "personal is political" aimed to neuter the feelings of shame shrouding sexuality so that women could openly discuss, and thereby own, their biology. Privacy norms have been denounced in the same spirit for shielding marital rape and sexual harassment.

The underlying feminist argument for sexual politics was that since a specific man's domination over a specific woman in the private sphere simply instantiated men's domination over women, and thus had to be considered as a categorical and social issue, interpersonal and domestic life could claim no exemption from public scrutiny.[48] An extension of this logic can be found in the sexual harassment laws that retrenched the privacy protections of erotic encounters. For example, with the Molinari Amendment to the 1994 Violence against Women Act, the lawyers of plaintiffs in sexual harassment cases obtained the right to interrogate defendants about their history of sexual relations – regardless of the absence of evidence pointing to their nonconsensual nature – in the workplace. All sexual activity between employees, especially questionable in the case of rank differentials, needs to be made public so that courts can decide whether a crime has occurred. The Molinari Amendment was signed into law by Bill Clinton, who, ironically, became its most notable victim as he was dragooned in 1998 to testify about a consensual office affair, his prevarication instigating his impeachment by Congress.

Gay rights groups further sexualized the public sphere. Take the practice of coming out, the liberating act par excellence for gays, as well as something that aims to normalize and even celebrate homosexuality. Such publicization can be waged aggressively too – as in the outing of homosexual politicians who do not endorse gay marriage.[49] However oppositional it may seem, sexual politics has not only been deployed by anti-establishment forces. Since the 1970s, countless politicians have been taking advantage of the atrophy of modesty in American society by publicizing elements of their private lives – including sexual ones – to establish a personal rapport with the masses or to assert moral superiority over rivals. Some activists, as well as television hosts, in America believe that publicized sexuality has an emancipatory dimension. There are even those who stress its therapeutic effects: according to certain "abuse advocates," sexually traumatic events in our past will never cease debilitating us unless we confront them in a public context.[50]

Nonpolitical actors in civil society can push expansion of content as well. A typical way to do it is through scandal. Publicizing sexuality can generate negative reactions, even scandal; but scandals, when repeated with impunity, will end up normalizing what was previously deemed transgressive. The stage will be set for publicizing something still more outré. An obvious example comes from art.[51] Nudity has always had a place in Western art because it could not be avoided in the treatment of many subjects in Christian iconography. Yet artists did not have carte blanche; the naked human body, implicitly or explicitly, posed a moral peril. One way to deal with this problem was to represent bodies not as objects of lust but as perfect figures incarnating ideals.[52] Another was to distance sensuality. Placed as they were in an imagined, alien Orient, the sultry odalisques of Ingres were fine for the artistic establishment as institutionalized in the French Academy. It was when nudes finally got more realistic in the nineteenth century – such as Courbet's earthy models or Manet's *Olympia*, the first painting since the Renaissance in which a naked woman was placed in a seedy setting – that they started to create genuine scandals. Yet academic traditionalism lost in the end. Whores became a favorite topic among painters; nudes grew rawer, raunchier. The gamut of sexual experience that art represented widened exponentially. Content got ever more indecent in the course of the twentieth century as artists bested one another in their public contempt for nonaesthetic standards set by moralizing outsiders. Masturbation, homoeroticism, fetishism, sadism, and even prepubescent sexuality, as in the work of Balthus, came to be fit for display.[53]

But content expansion in the public sphere is not a simple question of will. We cannot change the visibility norms by fiat; not all scandals of provocation work. General sentiments regarding what cannot be made public should not be overwhelmingly unanimous. There should be some – real or anticipated – positive responsiveness. Activist content expansion is therefore usually enabled by an attitudinal change in society. And this change is, in part, the product of organizational and cultural transformations. In other words, we need to consider not only the supply but also the demand side in accounting for the content expansion in the public sphere.

We can observe these forces at work again in the rise of sexual politics. Its victories were made possible by large-scale developments that increased public toleration – indeed demand – for publicized sexuality. An increase in the number of young people, rising female participation in the labor force, and the ideology of expressive individualism coincided in the 1960s to blunt traditional sexual morality. Only less than a quarter of Americans approved of premarital sex in the late 1950s; by the late 1970s, this was the percentage of those who found such activity to be wrong. Marriage age climbed; fertility rates tumbled. Divorce and cohabitation rates skyrocketed from the 1960s onward, undermining marriage as the normal living arrangement in society. A far-reaching, albeit not always recognized, upshot of the growing autonomy of sexual activity from the nuclear unit, especially with surging divorce and premarital sex rates, was that demand for sexual content in the media hiked.[54] Sexual liberalization also dented the modesty and reticence norms which had hitherto kept high- and middle-status media with high publicity on the whole innocent of explicit material. Sexual politics would radicalize the carnality of the American public sphere in the 1970s, but the sexualization process had already come a long way by then.

The country used to be much more reticent before the 1960s. As fantastic as it sounds today, as late as 1962 one could not say "venereal disease" on national television.[55] Until the early 1960s, Hollywood was muzzled by the 1934 production code, which rendered sexual content verboten. Film noir could well be suggestive; mainstream American cinema, on the whole, churned out sexless pictures in which not even married couples shared beds. The legitimation of the public representation of sexuality in literature was contingent on artistic intent, and a book with purple language like *Tropic of Cancer* could not be published until 1961. Neither the judges nor the ACLU regarded literary depictions of sex as a First Amendment issue until the fifties.[56] Soft-porn magazines such as *Playboy* took strides in publicizing sex. Still, many states had stiff obscenity laws, and respectable media kept their high-mindedness and adhered to the reigning modesty norms after World War II.

It was in the course of the 1960s that sexual material started to flood the American media. The mainstream press jettisoned circumlocution in sex talk, and popular music was suddenly full of explicit lyrics. A rarity in the twentieth century before the Chappaquiddick affair of 1969,[57] sex scandals regarding political figures came to glut the front pages of newspapers. Nudity now a common staple in Hollywood, commercials turned ever gamier; television followed suit.[58] American law gave the go-ahead to the sexualization of the public sphere. From its *Ulysses* decision in 1933, the Supreme Court had been contracting the scope of obscenity. As the Warren Court asserted the appositeness of sex for general consumption, what was erstwhile restricted to fringe, infra dignitatem precincts (underground pornography, red-light districts, etc.) now diffused into the center of the American public sphere. Frontiers of indecency were pushed back. It was the attenuation of modesty and reticence, caused partially by the social and cultural forces discussed earlier, that enabled the unfettered politicization of sexual matters in the public sphere during the 1970s. Crimes like rape could only become a public concern in a society that permitted people to talk about sex viva voce. Sexual content had to have already made forcible forays into public spaces, as a result of changing social attitudes, before it could be successfully politicized by moral entrepreneurs. But, of course, politicization quickened the erosion of modesty and reticence. The sexualization of the American public sphere was further hastened by technological innovations in the following decades that decreased publicization costs and facilitated access.

Contraction

Political actors, both when they are engaging in political action and when they are attempting to change the contents of public sphere, are themselves constrained by what audiences are willing and able to look at. Particularly potent in puritanical cultures, visibility norms mold political activity too. Victorian modesty trammeled moral crusades: the antiprostitution campaign that the irrepressible journalist William Thomas Stead embarked on in *Pall Mall Gazette* was lambasted by the London establishment as shameless, as terrible as what he was going after.[59] Victorians did not deny or repress carnal pleasure as long as it was sought within the confines of the nuclear family. They condoned underground pornography,[60] but not its wide-scale publicity.[61] Both Shakespeare and the Bible had to be expurgated of passages unsuitable for children, elite newspapers were very discrete about carnal matters, legal officials underenforced the sex laws to forefend scandals, and adultery scarcely figured in the English novel.[62] The publicized sexuality of specific individuals was particularly anathema. After the Divorce Act of 1857, divorce cases by upper-class couples, often involving adultery, enjoyed blow-by-blow narration in the pages of the *Divorce Court Reporter* and the *Illustrated Police Reporter*. Yet these newspapers targeted lower-class audiences; upright Victorians were – at least publicly – uncomfortable with such stories.[63]

Visibility norms in society can even constrain states, which cannot change or establish them as they please. An important – but not the sole – reason for the disappearance of public executions in modern Europe was the normative change toward the publicity of suffering.[64] Punishment, as we saw, has from time immemorial been linked to publicity. Christians were thrown to the lions in the Roman Coliseum; the Aztecs ripped the hearts out of their war prisoners at the summit of their temple pyramids; hapless heretics ended up being burned alive at the auto-da-fé of the Inquisition. In the Muslim world, capital punishment not only still exists but involves publicity as well. In Saudi Arabia people are executed in public; in Iran, while death penalties are administered within prison walls, the photos of the executions are distributed. Terrorist groups in the Middle East disseminate the videos of the beheadings of their hostages through the internet.

Until well into the modern era publicity was the warp and woof of most punishment. In Europe, executions in the sixteenth and early seventeenth centuries were public. Indeed, they were festivals: taking a day off, people came with their kids and sweethearts. And bearing out Nietzsche's dictum, "no festival without cruelty,"[65] the executions frequently featured disfigurement and mutilation. These violent spectacles seem wicked to us; yet many Europeans approved of long, torturous, public death for it gave the condemned an opportunity to repent and save his immortal soul as he was parting from his worldly body. Guillotine, some would protest later, killed too fast.

Less serious crimes deserved visibility as well; in fact, most public punishment was not capital at all. Hog theft earned the thief in colonial New England twenty-five lashes at the public whipping post; for the second offense, one was pilloried for two hours with both ears nailed.[66] Prostitutes were stripped naked and birched through the streets with whips and brushes.[67] More visible punishments included branding and letter-wearing, whose effects were more permanent. Letter-wearing à la Hawthorne was not exclusively for adultery: those accused of incest were ordered "to stand or sit upon a high stool" in public "with a paper upon each of their heads with their crime written in capital letters."[68] Burglars were branded or had their ear chopped off. The fate of rapists was frequently the iron collar. Mutilation was common in all premodern societies, especially for poor criminals who could not pay fines – this making the blind, the defaced, the branded, and the scarred, with their interminable suffering, an unexceptional urban sight. It is reported that wherever one turned there were maimed beggars in Constantinople during Byzantine rule.[69] Punishment in Europe was also often accompanied by a confession or a prayer by the convict, creating a chance for spiritual renewal for all attending.

In the course of modernity, however, public punishments, from executions to the pillory, gradually petered out. More and more, they were perceived as antithetical to a dignity that even the most horrific criminals had a right to. In any case, publicity could function as an effective accretion to punishment in earlier societies, in part, because many people lived in small communities where everyone knew everyone. But with urbanization the world grew increasingly anonymous. Sloughing off its chilling trappings, punishment eventually vanished out of sight. This was a slow process, varying in speed from country to country.[70] In England, mutilation, the staple of public executions under the Tudors, fell out of fashion in the seventeenth century. Blinding and cutting off limbs were becoming things of the past. All across Europe, scaffolds came to be erected in a way so that they would be unreachable by the spectators. Wooden ones, much less permanent, replaced stone ones. Public torture was abolished as the eighteenth century advanced; the corpses of capitally punished criminals were no longer exposed. Brands became less discernible, applied on the back of convicts – before they disappeared. Public hangings survived until the mid-1800s, but they were no longer preceded by a procession to the gallows. Even nonlethal corporal punishment moved into private quarters during the nineteenth century.[71] Physical publicity gave way to virtual publicity: in the United States, indoor executions were grisly detailed in the press, and images of lynchings, however extralegal, decked postcards.

Regardless of international variations, the general process has been that violence in the Western public sphere gradually shifted from physical public spaces to virtual ones to become something milder and formalized (as in sports) or something that could only be represented (as in the press, literature, and movies).[72] How to make sense of such a momentous transformation? Authorities in early modern Europe had resorted to publicity as they punished to deter and to signal their might to third parties. But they could only do so only as long as people did not mind seeing such bloody spectacles. Ultimately, however, these events came to be deemed horrendous, unfit for sight. This attitudinal shift was part of a more profound civilizing process, documented by Norbert Elias[73] and Philippe Ariès,[74] a master transformation within Western modernization that involved the gradual elimination of death, violence, and suffering from the public sphere – naturally in their physical actuality and not in their virtual representations, which only proliferated with the rise of mass media.

Europeans used to be much less squeamish than us.[75] From simple peasants to Marie de Medici, women gave birth publicly, the sight and sound of their unmitigated pain a habitual occurrence of everyday life, the event frequently ending with the loss of the mother or the child. Death – also not dampened by myriad medications that we cannot do without – was highly visible as well: Louis XIV as well as the regular commoner passed away in the open, not infrequently in piercing pain. One could freely enter a dying man's bedchamber in medieval Europe: as late as the early nineteenth century, passers-by would form a procession and accompany the priest bearing the last sacrament into the sickroom.[76] Death, even the death of common people, was a ceremony. One often died only after making a public confession; many mouthed reproaches at those who had maltreated them.[77] The dead did not exit public life after death either. Surrounded by shops and market stalls, churchyards were not yet the saturnine sites they eventually would turn into. Cemeteries, usually located in city centers, incorporated ossuaries where the skulls and limbs of the interred were displayed as ornaments.[78] Corpses of criminals were exposed along interurban routes as well as in public anatomy lessons. It is not surprising that in such a culture a great deal of killing could take place in open view without much ado. Animals were killed ceremoniously too. And not just for food: in eighteenth-century France, cats were burned just for fun in the summertime with the royals and the hoi polloi in full attendance.[79] Yet with modernity the bourgeoisie waxed fussier. Cemeteries migrated to the outskirts of cities after the mid-eighteenth century; death became a private event, a taboo even. Public anatomy lessons fell out of fashion. What Ariès called "the promiscuity between the living and the dead" gradually ceased to be.[80]

There are several interconnected reasons for the decline first of suffering and then of killing in public. With modernization, governments monopolized violence, which increasingly became a professional activity. Fewer people could, or had to, have recourse to violence in their everyday lives. Societies were disarmed with the rise of Leviathans with their mighty militaries and, later, swelling police forces.

Modernization required specialization in all forms of violence: fewer people butchered their livestock. States, needful of healthy soldiers, took measures to cleanse physical spaces of death and sickness. With improvements in medicine, people died more and more in hospitals, their ailing bodies and agonized voices no longer seen and heard in public. As violence and suffering progressively migrated out of the physical public sphere, habituation to them weakened. Literary, journalistic, and artistic representations took their place.

The first groups that were affected by – and in part drove – this transformation were members of the elite, even though the masses would ultimately ape them. According to Elias, the higher classes underwent a civilizing process that consisted of an ever-plunging threshold of shame and disgust regarding violence, sexuality, and biological functions.[81] Standards of civility took root in the aristocratic and middle classes in early modernity. Modesty and reticence are, on the whole, correlated with hierarchy and formality. By contrast, egalitarianism and intimacy require and are fortified by candidness, if not crassness: think of interactions among privates in military barracks or between an old couple. But the nascent norms of civility, emerging during the changes mentioned earlier, gradually spread from the higher classes to the populace. Finally, killing in the open disappeared not only because the public would not tolerate it anymore but also because the governments had less of a need for it: the successful centralization of political authority rendered violent shows of power to internal contenders less necessary. Mandeville, among others, fretted that executions frequently slipped into pandemonium. And rather than deterring, they gave notoriety to criminals, who were sometimes cheered on by the crowds.[82]

All this was undergirded and motivated by an even more general, *longue durée* sea change. In addition to the naturalness with which death and suffering were in constant open view, the medieval world was one that strongly favored physical publicity. Well-nigh all life was to be displayed, the more ostentatiously the better. Huizinga describes it most vividly:

Then, again, all things in life were of a proud or cruel publicity. Lepers sounded their rattles and went about in processions, beggars exhibited their deformity and their misery in churches. Every order and estate, every rank and profession, was distinguished by its costume. The great lords never moved about without a glorious display of arms and liveries, exciting fear and envy. Executions and other public acts of justice, hawking, marriages and funerals, were all announced by cries and processions, songs and music.[83]

Christianity – especially Catholicism, a much more visual religion than Protestantism – dominated public life with all its rituals and symbols. Passion plays were so popular in the fourteenth and fifteenth centuries that shops were closed during performances. Lewis Mumford is correct: "Whatever the practical needs of the medieval town, it was above all things, in its busy turbulent life, a stage for the ceremonies of the Church."[84] But secular municipal ceremonies, featuring a farrago of professional and other groups, all with their distinctive garments, were a vital part of urban life as well.

And such events, just like public executions, posed disorder hazards for the centralizing political authorities of early modernity. Jean Bodin cautioned, "Every procession of all the ranks and all the professions carries the risk of conflicts of priority and the possibility of popular revolts." So he urged, "Let us not overdo...ceremonies of this kind."[85] More important is the fact that with modernity emerged a valorization of the private sphere – notably as the nuclear family rose in the eighteenth and nineteenth centuries as an autonomous financial and emotional unit that had to be sheltered from public view and interference. Ariès famously claimed, "A sociability centered on the family or even the individual" supplanted "the anonymous social life of the street, castle court, square, or village."[86] The French historian exaggerated. Public life in modern times did not disappear at all. In fact, the street got more anonymous, and in a way more public, while the home became more and more protected and exclusive to close kin. The boundary between the home and the street thickened. The aristocratic household lacked much of the physical privacy that we are used to now: all sorts of people went in and out of most of its rooms with great ease. This was a time when a town crowd would put a couple into their matrimonial bed on the night of their wedding, only to come back to greet them the following morning.[87] By the same token, a sizable portion of medieval public life, especially in small towns, was lived among acquaintances instead of among perfect strangers in an anonymous fashion – as it is mostly the case in modern cities.

This world where so much took place in public was one of outbursts and abandons of emotions. With the Renaissance in Europe, however, the middle and upper classes turned discreet. Silent reading at home replaced reading out aloud,[88] just as written culture supplanted oral medieval literature.[89] The obscene and scatological tenor of the baroque novel – exemplified in Rabelais – was superseded by a more restrained, more sublimated mentality. Manners grew strict and uniform. Civility manuals, based on the bestseller of Erasmus, came to provide the firmament of all education. Until the nineteenth century, tears were permissible in public; the cultural elite, particularly, could thereby freely express and communicate its "privileged sensibility."[90] But crying in front of everyone looked affected, excessive later on. The shame threshold for biological activities declined throughout modernity. Sixteenth-century etiquette books exhorted aristocrats not to urinate or defecate in the open; the proscription would eventually spread to all society. Even though urine had long served as a bleaching agent and human feces had provided free manure, the imperative of banishing foul odors from the Western public sphere in the nineteenth century put an end to their practical use.[91]

6

Visibility in Society

People usually don't want to frequent restaurants where there is no one dining – even if they already know that the food is good – because the sensory presence of others is an integral part of eating out. Same logic with going out for a stroll: we tend to seek streets with people. But we don't want to be on the street with just any pedestrian and we don't want to be in a restaurant with just any patron. An intolerant concern about who and what can appear in public is a general matter, not an exclusively political one. Restaurants refuse service to those with improper garb.[1] Patrons themselves choose restaurants based on the appearances of other patrons. Intolerance here has little to do with a reluctance to interact with undesirables: we rarely interact with strangers in restaurants, yet we do care about what kind of people will be visible to us while we eat. Even though people don't necessarily prefer homogeneity in this regard – in fact some variety is typically preferred – profiling activity in the public sphere is at the root of much of everyday discrimination and can wreak havoc on the members of subordinate groups.

Groups

As it is the case with political actors, the visibility of groups – and of social categories – has complex effects on their life chances. Domination is frequently a matter of controlling and limiting visibility. A paradigmatic case is that of women, whose visibility, often regarded as perilous to feminine virtue, has in all times and places been regulated more than that of men. Until the nineteenth century European women could not appear on stage. Simply attending a spectacle was problematic: a woman by herself could watch a show in the theater only from a box. She needed a male escort if she wanted to sit elsewhere – that is, in a place that afforded more visibility – lest her morals be questioned. Rousseau noted approvingly that in Ancient Greece women were seated at the theater in a high gallery called the *cercis*, a place "convenient neither for seeing nor for being seen."[2] None other than Bentham, a paladin of publicity who insisted that all parliamentary deliberations be open to general scrutiny, barred women from the audience.

Such restrictions could even be more draconian. The women of Athens were largely confined to indoors and had to wear ankle-length tunics on the street. Women are still largely sequestered in parts of the Middle East to the private sphere, not only in their speech but also in their simple physical appearance. The institution of *purdah* (meaning "curtain" in Persian and referring in general to "concealment of women from men") excludes them from myriad activities in public – all the more if these come with high visibility. When strict *purdah* is not observed, women must put on some kind of a veil such as a burkha (a long garment that covers a woman from head to toe) or, in ideologically more moderate countries, a headscarf atop an overcoat. *Purdah* and veiling are underpinned by discourses that either impute perturbing powers (*fitna*, which means "disorder within the community") to the public appearance of femininity or sanctify a virtuous womanhood that cannot be but defiled by the lustful gaze of the male stranger.[3] Muslim jurist Ibn Taymiyyah stated that God ordained women to be "both protected and cordoned off."[4] Concealment of the woman can apply to all her public representations, even those produced by others. Calling out a woman's name so that people can hear it, an Egyptian saying goes, violates the sanctity of a house.[5] On the other hand, in some traditional Muslim communities, men are expected on the morning after their wedding to display to the community bloody sheets – an indexical sign of the penetrated hymen (called *hijab*, which also means "head covering" in Arabic) of their brides.

Women may agree, or pretend to do so, with the ideology of *purdah* and actively limit their visibility to secure high moral standing and better marital prospects for themselves and their daughters. The veil has signified social standing for women in many societies throughout history. In Ancient Assyria, only respectable women – those who were under the protection of a man – were permitted to wear veils in public: prostitutes and slaves, who were not granted the privilege, were, as a result, fair game.[6] Similarly, women from wealthier families in some Muslim societies are more likely to engage in *purdah* simply because it is easier for them to do so: they can retain poor females to do public tasks, such as washing clothes in the pond and gathering wood, for them.[7] Veiling, on the other hand, can enable women, who would otherwise be cloistered to domesticity, to venture into the public sphere – not just to the streets but to universities and workplaces as well – with their virtue theoretically intact. Veiling thus becomes a way to deal with modernization and urbanization in the Muslim world. Ironically, it can even allow women to openly engage in political action.[8] Some can have a public voice as long as their bodies are invisible.

Yet such a position is a tenuous, if not an untenable, one: public voice being ineluctably an index of the body, politically vocal women – no matter how stringently veiled and advocating maximalist Islamist theses – cannot evade suspicion and often face scorn. And for many observers and women living in these societies, *purdah* and veiling are self-evidently oppressive.[9] They help reproduce inequality too. Prevalent in numerous Muslim countries, polygamy reinforces the dominium of affluent men by letting them monopolize women, and thereby the means of reproduction, which is a big advantage in a society where family is the main economic and political unit. Naturally, polygamy also yields a surfeit of sexually frustrated low-status men without the wherewithal to get married, this creating high monitoring costs for husbands with multiple wives. Thus, veiling, by desexualizing women, mitigates, but by no means eliminates, the perils that polygamy induces for the magnates. In societies that are not governed by sharî'a law, veiling can take on an additional political meaning. Whether freely chosen or imposed by men, the veil – since it only hides the woman to the extent that it accentuates her religion to the outside world – will operate there, for some, as a highly discernible symbol of the desire and confidence to establish the rule of Islam.[10]

More than their simple visual appearance, women's public discourse and, to a lesser degree, their ability to access public discourse have been restricted in almost all cultures. Masculine speech – low-pitched, stentorian, objective – was erected as the norm in political discourse as early as in *The Odyssey*. In the first book of the epic poem, Penelope rebukes a bard singing a plaintive song about Greek heroes to her suitors in the great hall. She complains that the music is bringing down everybody's spirits. Her son, Telemachus, of all people, interjects rudely:

> You should go back upstairs and take care of your work,
> Spinning and weaving, and have the maid do theirs.
> Speaking is for men, for all men, but for me
> Especially, since I am the master of this house.[11]

Although the episode takes place in the household of Odysseus, the great hall is the part of the Greek *oikos* where outsiders – in this case, suitors – are let in. Homer is thus describing a public moment. By contrast, Telemachus sends his mother to the most secluded part of the household, reserved for women and slaves. The speaking that is referred to here is *muthos*, which means in Homeric Greek "authoritative public speech" – the opposite of chatter and gossip, the opposite of private speech appropriate for women.[12] There were indeed few opportunities for Greek women to speak in public: as victims or martyrs; or while defending their home, family, or the other members of their sex.[13] To appear in public even through words uttered by others was problematic. Perikles at the end of his funeral oration proclaimed to women, "Great will be your glory in not falling short of your natural character; and greatest will be hers who is least talked of among the men whether for good or for bad."[14] Apparently not everybody agreed. Women are remarkably assertive in Aristophanes's comedies, for example.

And one can exercise significant power without public speech. After all, kings tend to be laconic in public. In fact, public speaking – like all speaking – can create a certain, albeit one-sided, familiarity between a speaker and his audience, between one and many, which could well erode the prestige of those whose power is mainly iconic. Until the late 1970s, people knew little about the private lives of the British royal family, who rarely spoke in public and enjoyed high popularity. As they grew vocal – not to say garrulous and confessional – in the following decades, much of their aura vanished.

Speaking, due to its highly revelatory nature, is risky in public, where it is harder to control the meaning of one's utterances. At any rate, being freer, speech in private – something that women have often excelled in to wield formally denied power – can be more consequential at times. Consider prerevolutionary France, where intrigue was a principal mode of politics undertaken in private by women as well as men. In effect, a few French women dominated the salons of the eighteenth century, which, blending the aristocrats and the third estate, were as instrumental as Habermas's coffeehouses in producing enlightened public opinion – if not more so.[15] Speech in the public sphere, particularly when it is political, is usually addressed to and deals with collectivities or the individual citizen, which are both abstractions. By contrast, communication in the private sphere – dialogue – is about singular, unfungible individuals with flesh and blood. In politics, this is at times equally decisive as public speech. Moreover, just as public silence does not necessarily signify powerlessness for women, public visibility will not automatically make them better off – especially if they become visible against their will, with little control over the way they are represented. A great deal of the political libel in the French Ancien Régime made the female members of the aristocracy as well as the queen herself highly visible by portraying them as dissolute schemers.[16]

In liberal democracies, by contrast, visibility can yield advantages for social groups. Contemporary political actors of all hues clamor, therefore, for changes in visibility rules to secure physical and representational access for themselves and their groups to spaces that enlist large publicity. The idea is that being ignored is as bad as being oppressed or that ignoring is simply another, maybe more insidious, form of oppression. Those who are noticed acquire confidence and strong identities. Struggles for attention are the very nub of contemporary identity politics.[17] So the spokespeople of minority racial and ethnic groups in the United States routinely deplore their invisibility on television, in Congress, and at elite universities. Gay and lesbian groups, by exposing their lifestyles to the general population, have endeavored to legitimize what was previously deviant with significant success. Visibility normalizes when it is widespread and repeated with impunity, above all in central public spaces.

There is a popular strand of thinking in contemporary social sciences and humanities – one that usually has activist aims – that stresses how dominant groups "other" subordinate ones through various public speech acts. Such discursive practices that name and define the powerless are deemed crucial not only in maintaining hierarchy and producing hegemony but to the self-understanding of the dominant group itself as well – since social identities are seen as relational constructs. Edward Said's attacks on "Orientalism,"[18] Pierre Bourdieu's concept of "symbolic violence,"[19] and Judith Butler's work on "excitable speech"[20] are some expressions of this thinking which champions the powerless caught in the grips of linguistic hostility.

But official discourse does not convince everybody. For example, George Chauncey, in his historical account of the New York gay world, offers much evidence that many homosexuals ignored what psychiatrists said about them and did not think of themselves as sick, perverted, or immoral.[21] Further, there is here a highly debatable assumption that the dominant is constantly paying a lot of attention to the subordinate, whereas, in reality, more often than not, the former barely notices the latter. Brute exploitation, violent domination, or social hierarchy does not always require the powerful to think or say much about the powerless. In fact, the discourse, but also the gaze, of the dominant group – insofar as it is confident of its superiority, whether seen as ascribed or acquired – will be narcissistic. The dominant will largely ignore the subordinate; the wider the status differential, the more this is the case. Contrary to Hegel,[22] the master does not need to be recognized by the slave for validation. Masters are more likely to demand recognition from one another or from other free people.[23] As Frantz Fanon cynically pointed out, what the master wants from the slave "is not recognition but work."[24]

The relationship between the dominant and the subordinate (say, between whites and blacks in twentieth-century United States) is often characterized by a severe asymmetry. In Jakobson's terminology, we can say that the dominant group is unmarked, and the subordinate marked:[25] the former is the rule, the latter the exception. That is, the subordinate is constituted in his difference from the dominant, but not vice versa. James Baldwin brooded in *The Notes of a Native Son* that while his difference from the white man is a central element of the identity of the black man, the same does not apply to the white man. It is indeed frequently this one-sidedness that is at the bottom of the frustration and tragedy of the subordinate identity, experienced particularly by the elite stratum of the subordinates, who are more likely to compare themselves with the dominant group.[26] Real emancipation for the subordinate group, in the long term at least, is contingent on the creation of an autonomous identity that is not simply relational to that of the dominant group, because relationality – however seen by many social scientists as a structural characteristic of all identities – cannot but be lived as a dependence, if not as an diminished existence. Now, the difference of the subordinate group, as we will see especially with the case of Jews, can sometimes generate a salience in the public sphere. But for most subordinates the asymmetry described here fosters a stark nonreciprocity of attention. Further, usually the dominant will dominate the spaces that get a lot of publicity. The lot of the subordinate is frequently sheer indifference and invisibility. In the words of Ralph Ellison, writing as an African American in the 1950s,

> I am invisible, understand, simply because people refuse to see me. Like the bodiless heads you see sometimes in circus sideshows, it is as though I have been surrounded by mirrors of hard, distorting glass. When they approach me they see only my surroundings, themselves, or figments of their imagination – indeed, everything and anything except me.[27]

The African-American individual is invisible because he cannot appear in the central regions of the public sphere; because if he is ever seen, he is reduced to the white American's prejudices about blacks in general; and because even when he is noticed, he is not recognized. Elaborate public discourse by the dominant about the subordinate is usually produced when the former starts to fear or resent the latter because he is getting more visible or powerful, or when indifference is somehow not possible or optimal, or when there is a need to morally justify the inequality between the parties. Or such discourse is the product of curiosity, as it was the case with most of the Orientalist literature and human sciences unfairly demonized by Said and his acolytes.[28]

Invisibility has obvious real and symbolic disadvantages. On the other hand, visibility will not always translate into gains – at least not in the short run. In fact, in repressive contexts, an increased presence in the public sphere can further hurt already stigmatized groups. Should, for whatever reason, the dominant group notice, or decide to notice, the subordinate group in a serious way, then the members of the latter will risk coming across as offensive, arrogant, or disruptive – and not just lower in status. Fear, founded or not – and sometimes strategically fabricated – can be a reason why the dominant starts to focus on and talk about the subordinate. But this is a process that may well accentuate the fear experienced by the dominant group, which may well then lead to outright oppression, and even violence. And the more noticed, the more talked about the subordinates are, the easier they will be targeted. In many cases, this is because the subordinates will have little control over the way they appear. But public voice will not always be beneficial either; it may simply heighten the group's visibility without necessarily improving its overall appearance. It may set off various unintended, harmful consequences. The words of a member will give that group in its entirety higher visibility. Yet others in the group may prefer the real advantages, the relative peace and tranquility that come from being ignored. Moreover, given the synecdochic semiotics of the public sphere, the most visible, especially the most vocal, will be seen as representing the obscure, silent ones. In effect, all minority groups tend to be held collectively responsible for the behavior of their members – but, of course, only when that behavior is visible. This tendency is worsened the more the group can be distinguished visually and the more it is isolated from the general community.[29] Jewish groups in medieval Europe, for example, often had to pay damages for thefts committed by individual Jews. The notion of collective responsibility solidified into a rule with the establishment of the Ghetto – though it hardly disappeared after the emancipation.

Increasing visibility may, then, wittingly or not, blight a group – particularly an already persecuted minority. Forcing people to wear something indicative of their group in public has historically been a typical way to demean and target them. Consider the Magen David of Jews under Nazi-occupied Europe. Or the medieval heretics with their yellow crosses sewed on their clothing, the insignia of ignominy imposed by the Inquisition, as mortifying as flagellation in the canonical hierarchy of punishments. Stigmatizing insignia can have a psychological hold over the stigmatized too: some Avignon Jews did not want to give up the yellow hat after their emancipation by the French Revolution.[30]

Such requirements readily reduce the individual to his maligned group, rendering him vulnerable to further stigmatization. This can only happen because unusual dress or insignia – imposed or not – depersonalizes the person by its very salience. We don't look at nuns' faces on the street, because their uniforms make them nonpersons.[31] Similarly, an urban camouflage favored by the FBI is Hasidic dress, which gives the agents the facial inconspicuousness that they need: they instantly become ultra-Orthodox Jews and nothing else. Skin color for minorities can also have a similar effect: for the majority groups, all minorities with a different color tend to look alike.

The principle can be used for sheer degradation. Hence the *sambenito*, the rough garment of shame that the convicts had to put on in the Spanish Inquisition during their procession to the square where the auta-da-fé was to be held. The *sambenito* had different colors depending on the moral status of the convict: yellow for those who repented before their sentence; red for those who did the same before their execution; and black, decorated with figures of friars, dragons, and demons, for the impenitent, who were to be burnt alive on the stake. The penitent who was lucky enough to escape punishment still had to put on the *sambenito* on certain days or all the time afterward. The *sambenito* depersonalized so much that the term came to refer not only to the garment but equally to the wearer himself.

Sartorial impositions can be all the stringent to the extent that there are no visible signs that would clearly differentiate the dominated group from the dominant one, this leading to undesirable misunderstandings and interactions. Hence the 1215 decree of the Fourth Lateran Council of Pope Innocent III:

In the countries where Christians do not distinguish themselves from Jews and Saracens by their garments, relations are maintained between Christians and Jews or Saracens, or vice versa. In order that such wickedness in the future be not excused by error, it is decreed that henceforth Jews of both sexes will be distinguished from other peoples by their garments, as moreover has been prescribed unto them by Moses. They will not show themselves in public during Holy Week, for some among them on these days wear their finest garments and mock Christians clad in mourning. Trespassers will be duly punished by the secular powers, in order that they no longer dare flout Christ in the presence of Christians."[32]

Visibility can hurt groups, even when it is not coerced, even in democratic settings. Anti-Semitism, for instance, rose in nineteenth-century and early twentieth-century Europe as Jews became more visible, despite the fact that a lot of them were concurrently assimilating culturally.[33] Earlier, Jewish life had been in many countries largely confined to the Ghetto, which, coupled with the desire to not attract attention, had rendered its inhabitants relatively invisible to larger society – except during crises when they could serve as convenient scapegoats to be massacred and expelled. In eighteenth-century Berlin, for example, the floor of their synagogue had to be laid several feet below street level. The Ghetto, in its origin, was voluntary; only later would it become compulsory.[34] Of course, some Jews worked outside of it, and the wealthier ones had Gentile servants; they were not completely invisible. But even a sympathetic chronicler, the nineteenth-century German historian Gregorovius, wrote about the Jews of Rome that they lived "virtually shut off from humanity."[35] This quasi-concealment occasionally prompted the Gentiles to come up with miscellaneous conspiracy theories to be put in practice in sporadic attacks and pogroms.[36] But, overall, the seclusion of the Ghetto, in part because it made Jews less visible, protected them. It also gave them quite a bit of self-confidence. With the Ghetto, Judaism became an increasingly closed system of thought, proud of its ancient history and indifferent to Christianity, not bothering after the sixteenth century to engage in any kind of polemics against it. Much as they were in objective terms a subordinate group, their seclusion allowed the European Jews to not define themselves in relation to Christians, as they had, in part, done before.[37]

With the emancipation, however, things changed. There were now an increasing number of Jews in large cities going about their lives alongside Gentiles. In 1850, only 9,000 Jews lived in Berlin; this figure shot up to 172,000 in 1925.[38] In Vienna, the number of Jewish residents reached 200,000 during the same period, even though there had only been 1,000 of them in the second half of the eighteenth century.[39] Now, the exodus from the Ghetto was for many Jews a most exciting event. It enabled – and unleashed – tremendous creativity in all spheres of life. Many Jews excelled in economic and professional life as well as in the worlds of art and science. Not content with being simple citizens, some even made it to the political arena. There was cause for great optimism.

But the emancipation also meant that Jews lost the sensory protection of the Ghetto. And the more they were visible as a different group, the more their political equality with the Gentiles gave offense. And as many Jews, thanks to emancipation, became successful and thus prominent, their Jewishness, often easily identifiable by their names or other markers, gave even more visibility to their brethren. Naturally, most Jews had to come up with ways to not be noticed, to look like everybody else. Many espoused Jean-Pierre Claris de Florian's precept, "Pour vivre heureux, vivons cachés," as the golden rule of the Diaspora to avoid persecution.

Take the German-speaking lands. A number of notable Jews including Heine and Mahler converted.[40] Others – thinking that any public mention of it would be indiscreet – sought to relegate their Judaism strictly to the private sphere,[41] if necessary by stealth or deception, so that they would be only citizens, abstract beings, "men without qualities." There were still those who endeavored to become more German than Germans: consider Felix Mendelssohn's tireless efforts to revive early German music or his Reformation Symphony. Another strategy, adopted by some Jewish intellectuals and still in use in our day, was to conceive of – and present – Judaism as a system of universalist ethics that would be compatible with the public morality of civic liberalism.[42] Yet the most common response by European Jews was discretion or concealment. "Be a Jew in your home and a man in the street," wrote Judah Leib Gordon, a signal spokesman of the Jewish Enlightenment in Russia, in his poem, *Hakitzah Ami*. Many altered their names and tried to pass as Gentiles. Those who kept to Jewish traditions equally made sure that they would not be noticed. To the annoyance of the Dreyfussards who clamored for a cause célèbre, the Dreyfus family preferred to operate surreptitiously, apprehensive that the more fuss was made about a Jew, the less they stood a chance of saving their convicted son.

Even in a pluralistic country like the United States, Jews strived to keep a low profile in much of the twentieth century. The Jewish producers of Hollywood were opposed to Jewish characters in movies. Samuel Goldwyn and other Jewish executives pleaded with the Gentile Darryl Zanuck not to produce *Gentleman's Agreement*, which would later be directed by Elia Kazan in 1947; they feared the film, which took on anti-Semitism in genteel America, would only "stir up trouble." A gaggle of Jewish bigwigs met with Franklin D. Roosevelt in 1939 to dissuade him from putting Felix Frankfurter on the Supreme Court; such visibility, they maintained, could not but stoke anti-Semitism.[43] The *New York Times*, owned by a Jewish family, usually refrained from reporting on the Nazi death camps during World War II.[44] When the paper did mention Nazi atrocities against Jews, the victims were referred to as persons, refugees, or civilians – rarely as Jews. Only in the contemporary United States have the Diaspora Jews finally lost their dread of visibility; even there, the phenomenon is relatively recent and partial.

These strategies proved fruitless in Europe; Jews could not help crystallizing in discourses produced by the left and the right alike as a demonic reference, as the covert cause of all the social, political, and cultural predicaments of the Old World. Of course, it is well known that the physical presence of Jews is not a requisite for anti-Semitism, as the post–World War II Polish case shows. Jews have always been beset by a catch-22. If they are visible, this bespeaks of their bald-faced arrogance; if they are not, this can only mean that they must be plotting behind the scenes. Once a Jew appears in public, voluntarily or not, as a Jew, he is nothing else but a Jew – a suspicious figure. Not surprisingly, then, many Jews tried to relinquish the signs that could mark them as different in public. But this was no easy feat. And the private, hidden, or even converted Jew remained a Jew – maybe a more suspicious, indeed dangerous, Jew. As Édouard Drumont spelled it out in the Bible of French anti-Semitism, *La France juive*,

> Every Jew one sees, every professing Jew is relatively harmless, he is sometimes even estimable; he worships the God of Abraham, this is a right that no one would dream of disputing, and as one knows what is believed on this score, it is possible to supervise him. The dangerous Jew is the shadowy Jew... This is the dangerous animal par excellence and at the same time the uncatchable animal... He is the most powerful trouble-maker element the earth has ever produced, and he thus passes through life with the joy which awareness of having, in various ways, harmed Christians, gives Jews.[45]

Visibility has equivocal effects on groups. In line with the synecdochic logic of the public sphere, if a few members of a minority group are highly conspicuous, while the others are not, then outsiders can make general inferences from these tokens. All would naturally be hurt if the inferences are negative. An example comes from the history of homosexuality in the United States. There used to be a somewhat visible gay culture in New York City from the 1890s to the 1930s, one that was played out in a cornucopia of spaces such as drag balls in Harlem, clubs in Greenwich Village, and male beauty contests in Coney Island. Gays were not only noticeable on certain streets with their red ties and bleached hair; they could even be represented – usually implicitly yet not always too negatively – in newspapers and films. All this would come to a close with the Great Depression, though. With social attitudes hardening against gays, homosexuality went into hiding. The situation further worsened after World War II. In the 1950s, responding to souped-up homophobia that culminated in purges in the government, many gays decided to pass as heterosexual. That is, in public contexts, they embraced the physical cues of straights or at least shied away from anything that would give away their sexual orientation. They became invisible as gays.[46] Yet some did not. Among those was a subgroup that was remarkably conspicuous: "swishes," that is, "gay men who appropriated female gender mannerisms as visible markers of their sexual identity."[47] Swishes were greatly resented by other gays: by the attention they got, they contaminated all of the homosexual community. A leader of the Homopholies – America's first gay civil rights movement – W. Dorr Legg bellyached about them in a letter: "The 'man in the street' instantly classifies all homosexuals as swishes with long fingernails, painted eyebrows and exaggerated clothing."[48]

Once stereotypes about a group have been solidified, then the visible tokens' behavior – as discrepant as it may be from these stereotypes – will be seen under that light as well. Psychologists Shelley Taylor and Susan Fiske have found that the evaluation of someone hangs on whether he is a token of his group in a particular context. The tendency is particularly pronounced if the token cannot help giving off salient visible cues – such as skin color in the United States – linking him to his group. If one is the only black person in the office, one is more likely to suffer from the stereotypes about blacks in America.[49] At the same time, the token's performance is supposed to have implications for the rest of the group members.[50] When Walter Rathenau, who would later be assassinated by German ultra-nationalists, agreed to serve as the foreign minister of the Weimar Republic after World War I, his fellow Jews, Zionist leader Kurt Blumenfeld and Albert Einstein, paid him a visit to change his mind. "You see only yourself. You don't realize that every Jew will be held accountable for your actions – and not only in Germany. You have no right to do this," Blumenfeld implored unavailingly.[51]

The recent history of Jews is full of examples where those who want to remain invisible are, or feel, affected adversely by their visible brethren.

The first group can also include more assimilated Jews who adopt the condescension of the Gentiles toward their coreligionists. Such a position has often been described as Jewish self-hatred, but there may equally be a certain dose of snobbery in it. A perfect example is Walter Lippmann, a leading American intellectual – who happened to be a Jew, though he rarely talked about it – griping in 1922 about his people:

> The rich and vulgar and pretentious Jews of our big cities are perhaps the greatest misfortune that has ever befallen the Jewish people. They are the real fountain of anti-Semitism. They are everywhere in sight, and though their vices may be no greater than those of other jazzy elements in the population, they are a thousand times more conspicuous... When they rush about in super-automobiles, bejeweled and be-furred and painted and overbarbered, when they build themselves French chateaus and Italian palazzi, they stir up the latent hatred against crude wealth in the hands of shallow people: and that hatred diffuses itself. They undermine the natural liberalism of the American people... The Jew is conspicuous, and unless in his own conduct of life he manages to demonstrate the art of moderate, clean and generous living, every failure will magnify itself in woe upon the heads of the helpless and unfortunate.[52]

To be sure, Lippmann notes that the Jew is not responsible for what makes him conspicuous: "The Jews are fairly distinct in their physical appearance and in the spelling of their names from the run of the American people. They are, therefore, conspicuous." But he then proceeds to attack them for making themselves even more conspicuous by their nouveau-riche materialism and gaudy consumption habits: "Sharp trading and blatant vulgarity are more conspicuous in the Jew because he himself is more conspicuous." And the more the New York Jew behaves likes a Gatsby wannabe, the more he is conspicuously Jewish. No wonder Lippmann was distressed by the high number of Jewish students at Harvard in the 1920s; he wished they would go somewhere else, though he drew the line at supporting a quota.[53] "Lippmann, in his Wall Street suit and carefully controlled manners and appearance, looks just like every one – or so he hopes," notes Sander Gilman sarcastically.[54] Or so he hopes, indeed, as Lippmann would himself be the target of anti-Semitic attacks later in life, his self-satisfied universalism proving not at all a lesser Jewish sin in the eyes of hostile Gentiles.

In other instances, the token may feel more positively about his group and act in solidarity with it. Wyat Cenac, the only African American on the writing staff of *The Daily Show* from 2008 to 2012, thought he had to speak out against an impression by Jon Stewart that seemed to him racist – at the cost of earning the host's wrath:

Something like this, I represent my community, I represent my people, and I try to represent them the best that I can. I gotta be honest if something seems questionable, because if not, then I don't want to be in a position where I am being untrue not just to myself but to my culture, because that's exploitative. I'm just allowing something to continue if I'm just going to go along with it. And sadly, I think that's the burden a lot of people have to have when you are "the one." You represent something bigger than yourself whether you want to or not.

That the most visible member will typify his group is a fairly general rule. But insiders may think differently. Andrew Abbott shows that it is often precisely the most visible members of a profession that tend to enjoy the least prestige in the eyes of the insiders.[55] For outsiders, the most exemplary, the most glorious lawyer is the most visible one – the litigator. Within the legal community, however, highest praise is reserved for those who are the least visible – such as tax lawyers – because their work is regarded as the purest, as the least contaminated by contact with outsiders. For the general public, the best professor is the most prominent lecturer; for the professors themselves, too much teaching – especially at the undergraduate level – is a sure sign of lowliness.

Another important point is that the high visibility of the internal doings of a collectivity – a family, a religious group, or an organization – can have negative effects on its integrity, both in the moral and nonmoral senses of the term. The more its operations are placed in the public sphere, the more the solidarity of the group will be at risk of dissolving. Each group, each organization, in fact, each social relationship requires some level of freedom from scrutiny. Without confidentiality, without protection against the foreign gaze, a collectivity cannot claim autonomy, which has the following consequences: members cannot trust one another, discipline cannot be sustained, and a unitary identity cannot be maintained. The vertical as well as the horizontal unity of groups and organizations may particularly suffer when a member other than the appointed spokesperson engages in public voice – doubly so if he airs dirty laundry. Indeed, control of voice is indispensable both to the internal solidarity of organizations and their capability to appear reliable and accountable.[56]

Here is an example showing how increasing visibility can undermine hierarchy within groups. Before the 1960s, senior senators and representatives controlled the legislative proceedings in Congress.[57] And much of policy making was hidden from public view, for most legislative deliberation took place in camera. In the words of Woodrow Wilson, "Congress in session is Congress on public exhibition, whilst Congress in its committee rooms is Congress at work."⁵⁸ These two principles – hierarchy and secrecy – went hand in hand. The system, however, came under attack in the 1970s and 1980s from young congressmen such as Newt Gingrich. These new guns strove to circumvent party hierarchies through the use of media. Speaker Rayburn had banned television cameras precisely to strengthen the House leadership.⁵⁹ The ban could not last; very soon, low-level, rank-and-file congressmen and congresswomen became common fixtures of news programs, as common as party bosses. Another development, which further increased visibility, had to do with voting. Before the 1970s, no publicly recorded voting was permitted in the Committee of the Whole, the entity that materializes when the whole Congress operates as a single committee. Only the total vote was made public, not the individual votes, which had momentous consequences. As the legendary Democratic Speaker of the House Tip O'Neill admitted, "It was embarrassingly easy for a member to duck a vote because he had made promises to both sides – and even to lie about it later, because there was no way anyone could check."⁶⁰ With the Legislative Organization Act of 1970, votes in the Committee of the Whole were made public. The incentive to vote was thereby bolstered.⁶¹ On the other hand, the recording of votes fortified parliamentary surveillance and accountability along with the power of constituencies, including interest groups, over party superiors. As congressional activities – voting and political speech – grew more visible in the 1970s, the role of House and Senate floors in policy was enlarged at the expense of the secretive and hierarchical committees. Increasing visibility rendered congressional decision making more collegial.

Surveillance

Visibility is obviously related to surveillance, and Michel Foucault is perhaps the best-known theorist of surveillance in recent history. It is therefore useful to consider in broad terms his account. Foucault famously asserted in *Discipline and Punish* that modernity entailed a transition from the visibility of power to the visibility of subjects. Until the late eighteenth century their visibility – which was engendered especially by ceremonies and violent punishment rituals among other similar public events – endowed rulers with might and grandeur. By the same token, subjects remained in the shadows, not seen and, consequently, not known. Mere spectators, their role was to watch. With modernity, we observe a reversal in toto. Power becomes invisible; it now functions by making its subjects visible so as to monitor them, to create knowledge about them, and to individuate them. According to Foucault, the Panopticon, a model prison devised by Bentham, where the prisoners are constantly visible to the guards who remain invisible to them, was the avatar of the new regime: "disciplinary power." Here, "power marks its signs on the objects instead of emitting signs of potency."[62] Visibility, no longer a privilege, becomes synonymous with domination. Foucault argued that the new regime of power was not limited to the prison; it quickly spread to all modern institutions, including hospitals, schools, army barracks, factories, and asylums. In these settings, inmates are, at once, individuated, subjected, surveilled, and turned into objects of science – all intertwined processes, the French philosopher wrote.[63]

Foucault's narrative has been no less influential than Habermas's model of the public sphere. It is, however, not devoid of problems – quite a few widely recognized, others less so. As many of his critics have noted, no truly Panopticon-type prisons were built during or after Bentham's lifetime, the philosopher and his followers failing to persuade the powers-that-be of their necessity. Prisoners retained some of their privacy in their cells. Surveillance is, after all, always costly: arranging the space so that the surveilling guards would not themselves be visible to the prisoners proved very difficult. At any rate, power in actual prisons does not require a high degree of surveillance. "If you control the entrances and exits, you don't have to look," is the succinct summary of Fred Alford's ethnography of prison life in the United States.[64] Most guards are oblivious to what happens behind the bars – at times to the dismay of inmates, who as a result, face violence from one another unless they have protection. Were Foucault right, there would be neither rape nor gangs in American prisons.

Another problem is that modern political power, however institutionally complex, is far from invisible. In fact, with modern media, leaders are more visible than ever. Governments and their procedures have become more transparent to the general population: *raison d'État* justifications of official secrets are increasingly regarded as invalid. Authorities have a hard time keeping even their legitimate secrets out of the public sphere: consider the data that have been unleashed by Wikileaks in the recent years, an amount so massive that it defies categorization as well as effective political use. The visibility of political actors and institutions has ambiguous effects on their power: as we saw, visibility can enhance as well as degrade. And neither the visibility nor the invisibility of the rulers or the ruled is clearly correlated with political repression.

More important, a good deal of current research and thinking about surveillance, which originate from Foucault's work, conflate vertical and horizontal surveillance: what the authorities vs. our neighbors know about us.⁶⁵ Modern societies function by high vertical surveillance with limited horizontal surveillance. Governments may know all about our financial transactions and have access to our emails; Google may keep a record of our searches and may even give information about them to third parties; health industry may collect our medical data. Yet all this information is ordinarily not in the public sphere. In all these instances, the one being watched is often unaware of the surveillance that he is subject to – such awareness being the very gist of publicity. Further, other citizens don't have access to our information, except the ones whom we share it with. It is true that we are at the mercy of our sharers, and our sharers can use new technology to publicize with greater facility, say on Twitter, what they know about us. But sharing is a private act; so is usually the betrayal of our sharer. And even when our sharers publicize our information, the publicity that is created is not the direct result of vertical surveillance. Surveillance by our peers is not necessarily preferable to surveillance by authorities. To a significant degree, many of our freedoms in contemporary society derive from the fact that horizontal surveillance has, relative to earlier times, waned for regular people (i.e., those who are not public personalities). Our neighbors know less about us, we are not under their constant gaze, we have much more control over what we reveal to them.

Foucault's prime bugaboo was surveillance by technocratic authorities; he was not worried about general visibility. We see this mostly clearly in his first major work, *The History of Madness*. Prior to modern times, Foucault contended, the conceptual boundary between reason and madness was not a thick one. The insane could even be attributed a wisdom that was denied to others, a capability to pierce through appearances. However tragic or ludic – sometimes both – they were always in a dialogue with the sane. Constituting the limits of society, they were, nonetheless, still not placed on the outside of it. There was no physical separation between them and us: the insane, profiting from tolerant attitudes, were largely visible on the streets.

According to Foucault, modernity discovered, in the same movement, reason and its foil, madness, which became a medical category, an illness by the end of the eighteenth century. The dialogue between the sane and the insane was muted by the novel language of psychiatry, "a monologue by reason about madness."⁶⁶ The insane were now a threat, not unlike the prostitutes, the vagrants, and other social misfits. They had to be treated, and their treatment could only take place far away, in asylums on the outskirts of cities. But if the insane were less and less visible in general society, they became completely, constantly, compulsorily visible in new enclosed institutional spaces. Horizontally invisible to the sane, they were now vertically visible to the disciplining experts.

Foucault's story, suffused by a nostalgia for a more humane time while driven by some sort of nihilist politics,[67] is not quite correct, though. Visibility was not empowering for the madman: in fact, it rendered him vulnerable. Marcel Gauchet and Gladys Swain – among others – have shown that he was not considered a kindred spirit, an alter ego, before the emergence of the asylum and modern psychology. The madman was, in fact, someone so different in nature that he could serve as the perfect object of spectacle: a *monstre de foire*, a fairground freak.[68] Shackled in grimy cages, he was displayed to tourists as a major attraction until the early nineteenth century in London. The early madhouses, which emerged in the beginning of the fifteenth century, remained open to spectators until the end of the eighteenth century. Before their closure, visitors could come and make fun of inmates confined in cages with windows on the street side.[69] This amusement was so popular that in 1657 its administrators had to close Bedlam on Sundays on account of huge crowds. Hardly a part of the social fabric, the lot of the insane was frequently expulsion. Accordingly, their subsequent enclosure in the asylum was not an exclusionary practice that served to "other" the insane. Modern psychiatry, in fact, placed madness within the vast human experience. And the asylum, at least in principle, was a humanitarian enterprise, enabling the insane to live and maybe even heal in their own space, far from the cruel eyes of society.

7

Justice and Morality in the Public Sphere

Law

The public sphere presents serious threats not only for the common good but equally for the individual. Take law. A sizable part of the judicial process is public in Western democracies, as opposed, for instance, to the secret inquisitorial penal procedure of the absolutist era in Continental Europe. Justice has always entailed some level of visibility, but it is with modernity that courts and legal procedure have become more and more public – and punishment less and less so. Openness serves to render legal actors accountable to citizens, reinforcing the defense rights of the accused. When the suspects are powerful people or institutions, publicity will deter officials from shelving investigations. A free press, along with other public venues where grievances and accusations can be voiced, should evidently succor the cause of justice when legal routes are barred.

The visibility of the judicial process can also facilitate the cause of victims. The first lawsuits against the Boston clergy for sexual abuse in the 1990s ended with settlements with confidentiality clauses serving to protect the privacy of those involved and to save the Catholic Church from scandal. But some plaintiffs and their lawyers wanted case files to be accessible, and the *Boston Globe* successfully sued in 2002 to have them unsealed. This allowed significant press coverage, and, as a result of the publicity of depositions and church files obtained through discovery, the issue molted into a major scandal implicating high-up third parties, namely bishops who knew about the offenders and did not do more than simply assign them to different parishes. Maybe more important, the publicity of these documents encouraged other victims, who had until then remained silent, to open lawsuits themselves.[1]

Yet the public sphere is not an unalloyed blessing for law and justice. High visibility can transform legal justice into popular justice – with prejudice and demagoguery as its currencies.[2] The more an investigation and trial will get publicity, the more the values, perceptions, and expectations of the spectators will mold the actions of legal actors. The more public the legal process is, the less evidence will be necessary for the conviction of a suspect: in a world of appearances, sheer allegations can quickly turn into verities. Anger at a suspect can be further aggravated within a public either through collective effervescence or through a feeding frenzy where people adopt progressively negative attitudes only to signal righteousness to one another. Further, since the public sphere has the tendency to reduce suspects to types, we may act as if an unproven allegation were true if it is consonant with our settled beliefs about the suspect's group, if non-response seems risky, or if sanctioning is costless. It was easier for the French of the Third Republic to assume the culpability of Alfred Dreyfus due to the then-hegemonic trope of the Jew as the devious traitor corroding the system from within. Promoting guilt by association, the public sphere always risks undermining the individualism of law. A well-publicized wrongdoing, even if only alleged, will compromise third parties associated with the suspect. A high-profile trial, occasioning a scandal, can contaminate an entire group. The political exploitation of these dynamics by totalitarian governments in the form of show trials to terrorize dissidents and social groups is well known.

Few trials get large publicity – the audience, if there is any, consists, on the whole, of family and friends. The more attention a trial gets, and especially the easier a trial can be publicized out of the courtroom, however, the more participants will be seen not merely as individuals but more like representations of collectivities. This principle, as we have seen over and over again, is inherent to the public sphere in general and operates in all public events, not just causes célèbres. So the more the O. J. Simpson case got publicity, the more it became about race – both for its participants and spectators. But there is a paradox here: while Simpson appeared increasingly black in the course of his trial, the reason why he received so much publicity in the first place was that he was actually the least representative black man. The legal woes of most blacks, who are neither rich nor famous, capture no attention ordinarily. Here is another paradox: the more public a trial is in America, the less it is objectively like other legal cases (an overwhelming of which do not even go to trial), but the more it will come to represent the legal system as a whole. The O. J. Simpson case was, for example, seen as representative for whites insofar as it showed the power of money; it was equally representative for blacks insofar as it showed the police mistreatment of blacks. Objectively speaking, however, the case was a very exceptional one by all regards. Not only did it end with a jury verdict, as opposed to a plea, but, owing to publicity, it took more than a year; murder trials rarely go over a month in the United States.

The publicity that a trial can generate is always dangerous for suspects. So when the crackdown on gays intensified in the 1950s and 1960s, as the police took to regularly raiding bars, tearooms, and highway stops, those who were arrested often pleaded guilty: they were apprehensive of public exposure in open trials.[3] Trials will be bad also for close relatives, especially in more traditional societies where family is everything. So in prerevolutionary France, to have their wayward members imprisoned without a trial, many families – notably, but not only, the distinguished ones – resorted to *lettres de cachet*: orders from the king to enforce unappealable yet discrete legal action. Prodigal sons, libertine wives, absentee drunken husbands, and fallen children were among the usual targets. The future revolutionary Comte de Mirabeau was one of the most illustrious victims of this practice; so was Marquis de Sade, whose mother obtained a letter against him after he raped and battered – and maybe even killed – several women.

Eventually decried as the most egregious illustration of arbitrary rule, *lettres de cachet* allowed families to sort out their intractable predicaments with as little din as possible and to preclude the opprobrium that would engulf them in scandalous public trials.[4] *Lettres de cachet* also protected the family from the infamy of public executions. Daniel Jousse, the great jurist of the eighteenth century, wrote, "Executions have to be undertaken in public because this manner adds to the pain and infamy of the accused as well as to the dishonor of his relations."[5] Only the king could eliminate the prospect of publicity, and only for the sake of the family; one way he could do it was through a *lettre de cachet*. The state could thereby secretly intervene in the domestic sphere to sever the bothersome member without damaging the privacy and respectability of the family. The letters were deemed illegitimate only when the authorities acted on their own initiative.

Another discontent of publicity is that it can turn legal actors into performers. The more publicity a trial gets, the more it will transmogrify into a circus, the more the prosecutor will be keen in making a name for himself, and the more ruthless his comportment will be – a potent propensity, particularly when they are pursuing high-status suspects, among American prosecutors, who are mostly democratically accountable and have political ambitions. So the average prosecutor will become – or at least could become – unduly concerned with how he appears instead of enforcing the law. And by appealing to the public – through leaks as well as statements – one can skate over the exigencies and technicalities of criminal procedure. Lawyers and suspects can equally play to the crowd[6] – as it is common in legal trials that acquire a political character. Among the Greeks, litigation before a judge, as any athletic event, was referred to as an *agon*.[7] Juridical process was in its origins a contest; it still remains so in certain respects, particularly in common law countries.

It is to offset these dynamics that many elements of the judicial process are kept out of the public sphere in the American judicial system. The right of access to judicial records is limited to court documents. Discovery and settlement negotiations are usually not public. Communication between an attorney and a client is confidential; so is the identity of police informants. Prosecutors cannot leak grand jury testimony. They cannot even communicate this information, without court approval, to another governmental agency.[8] A judge can decide that part of a trial will be held in camera and can bar all kinds of testimony from being aired in court. Very often, because it could undermine due process, commenting publicly on cases sub judice (Latin for "under judgment") is either inappropriate or simply an offense, which can provoke contempt of court proceedings. Some other countries like the United Kingdom have very strict regulations regarding the media coverage of crimes. A trial participant can be bound by a gag order issued by a judge, who can also seal legal motions.

And although their verdict must ultimately be divulged, jurors neither deliberate nor are expected to justify their decision in public. The secrecy of jury activity is central to American law:

> [A jury] has great power; indeed, it may hold life and death in its hands, but its deliberations are shrouded in mystery and it expresses its conclusions in the tersest manner possible: one or two words. Hence a jury can, if it wishes, change the (living) law, dispense with a rule, elide technicalities, but in a quiet, subtle, and subterranean way. Patterns of jury decisions can move the law in one direction or another. Legal systems need flexibility; and this is one way the common law gets it.[9]

All legal officials may be affected – positively or negatively – by publicity, particularly in high-profile cases. Take the prosecutors who appeared on the American public scene with the Independent Counsel Provision of the Ethics in Government Act of 1978, which remained operative until 1999. The Watergate scandal instigated calls to beef up surveillance on political actors to ensure that they would not be able to stifle ongoing investigations – as Nixon had tried to do in the so-called Saturday Night Massacre when he fired the prosecutor investigating the White House. The provision required the attorney general, when informed of possible misconduct by members of the executive branch, to ask a panel of senior federal judges to appoint a special prosecutor, an actor who would be rechristened as "Independent Counsel" in 1982. The objective was to avoid the appearance of a conflict of interest. The new prosecutors could be removed from their investigations only by the judges who assigned them and solely for grossly improper behavior. Armed with plenary powers in determining the length of their probes, they disposed of substantial resources – Kenneth Starr had a hundred staffers under him while he was going after Bill Clinton in 1998 – with which they could take on cases that normal prosecutors would not touch. As the American public would realize with the Lewinsky hullabaloo, they could investigate and prosecute almost any type of misconduct. From 1978 to 1999, these prosecutors pursued twenty investigations, several of them causing major disruptions in the political system.[10] One of these led to the impeachment of a president. Another came within an ace of ending Reagan's presidency; his secretary of defense, not as lucky, was indicted. The roster of those investigated or targeted comprised three presidents, one first lady, one attorney general, a former assistant attorney general, several chiefs of staff, and six cabinet secretaries.

A key aspect of these investigations was that they were much more public than pursuits by regular prosecutors. The targets or suspects were high-profile politicians, whose alleged transgressions, when publicized, instantly piqued interest. But equally important was the fact that while regular prosecutors take most of their decisions in private, all independent counsel reports had to be made public so as to stave off suspicions of political interference with the course of justice. This meant that journalists could publish any item in the reports, though most would eventually not make it into the indictments. Few executive officials implicated in the investigations were convicted; reputations were nonetheless muddied, mangled – at least temporarily. Increasingly the probes came to rove in terms of charges and suspects, instead of being restricted to the targets originally specified by the Justice Department. High publicity put ambitious prosecutors in the spotlight, providing an incentive to prolong the investigations, one of which lasted as long as eight years. Publicity could be a stick too. The independent counsel Kenneth Starr, for instance, had to turn over any "substantial and credible information" relating to impeachment, and this information was quickly made public.[11] With every detail in their reports exposed blow-by-blow in the media and with their behavior under cynical scrutiny, these prosecutors, willing or unwilling performers, felt compelled to come up with anything lest they be seen as irresponsible or tendentious. As it is the case with politicians, publicity makes it harder for legal officials to alter their positions in the course of their investigations.

Take what happened to Kenneth Starr, who is often portrayed as a bellicose right-wing fanatic out to get the president of the United States at all costs. The characterization is not self-evident. After all, on February 17, 1997, almost one year before the Lewinsky scandal broke, Starr had announced that he would terminate his probe of Whitewater, an affair involving charges of real estate fraud by the Clintons that he was assigned to three and a half years earlier. He said that the evidence was not there and that he wanted to take a teaching position at Pepperdine University. The editorial page of the *New York Times*, which had covered Whitewater extensively, reprimanded him two days later for his "selfish indifference to his important civic obligations." Chastened, Starr backtracked and, within a year, produced novel charges against the president, including perjury and obstruction of justice.[12] While the prosecutor was showered with plentiful flak for widening his investigation, the charges were not created out of whole cloth. The highly publicized and transparent nature of the independent counsel investigations not only made them drawn out and very hard to end, but also induced all kinds of people to pass all kinds of potentially discreditable information about the target to the prosecutor – all the more when the target was a sitting president. This is, of course, what the infamous Linda Tripp – the woman to whom Monica Lewinsky, an intern in the White House, had communicated the details of her dalliance with Bill Clinton – did. In the tapes slipped by Tripp to Starr were conversations between the two women that seemed to suggest an effort by the president to suborn Lewinsky to commit perjury in the Paula Jones sexual harassment case, in which Clinton was already entangled. The independent counsel learned from the tapes that a friend of Clinton was lobbying to get a job for Lewinsky in Revlon, which made it look like the president's end of a quid pro quo. Starr thus asked for an extension to expand the probe to possible obstruction of justice in the Paula Jones case. An independent counsel in his situation could remain unresponsive to the allegations of wrongdoing in such a high-profile investigation only at the burden of appearing to illegitimately succumb to political pressure. Once he received the tapes, Starr was obligated to take the matter to the attorney general, Janet Reno, who would have been massacred in the media had she not advised the special division to appoint a prosecutor to look into the activities alluded to in the phone conversations. It was publicity that in great part both forced and, later in the scandal, enabled Starr to be as fierce as he was. And publicity made such investigations so disruptive of the political process, finally climaxing in 1998 in a cataclysmic constitutional crisis, that the Independent Counsel Provision had to be annulled.

Moral Ambiguities

The public sphere is therefore not only the arena where selfless Zola defends poor Dreyfus. It is also where moral character is assassinated with scant evidence, where entire groups are unfairly disgraced. It is the breeding ground of frenzies and scapegoats. And there is a more general moral problem here. The public sphere is a world marked by an elemental inauthenticity: insomuch as it is public, all purportedly civic-minded behavior or talk can seem staged.[13] All moral qualities displayed in public, except maybe courage, are inherently disputable.

The very integrity of many private objects – such as an intimate letter – is jeopardized once they are made public. There is a certain sacredness about things intimate, not because they embody collective ideals, but in the sense that once they are subjected to the gaze of the strangers, they are somehow spoiled. Their protectedness is essential to their value. Lifted from its dyadic context, a private conversation is an alien entity; it is further objectified when publicized. When read or heard by a third party, our words will almost always seem suspect, compromising, if not worse – all the more if they were uttered freely to someone close. Not only can their original import not be comprehended by third parties, but it will now also be lost to the addresser and the addressee, who would find it impossible not to look at the exchange from the viewpoint of a spectating stranger. As Milan Kundera writes,

Man who was the same in both public and intimate life would be a monster. He would be without spontaneity in his private life and without responsibility in his public life. For example, privately to you, I can say of a friend who's done something stupid, that he is an idiot, that his ears ought to be cut off, that he should be hung outside down and a mouse stuffed in his mouth. But if the same statement were broadcast over the radio spoken in a serious tone – and we all prefer to make such jokes in a serious tone – it would be indefensible.[14]

Maybe the only true proof of a friendship is that one says things to a friend that cannot be defended in public. The closer the relationship between the parties in a private conversation, the more discomfiting, the more damning it will be for the parties if the conversation were to be made public. Any intimate relationship is a conspiracy; badmouthing third parties – inequitably, indecently – is essential to it. The private sphere is not only a protected area where we can reveal our vulnerabilities to intimates; it is equally where we are obligated to make ourselves vulnerable, to place ourselves in each other's confidence, often by bad behavior – not unlike gangs that require criminal activity for initiation. If what I say to a friend can be unproblematically made public, this could only mean that what I say is worthless, that I treat my friend as anyone, that he is no real friend. That we speak differently in private and public is at very core of the human condition, at once a fact and a norm: anyone who speaks to an intimate as if he were talking to a public would come across as cold, affected, fake. Nevertheless, it is equally true that the moment our private words are made public, our spectators – as human as we are – will be suddenly predisposed to judge us, especially to the extent that they are themselves visible to one another, unlike the way they judge their intimates in private situations and unlike the way they would like to be judged themselves. This hypocrisy is a part of the human condition, too.

It is true that what is rooted in personal experience can only be universalized through publicity. Much of literature and art, much of human wisdom is the end product of such a process. Yet the attempt to universalize can fail, resulting with an embarrassing discrepancy between the small import of what is publicized and the grandeur of the space where it is publicized.[15] And even when the attempt succeeds, something is lost. A novelist can, drawing from his own life, write a great novel that will enrich the entire humanity. From the standpoint of his friends and relatives, the text, simply because of its objectifying nature, will often not be any less an act of heartlessness, even if it does not – as it often does – distort and betray. In any case, the truths that we cherish, the truths that guide us are usually those that have been arrived at solitarily or through dialogue – that is, in private. If publicized by us or by others, these intimate convictions will always risk becoming cheapened, congealed, etiolated.

As deceiving, as false as they may be, appearances are all there is in the public sphere. Despite its blatant superficiality, however, the public sphere is a moral order of some sort. Many social practices with a normative component like religion take place predominantly in public. Injustices and sufferings become visible and audible only by dint of publicity, which also enables collective moral action geared to the welfare of strangers. And our very moral identity can be colonized by how we appear in public, thanks to our own collaboration. No one captured the sad irony better than Proust:

> But certain favorite roles are played by us so often before the public and rehearsed so carefully when we are alone that we find it easier to refer to their fictitious testimony than to that of a reality which we have almost entirely forgotten.[16]

Appearances can matter – morally – even when we know that they are representations that do not represent anything other than themselves. The more formal the setting, the more the principle holds. The main issue in a job interview is to see whether the applicant in a job interview can play the applicant in a job interview. Similarly, make-up does not lose its effect when it is visible as make-up; it should simply not be excessive. The same rule of moderation is equally valid for manners. We appear the way we do frequently for the benefit of our audiences; in return, they will, we hope, show tact whenever we fail to produce the appearances we want to produce.[17]

Indeed, no matter how skin deep and forced, appearances claim some moral authority. Even an ultra-rationalist such as Kant acceded to this – thereby negating the purism of his *Critique of Practical Reason*. He wrote in *Anthropology from a Pragmatic Point of View* that public virtues such as modesty, decency, disinterestedness, and politeness are often nothing more than appearances. While "everyone understands that nothing sincere is meant," appearing to have these virtues is still very important:

> Every human virtue in circulation is small change; only a child takes it for real gold. Nevertheless, it is better to circulate pocket pieces than nothing at all. In the end, they can be converted into genuine gold coin, though at a considerable discount... Even the appearance of the good in others must have value for us, because in the long run something serious can come from such a play with pretenses which gain respect even if they do not deserve to.

The issue here is not simple convenience or expediency. Consider the vitriol with which Kant denounced those who distrusted the appearances of virtue: "To pass them off as nothing but counters... is high treason perpetuated upon humanity."[18] We are indeed much of the time expected to take people as they seem. Some trust, unless there is any obvious reason to do otherwise or unless it seems parlous, is the default position in our dealings with strangers who evince the appropriate signs. Total distrust, for the most part, is neither reasonable nor moral in the public sphere.

8

A Defense of Spectatorship

There is probably no concept more exalted than interaction in social sciences and humanities, indeed maybe in enlightened discourse tout court. It is by interacting, everybody seems to say, that we all understand ourselves, grow, function. Interaction is what makes us truly human and cements society, helps us get the better of our prejudices. There is, of course, also bad interaction, but the panacea is still interaction, more interaction – of the good kind. The more diverse are the parties to an interaction, the more they are strangers to each other, the better it is. Its privileged site is the public sphere, since all civic participation is already, or is based on, some kind of social interaction. For Habermas and countless others, this is where dialogue among citizens – the civilized interaction par excellence – would enable collective decision making. Similarly, for many urbanists, this is where impersonal sociability among strangers – and especially among different ethnic, racial, and religious groups – will bring about tolerance and cooperation. For instance, just like Habermas idealized the civic communications of eighteenth-century Europe, Richard Sennett, in an otherwise penetrating book, romanticized the city of the same era and deplored the later urban transformations, in the course of which a space of interaction among strangers is to have transfigured into a world of spectacle.[1]

Spectatorship – the very opposite not just of participation but also of interaction – is indeed the nemesis of the conventional perspective on the public sphere. But its denigration has a longer pedigree in Western thought. Rousseau upbraided the urban culture of his day on the grounds that it only produced passive individuals voyeuristically assembled around spectacles. Unlike many contemporary intellectuals, however,

Rousseau recognized correctly that urban life by its very nature is more spectatorship than interaction – and thereby called the city the "abyss of the human species."² Still worse was the theater: the quintessential spectacle, derived from the Greek verb *theasthai*, meaning "to behold." He grumbled that people only went there to "forget their friends, neighbors, and relations."³ Lucretius had before him described in *De Rerum Natura* the wicked pleasure of watching a shipwreck from a place of safety, and Rousseau maintained that the theatrical experience was not any less obscene.⁴ Hence his support for censorship, although he was a playwright himself. What compared favorably with the theater were the popular festivals of his beloved Geneva, public events where people were at once actors and spectators.

This attack on spectatorship, which is still with us, is an attack on representation tout court. The city and the theater, both central public spaces, are built on the asymmetries between the representation and the represented, on the one hand, and between the representation and its spectatorship, on the other. It is these asymmetries that are at the source of the pathologies of much of public life according to Rousseau; contemporary diatribes on mass media and on urban alienation, from the left as well as from the right, say little else. The very same evil is supposed to plague politics as well: hence the theory that Rousseau developed in *The Social Contract* of a general will that can neither be divided nor represented by anything other than itself. For him, the general will and the popular festival had the same structure, the same lofty status, the same moral function.⁵ And even though general will fanaticism does not sit well with contemporary liberalism, any time we denounce special interests – intellectuals, journalists, and politicians of all persuasions do it without respite – we follow Rousseau more than we would care to admit.

A great deal of our daily life is spent is spaces in the presence of strangers with whom we can always technically interact in some way. This is also the case, to a certain degree, with virtual spaces including the internet, granting that it is easier to be completely invisible in a chat room than on a street. The philosopher Roger Scruton stated that "the public is a sphere of broad and largely unplanned encounter."⁶ This sounds virtuous, but also exhilarating: there is nothing nicer than meeting or running into people. Yet public interactions with strangers – when we shop, for example – tend to be superficial, ephemeral. Less interactions than transactions, such encounters largely take place between fungible beings. In any case, a good deal of our conversations in these situations are usually inaudible by third parties; they are therefore factually – and many times normatively, as we may be rightfully outraged if we suspect any eavesdropping – private.

More important, when we are out on the street, we are, for the most part, not interacting with anyone – however the public world may be lyricized in imagination, literature, and cinema as a world of infinite interactional possibilities. One does not interact with a newspaper or a book either. We may interpret them in our own way, and they may move, transform, overwhelm us; they do not remain any less unmoved, silent, same. For the most part, when we are in public or when we access things in public we do little more than look at people, objects, images, and words that do not look back at us. We don't interact – neither in urban life, nor in the world of culture in general. And this is not bad. Cities would be less stimulating places if there were more pressures in it for civic interaction. Literature would be a less liberating activity if we had to respond – especially in public – to what we are reading. Some movie producers do interact with the public while making a film when they test different endings on groups; it is far from evident that the practice improves the product. Any play that calls for participation from the audience – the so-called interactive theater – is just gimmicky.

Social scientists and philosophers have customarily ascribed typically unpleasant motives to the spectator. The book reader or the television watcher – all the more when what he is reading or watching is not approved by the commentator – is governed by some unpalatable interest or ideology. Or the spectator is under the spell of some hidden psychology: he is but construing an identity for himself, projecting his desires, playing out his neuroses and resentments, subjecting what he sees with his gaze.[7] Activists and others with a normative bent are wont to condemn spectatorship in general, considering it either as the stultified outcome of false consciousness or as a form of egoistic perversity that entails simply looking and not doing anything, even at the sight of suffering – a sin that is only aggravated when the pain of another affords the spectator a complacent catharsis, a moral self-aggrandizement, if not the vile delights of schadenfreude.[8]

In all this thinking, more often than not, the spectator's pathology is caused by the spectacle that he is faced with. And for countless contemporary commentators, not just for Debord or Baudrillard but equally for a garden variety of lower-brow intellectuals, spectacle is a peculiarly modern predicament that replaces genuine experience with representations, supplants reality with simulacra, generates alienation, and reduces us to passivity and powerlessness. Yet, as we saw, these things are inherent to the public sphere, physical or virtual, modern or not. A spectacle does not need any technology. One could even say that premodern times were more carnivalesque; urban medieval life was a cavalcade of spectacles, many of them infinitely more colorful than whatever we can see on television. Now spectacle is more of a media event, and, in a way, its effects are more modest since spectators have more distance – and freedom – from one another and from what they see. Still, it does not follow that that there is less participation now: premodern men and women were as much spectators as we are, in all realms of public life.

Moreover, the critique of the world as appearances is very old. We already saw it in Rousseau; it was first formulated maybe as early as by Plato. Among many other examples, here is Feuerbach's preface to the second edition of his *Essence of Christianity*, published in 1841 – well before the internet, reality shows, and smartphones:

> But certainly for the present age, which prefers the sign to the thing signified, the copy to the original, fancy to reality, the appearance to the essence, this change, inasmuch as it does away with illusion, is an absolute annihilation, or at least a reckless profanation; for in these days illusion only is sacred, truth profane.[9]

The discontents of spectatorship are those of the public sphere. As we saw, the reduction of the world to appearances poses a whole array of perils – but not the ones decried by most commentators – for those on display as well as for the spectators. There are good reasons why spectatorship is at times made into a moral issue and why visibility is regulated by taboos and censorship. Yet there is a positive aspect – at least potentially so – to spectatorship as well, especially when the spectator is anonymous and autonomous from other spectators. Voltaire was kinder, and more judicious, than Rousseau in his appraisal of spectacles and their spectators. People climb trees, he insisted, to look at massacres and public executions, not because of any ill will but simply out of curiosity – a passion that we share with monkeys and puppies:

> When little boys and girls pluck the feathers from their sparrows, it is merely from the impulse of curiosity, as when they dissect the dresses of their dolls. It is this passion alone which produces the immense attendance at public executions... Take a little dog with you in your carriage; he will continually be putting up his paws against the door to see what is passing. A monkey searches everywhere, and has the air of examining everything. As to men, you know how they are constituted: Rome, London, Paris, all pass their time in inquiring what's the news?[10]

It is often a natural, noninstrumental curiosity that makes us interested in other people's business (not to have a say in them but simply to know about them), look at other people on the street, read biographies and novels, zap channels on the television. Even though this orientation can harm through objectification, particularly when the gaze is collective, its impetus is nevertheless innocent. It is an orientation best exemplified in the modern figure of the *flâneur*: a character who strolls about the city, without interacting, without a concern for the common good, engrossed in the utter ecstasy of watching, governed by nothing except his ardent curiosity. He is "the true sovereign of Paris," wrote Anaïs Bazin, a nineteenth-century French essayist.[11] But it was Balzac who immortalized him in a famous passage:

To stroll [*flâner*] is a science; it is the gastronomy of the eye ... To stroll is to enjoy life; it is to indulge the flight of fancy; it is to enjoy the sublime pictures of misery, of love, of joy, of gracious or grotesque physiognomies; it is to pierce with a glance the abysses of a thousand existences; for the young it is to desire all, and to possess all; for the old it is to live the life of the youthful, and to share their passions.[12]

Baudelaire was the *flâneur* par excellence. Hence his hatred for the Belgian capital: "No shop windows. Strolling – something that nations with imagination love – is impossible in Brussels. There is nothing to see, and the streets are unusable."[13] Charles Dickens, a kindred soul, could compose his novels only while he meandered around London, ensconced in the persistent hum of the city. What the *flâneur* according to Baudelaire wants to see most, the perfect objects of his curiosity are people: "Anyone who is capable of being bored in a crowd is a blockhead."[14] He added,

For the perfect *flâneur*, for the passionate spectator, it is an immense joy to set up house in the heart of the multitude, amid the ebb and flow of movement, in the midst of the fugitive and the infinite.[15]

We have here then a one-sided relationship based on curiosity. The *flâneur* is drawn to the public. In fact, he is in public himself. Yet what draws him is also what allows him complete anonymity. "The spectator is a prince who everywhere rejoices in his incognito," emphasized Baudelaire. Owing to this low visibility, combined with his ability and desire to move from one spectacle to another, he can be detached, autonomous from what he is looking at, as well as from other spectators. While the *flâneur* looks objectively at the objective world – of which the crowd is an essential component – he does not become part of it. There is no moral or ideological identification with the object of his gaze, no desire to interact or participate. As Sartre observed in his biography of the *poète maudit* who wrote paeans to solitude in his poems, "Baudelaire, the man of the crowds, is also he who is most scared of crowds."¹⁶ And anonymity, allowing us to not interact with anyone, is the best protection against crowds.

Yet such a proud individualism is maybe not a necessary characteristic of the spectator. Take the *badaud* – the gawker, another urban figure again deftly delineated in nineteenth-century French belles-lettres:

> The simple *flâneur* observes and reflects, he can at least do that; he is always in full possession of his individuality. On the contrary, the individuality of the *badaud* disappears, absorbed by the outside world which ravishes him, which knocks him out to drunkenness and ecstasy. Under the influence of the spectacle which presents itself to him, the *badaud* becomes an impersonal creature; he is no longer a human being, he is the public, the crowd.¹⁷

The *badaud* loses his individuality not only because he unabashedly surrenders himself to what he watches. It is equally because his rapture is often a collective one, shared by other spectators. Voltaire fretted that these "useless people…gather at the first unfamiliar sight, to contemplate a charlatan, or two women of the people arguing, or a driver whose cart has overturned."¹⁸ We have here two types of spectators – or better, two modes of spectatorship that the same person can vacillate between. Remember that the crowd is not the mob, but simply a mass of people. Insofar as someone else is also looking at what he is looking at, the *flâneur*, simply by the semiotics of publicity, can come to resemble a *badaud*. The difference between the two figures should not be overstated. In both instances, the stance of the observer is not moral; it is one of simple curiosity. The *badaud* may be useless; so is the *flâneur*. In both instances, there is no real interaction, not even a mutual recognition: what one looks at remains a distant object.

The *flâneur* was for Walter Benjamin an alienated character; the cultural critic was dismayed that with the rise of consumer capitalism and its epitome, the department store, objects would replace individuals as the focus of his gaze.¹⁹ Decidedly a victim of his Marxism, Benjamin ignored that the people whom we see on the street or on the television, along with those whom we read about in books, are, just like the objects of capitalism or any other mode of production, already objectified simply because they are in the public sphere.

Simmel argued, it is well known, that the urban dweller, shielding himself against a surfeit of stimuli shelling him from everywhere, espouses a blasé mien marked by an indifference toward the distinctions between things. But the *flâneur* is interested in the specificity of everything; he does not choose between the obviously spectacular and the negligibly mundane. He is a collector of all appearances, small and big. His passion is indeed to notice what is taken for granted. The *badaud* is maybe not such a connoisseur, but for all intents and purposes he ends up accomplishing something very similar. Naturally, few of us are full-time *flâneurs*: we lack the time, the discipline. Usually, we go about our business on the street. Regardless, urban life affords us with the possibility of this most perfect form of spectatorship, and we all from time to time engage in it in our way, even though it is also a passion to be cultivated. *Flânerie* is sometimes associated with an aristocratic attitude toward the world. It is, in fact, deeply democratic – not because it is undertaken collectively (the *flâneur* tends to be all by himself), but because it is a capability open to all. And when we go about our business, even if we arm ourselves with a jaded façade, public life will still impose on us its innumerable appearances that we cannot but assess, make sense of, be delighted with.

There is an old liberal tradition that identifies the private with liberties and rights, and the public with obligations and duties. Even those in the conventional perspective who write about the liberating effects of civic dialogue also consider such talk as a duty of some sort imposed by society or reason. The contrast is off the mark. Both worlds have their proper freedoms and chains. As we saw, the public sphere can degrade. It can falsify our beliefs, our conscience. It has an indelible inauthenticity about it. It objectifies all its contents, including individuals. At the same time, the public sphere offers the spectator, in his senses if not in his body, a unique freedom – not the freedom to act, but rather a freedom, however momentary, to escape from the deep, heavy personal ties that bind and burden him in his private world. There is an emancipatory impulse in the *flâneur's* endeavor. He is strolling about because he wants to flee himself, his family, and all the other small prisons that make up the private sphere, even though these prisons provide most of the meaning of his life, to take temporary refuge in a world where he can flit from one sight to the next, from one face to another, interpreting and relishing appearances for their own sake, doing all this without being noticed himself. The public sphere is alienating, though alienating in a good sense: away from home, on alien territory, the spectator is seeking the spectacle that strangers stage as well as their indifference. To repeat: such a freedom, in its perfect form, requires an anonymous and mobile spectator and a condensed and vibrant public sphere brimming with strangers, all appearing somehow different in their own way.

This requires ideally a city – not a suburb. "Stadtluft macht frei," the city air makes us free – not only because of its political liberties, but equally because of its visual richness. For most of us, most of the time the only public space that we are visible in is a city, which is also where we see the most. And what makes urban life distinctive is not civic participation but its hustle and bustle, which is above all a sensory experience. Herein lies the most striking characteristic of the American public sphere: despite its matchless liberty and inventiveness, in much of the country there is little actual human presence. Driving for the slightest thing being the norm in sprawled geographical settings with low population density, American streets (other than in European-style cities such as New York or San Francisco built before the era of the automobile) tend to be deserted, desolate. Without sidewalks, pitch black at night without lamps, streets form the bleak penumbra of the American public sphere. The fact that there is no one on them is for many visitors and immigrants the very defining trait of the country.

The outdoors is synonymous with cars for Americans; driving is the quintessential public activity. John Updike put it best in *Rabbit at Rest*: "Driving is boring . . . but it is what we do. Most of American life is driving somewhere and then driving back wondering why the hell you went."[20] In much of the rural United States, where there are not even any malls, the only real physical public sphere, the only place where one can go and see people is Walmart: the true American agora combining individuals from all ethnic, racial, and religious groups engaging in all kinds of activities from shopping to eating to strolling to banking to sending mail.[21] But one can only get there by car, and many hang out in Walmart in their pajama pants, the private sphere outfit par excellence.[22]

An obvious reason why no one walks is the urban sprawl: there is no store, no school, no café, no restaurant, no library to walk to. Single-use zoning ensures that home, shopping, work, education, and entertainment are all endless highway exits apart from one another. Under these circumstances, there is surely something either mentally or financially wrong with anyone who walks; such a person is to be approached at one's peril. In any case, walking on the American street, without sidewalks or streetlamps for no one has any incentive to pay for them, is dangerous – especially for children, since the roads are designed to allow driving at fifty miles per hour.[23] Much of life is then spent in the car, hidden from sight, with nothing to see. True, one occasionally sees houses, when one is not on the highway. But there is usually no one on the front porches, and the yard that Americans prefer is the backyard. And things in the public sphere are only interesting to the extent that they involve or relate to people. Most houses and streets look the same anyway. When everything looks the same, one does not notice anything. The visual element, which is so important to the public sphere, is altogether lacking on the American street. Even beautiful suburbs with beautiful houses and beautiful trees are boring, not worth taking a stroll in, given the paucity of people on the street, given the general monotony. They are only good for jogging, but for that Americans prefer the gym – where one can at least look at the television monitor while sweating on the treadmill.

The problem is hardly restricted to nominal suburbs. Most of America is suburbia. Many places that are usually referred to as cities are indeed largely suburbs: their population density is low, activities are spatially separated from one another, one cannot go anywhere without a car, there is no one on the street. This holds largely also for many cities such as Seattle, Denver, Austin, Madison, Portland, Boulder, and Ann Arbor that are celebrated as vibrant, apparently because they boast of a wide range of ethnic food restaurants and liberals.[24] There is no clear differentiation between city and suburb in the American public sphere. It is true that we have witnessed a certain revalorization of downtown life – usually referred to as gentrification – in recent years. But the model is still a meager, bogus urban experience: simply a playground for young professionals, a homogeneous, thus monotonous, space in terms of activity, age, class, and – since this is America – race.

Now, virtual spaces, such as the internet or simply a library flush with books, also offer a promise for endless intellectual and sensual perambulations. After all, the virtual public sphere constitutes much of what we call culture. All but boundless, it is a richer world than the street in many respects. And it can be accessed for the most part from a protected, private space, allowing maximum liberty. Yet it should be added that in this solitary world, people only exist in their representations, which, to the spectator, are always somehow experienced as an absence.

There is a potential transcendence in spectatorship even when its unintended consequences may be terrible for those who are observed. All transcendence is but an escape.[25] Yet an escape from the shackles of our private lives, a negative liberty is not all that spectatorship can offer. It has a positive, affirmative side to it as well. Curiosity for the world, an orientation that can only be sustained for its own sake, is at once a most natural and a most sublime human capability. It is nevertheless outright passed over by much of social science, for which all behavior and dispositions are instrumental, expressive, or normative. Curiosity is none of these things. And without curiosity, there can be neither science nor art, neither in their production nor in their appreciation. Its cultivation is the true objective of liberal education. The Greeks – or rather at least some of them – thought that the spectator, motivated by his curiosity, was more insightful than the actor in the public sphere, who could not help being bounded, blinded by his very own lust for *doxa*, for fame and opinion.

Not all spectators are knowledgeable, it goes without saying. Many citizens are, for example, shockingly ignorant about political matters. And often elites equate this ignorance with incompetence, if not idiocy. Here is Schumpeter in *Capitalism, Socialism, and Democracy*:[26]

> Thus the typical citizen drops down to a lower level of mental performance as soon as he enters the political field. He argues and analyzes in a way which he would readily recognize as infantile within the sphere of his real interests. He becomes a primitive again.

But this is unfair. Much of the time, the typical citizen does manage to vote for the candidate or party that, when elected, does promote his perceived interests or values. Further, there is evidence he doesn't make worse political predictions than experts on television and in academia.[27] Many times he does better: 27 percent of all American voters – including 10 percent of those who voted for Hillary Clinton – correctly predicted that Donald Trump would win the presidential elections in 2016.[28] Compare this with the well-nigh unanimity among experts and pollsters that Clinton would triumph. Experts and other elites may have more information about the political system; this does not necessarily translate into deeper insight.

To the extent that he is not involved in what he sees, the spectator can freely appreciate and judge – so long as he is himself relatively free of visibility. His gaze cannot break into the surfaces, but surfaces are all there is in the public sphere. No wonder in Ancient Greek *theoros* meant a spectator: someone who would travel from one town to another to observe the world, his contemplations about what he had seen amounting in their sum to *theoria*.[29] The spectator can be emotionally moved. After all, this is what most theater and literature attempt. Pity and terror are what successful tragedy produce in the spectators, Aristotle claimed in *Poetics*. And other emotions – including foul ones such as schadenfreude at the fallen ones in scandals or sadistic glee during a capital execution – can inhabit the spectator too. A moral stance can be mixed with his affective state: he may be outraged by what he reads in the paper or, less rarely, by what he sees on the street. When visible to others, he may feign fury, his feint then growing only too real to his focus as well as to himself and others. He may even be finally propelled to some action, by his conscience or publicity.

Nevertheless, his emotions and morality are not what make the spectator a spectator. We find them in the private sphere as well. They are not the primary source of his interest in the world; the spectator can very well do without them. In any case, they do not prevail and rarely lead to genuine involvement. They are additives to his natural curiosity – although there are times, especially because of publicity, when these additives can overpower the essential ingredient, which is less a constant habit than a capability to be cultivated. Curiosity, implying an uninvolved yet attentive outsider who wants to know things for their own sake,[30] is an orientation that is mostly specific to the public sphere: it is morally problematic to be just curious about the intimates whom we interact with in private. This is why it is essential to keep the public sphere – and thereby urban life and culture in general – as free from politics as possible. What appears in public can always be politicized, and politics is itself a heavily public practice. But the more politicized the public sphere is, by citizens or others, the more it risks becoming dull or oppressive, usually both.

The life of the mind is not one of introspection; it is oriented to the outside, but without a desire to react against or change what it captures through cognition. Simple curiosity is at times deemed reprehensible: it frequently does not lead to action when inaction would seem inhumane, and it objectifies when objectification can be degrading. Even with good intentions, spectatorship can end up generating hurtful effects on what it focuses on – above all when there is wide publicity. Still, when the spectator is anonymous and mobile, when he is able to cultivate his natural curiosity, when he can somehow withstand the conformist pressures of the public sphere, when he is presented with something interesting to watch, his amoral interest in the world is equally the foundation of much that is joyful and worthwhile in life. It is one of the positive aspects of modernity that it has largely secured the anonymity of the spectator as he attends to physical as well as virtual spaces. Spectatorship is often viewed as a degraded, secondary existence. Yet it is what we do most of the time – in our everyday urban experience as in our cultural life. Moreover, unlike participation in the public sphere, which is invariably inegalitarian, there is a strongly democratic dimension to spectatorship. Finally, the spectator is always more authentic than the participant, who cannot be but putting on a show.

There is a further, equally underappreciated, transcendence to the public sphere. The gaze of the spectator, his reviled voyeurism, is not only too human; it is also aesthetically oriented. And the aesthetic orientation, in the words of Geertz, involves "an eager dwelling upon appearances, an engrossment in surfaces, an absorption in things, as we say, 'in themselves.'"[31] This absorption entails a certain losing oneself in what one spectates – rather than imposing one's interpretation on, or adopting a utilitarian attitude to, it.[32] Just like spectatorship, the aesthetic orientation has been dismissed or maligned by social sciences. It has been reduced either to a reflection (of one's social class or background) or to an instrument (to look down on others and exclude them). Pierre Bourdieu accomplished both of these reductions at once – inconsistently – in his famous *Distinction*.[33] But the sociologist is only one among many who miss the an-end-in-itself nature of the aesthetic experience.[34] Such reductionism equally misses the fact that even if we have different tastes, which mostly stem from our upbringing and exposure, the aesthetic orientation toward the world is itself universal. Pure aestheticism is rare and difficult; other inclinations will tend to creep in. Yet the shape and form of whatever may appear in the public sphere – objects, words, images, or people themselves – matter momentously to the spectator, no matter who he is, where he hails from, what his taste is. Nothing, nobody, no action in the public sphere, where appearances reign supreme, can evade being judged aesthetically.[35] This can evidently be troubling from a moral vantage point. But the beautiful is just as transcendental as the good, the just, and the sacred. And there is always a pursuit of beauty in the gaze that the spectator lances on the public sphere, a pursuit all the more honorable as the quarry can never be appropriated.

Endnotes

Chapter 1. A Critique

1. Habermas 1997: 105.
2. Habermas 1989.
3. Habermas 1996.
4. The decline trope can be found passim in the public sphere literature. See, for example, Aronowitz 1993, Dahlgren 1995, Hoynes 1994, Robbins 1993, Sennett 1977.
5. Habermas 1989: 171.
6. Benhabib 1996: 75, 80.
7. The sociologists Pamela Oliver and Daniel Myers, for instance, call the public sphere the "abstract space in which citizens discuss and debate public issues" (1999: 38). In a typical formulation, Myra Marx Ferree and her collaborators state, "Democratic theory focuses on accountability and responsiveness in the decision making process; theories of the public sphere focus on the role of public communication in facilitating and hindering this process" (2002: 289). See also, among many others, Alexander 1998; Eliasoph 1998; Emirbayer and Sheller 1999; Koopmans 2004; Lichterman 1999; Somers 1993; and Soysal 1997.
8. Putnam 2000.
9. See, for example, Calhoun 1992; Hohendahl and Silberman 1979.
10. Zaret 2000.
11. See, for example, Baker 1990.
12. Koselleck 1988.
13. Schudson 1998.
14. See, for example, Black Public Sphere Collective 1995; Eley 1992; Farge 1992; Fraser 1992; Landes 1988; Negt and Kluge 1993; Warner 1990.
15. This is a common theme in postcolonial theory and subaltern studies.
16. For example, see Benhabib 1992; Elshtain 1981; Pateman 1983; Ryan 1990.
17. Calhoun 1992, 1993.

18. For instance, Schudson 1998.
19. Eliasoph 1998: 16. Giafranco Baiocchi, another sociologist, similarly calls the public sphere "an instance of open-ended and public-spirited communication" (2003: 55).
20. Alexander 2008: 31. Alexander does not quite spell out how the civil sphere is different from the public sphere, except that he seems to want to avoid the face-to-face implications of the latter concept. But, in the main, his book is situated within the conventional perspective because the civil sphere is, for him, defined by universalism.
21. This is a point driven home by Alan Wolfe (2008) in his critique of Jeffrey Alexander's concept of the civil sphere (2008), which is mostly crowded by progressive movements. An advocacy spirit permeates public sphere studies in general.
22. For example, see Stamatov 2000.
23. Silverstein 2003: 18.
24. Mendelberg 2002; Sunstein 2001.
25. Young 2003: 20.
26. Kaufman 2002.
27. Compare this with Jeffrey Alexander's civil sphere: not only "a world of values and institutions that generates the capacity for social criticism and democratic integration at the same time," but also a sphere that "relies on solidarity, on feelings for others whom we do not know but whom we respect out of principle" (Alexander 2008: 4).
28. Knight 1933: 7.
29. Healy 2016.
30. Since it is identified with citizenship, the public sphere, in most analyses, is a national entity. But some social scientists also herald the ascent of a global citizenship and a corresponding "transnational public sphere" (Guidry et al. 2000: 6–7).
31. Fraser 1992.
32. Kuran 1995.
33. Sartre 1972: 12.
34. For example, Zaret 2000. Ikegami (2005) provides a masterful account of an aesthetic public sphere in Tokugawa Japan.
35. See, among others, Berman 1997; Kaufman 2002; Laitin 1995; Stamatov 2000.
36. Skocpol, Ganz, and Munson 2000; Tarrow 1998.
37. Starr 2004. State involvement in the media sector, such as regulations and subsidies, can also mitigate the unrestrained commercialism that Habermas laments. See Benson 2004.
38. Aronowitz 1993; Calhoun 1992, 1993; Elshtain 1981; Fraser 1992; Hohendahl and Silberman 1979; Hoynes 1994; Landes 1988; Pateman 1983; Warner 1990.
39. Hirschman 1982.
40. Zaller 1992; Converse 1964.
41. Putnam 2001; Milbraith 1965. Neuman (1986: 11) divides Americans into three groups: those who are politically active constitute 10 percent of the

population, those who are apathetic make up 30 percent, and the remaining 60 percent are simply spectators.
42. Prior 2007.
43. Neuman 1986.
44. Somin 2004: 4.
45. Berelson, Lazarsfeld, and McPhee 1986. Ignorance is not specific to Americans (Converse 1975: 79).
46. See www.annenbergpublicpolicycenter.org/americans-know-surprisingly-little-about-their-government-survey-finds/.
47. Neuman 1986: 17.
48. See, for instance, Putnam 2001.
49. Skocpol 2003.
50. Skocpol 2003: 222.
51. See, for instance, Altschuler and Blumin 2001.
52. Dahl 1961: 279.
53. Schudson 2006.
54. Mutz 2006: 130.
55. Huntington 1968.
56. Berman 1997; Eley 2013.
57. Mansbridge 1983.
58. The discussion of blogs and Twitter comes from Healy 2016.
59. Gianpaolo Baiocchi (2003: 65–6) remarks correctly that community meetings can be used for reputational ambitions. But he sees this as antipodal to the essence of the public sphere, which, according to him, is "public-spiritedness."
60. For an extended treatment, see Adut 2008.
61. Adut 2008; Lang and Lang 1983; Thompson 2000.
62. Bredin 1986; Griffiths 1991.
63. Sennett 1977: 239–51.
64. One way to think of scandals in the conventional perspective is as rituals. An example is Jeffrey Alexander's treatment of Watergate. According to the sociologist, the famous scandal – the episode that began with the botched burglary and ended with the resignation of Nixon – was a ritual of renewal in which, via civic discourse, the central categories of American civil religion were reaffirmed (Alexander 1989). Despite his trenchant account of the sacred element in American politics, Alexander downplays the very essence of the scandal. We find very strategic, partisan actions in the course of Watergate by all actors, not just by Nixon and his minions. The investigation of the *Washington Post* journalists, for instance, would have surely stalled absent tips from Mark Felt, a.k.a. Deep Throat, the number two official in the FBI who capitalized on the scandal to best his opponents in the infighting within the organization that broke after the death of J. Edgar Hoover (Woodward 2005). The public was not altogether impartial and nonstrategic in its thinking, either. Attitudes were predicated on party affiliations during much of the scandal. Regardless of their beliefs as to what Nixon had done, Republicans overwhelmingly supported their president until quite late in Watergate. More important, the Independents behaved similarly. Watergate was therefore no

ritual of renewal. On the contrary, it engendered an enormous contamination in American public life. The scandal was lived as a sordid affair: when Ford took office, the first thing he said was, "Our national nightmare is over," and most Americans agreed. Not surprisingly, confidence in public authority declined both during and after Watergate. These negative dynamics are not specific to Watergate. See an extended treatment in Adut 2008.

Chapter 2. A Realistic Perspective

1. Quoted in Emirbayer and Sheller 1999: 45.
2. Peirce 1940.
3. For example, Glazer and Lilla 1987; Jacobs 1992; Lash 1979; Sennett 1977.
4. The notion is consistent with everyday language use. Linguists George Lakoff and Mark Johnson (1980: 31) point out that "we conceptualize our visual field as a container and conceptualize what see as being in it." As I will argue shortly, the public sphere is mostly a visual entity, but auditory fields are also considered as containers in language, for example, when we recount what was said in a conversation.
5. Jacobs 1992: 35.
6. See, for instance, Simmel 1972; Gitlin 2002.
7. Weintraub 1997.
8. Rozell 2002.
9. Smith 1976.
10. A classical reference on the role of personal networks in the formation of political ideas is Klapper 1960. See also Granovetter 1973.
11. Collins 2003.
12. Gitlin 1981.
13. Arendt used the concepts public sphere, public life, public world, public realm, and public space interchangeably. See, for example, Arendt 2007: 14. And while her followers have mostly written on discursive citizenship, Arendt was herself very much uninterested in civic talk. Yet she reflected quite a bit on the actual public sphere – not just on the agora but also on less exalted spaces such as buses, hotels, and restaurants. The church, to her, constituted the only public place where appearances did not count (1959: 52–3).
14. See especially Arendt 1958: 57.
15. Arendt 1958: 41.
16. See the excellent account in Benhabib 1992.
17. Camp 1986. "Almost any function might be performed [in the agora]," noted the urban historian Lewis Mumford (1961: 162).
18. Aristotle 1996: 183.
19. Mumford 1961: 150.
20. Burkhardt 1998.
21. Ober 1989. Even Arendt had to acknowledge that the agonal spirit made alliances among Greek city-states impossible and generated envy and hatred within the citizenry (Arendt 2007: 16).
22. Aristophanes 2012: 18.

23. Huizinga 1955: 146.
24. Veyne 1987: 22.
25. Braudy 1986: 73.
26. Morstein-Marx 2004.
27. Nietzsche 1974: 38.
28. There are some social scientists who incorporate sensory access into their understanding of the public sphere. One example is Louis Quéré (1992) and his pragmatics of visibility. Another example is Nilüfer Göle (2015), whose work is largely on Islamic visibility. But hers is still a politicocentric, dialogical vision, situated largely within the conventional perspective. She writes, "The public sphere provides a stage for bringing together and reassembling citizens of different cultural and social backgrounds. The public sphere is linked to the democratic experience of pluralism" (7–8). It is a space devoted to the "exploration of norms and ways of living together," one that "provides a democratic site where newcomers can argue over their places and their norms" (8).
29. For the link between intimacy and confidentiality, see Zelizer 2007.
30. Geertz reported that in traditional Javanese society, where the household comprises both the nuclear family and the extended kin, people exercise extreme restraint, follow decorum, and demonstrate a lack of candor in speech and behavior to make up for the absence of physical privacy. See the discussion in Westin 1967.
31. And intimacy is not always put in practice in private: many couples sometimes relish being visibly, if not ostensibly, affectionate with each other in public settings – with varying levels of social approbation.
32. Arendt 1982: 76.
33. Smith 2011.
34. Smith 2011: 81–2.
35. Debord 1994: 17.
36. Plato 1986.
37. Geertz 1980: 135.
38. At the same time, a triad could well be more interesting. In a dyad, one often already knows the response of the other. When there are four people, however, the interaction is apt to devolve into multiple parallel conversations. See Knight 1933.
39. Wittgenstein 1973; Geertz 1977. See also Nagel 1986: 22–3.
40. As Thomas Nagel writes, "some things can only be understood from the inside" (Nagel 1986: 18).
41. Schoeman 1992.
42. White 2009: 277.
43. Kundera 1999: 105–6.
44. Geertz 1977.
45. Ebrey 1933: 40–2.
46. Ford and Beach 1951.
47. Hobbes 1981: 156.
48. Burke 2008: 26.
49. Camp 1986.

50. Peirce 1931: 2.228.
51. Kant 1965: 65–7.
52. McLuhan 1964; Eisenstein 2012.
53. Collins 2000.
54. Size matters, but what is conspicuous is not always obvious. French law regarding what can be worn in high schools differentiates "discrete" signs such as small crosses and hands of fatima from "conspicuous" ones such as the Jewish yalmulke or Sikh turbans. Needless to say, not everybody will agree with this categorization.
55. Goffman 1963b: 49.
56. Schickel 1985: 127.
57. Black 1983.
58. Fisher 1981; Goffman 1963a; Lofland 1985.
59. Jeffrey Alexander (2008: 250) should be commended for studying performances in the "civil sphere." His focus is nevertheless the civil and civic-minded discourse (especially its moral categories and heroic narratives) that undergirds performances. The raison d'être of performance is dramatizing "ethical positions and political programs."
60. Hamermesh and Parker 2003.
61. Baumgarten 1954.
62. Boltanski 1990.
63. Marx 1988.
64. Katz 2001.
65. But even then the signification is not completely over: while his detractors cried blasphemy, the artist himself promulgated that his work was about how capitalism debased religion. See the discussion in Steiner 1997.
66. Hallin 1989.
67. The indeterminacy of meaning produced by visual cues can be unnerving. As Simmel points out, "The majority of the stimuli which the face presents are often puzzling; in general, what we see of a man will be interpreted by what we hear from him, while the opposite is more unusual. Therefore the one who sees, without hearing, is much more perplexed, puzzled, and worried than the one who hears without seeing. This principle is of great importance in understanding the sociology of the modern city" (quoted in Benjamin 1999: 433).
68. Eliot 1968: 19.
69. Barthes 1978: 38.
70. Simmel 1972: 324–40.
71. "Before the appearance of omnibuses, railroads, and street cars in the nineteenth century, men were not in a situation where for periods of minutes or hours they could or must look at each other without talking to one another" (Simmel 1969: 360).
72. Breviglieri 2002.
73. Carothers 1956: 311; Ong 1967.
74. Goody 1977: 37.
75. Quoted in Vincent 1998: 65. But, naturally, anonymity was also criticized for facilitating defamation.

76. Jonas 1966: 139, 145.
77. Buber 1958.
78. Keller 2010.
79. Goody 1977.
80. Derrida 1967.
81. Eisenstein 1993: 93.

Chapter 3. Publicity

1. Compare to Dewey 1946; Park 1972; Lippmann 1965.
2. Goffman 1963a.
3. Quoted in Eisenstein 2012: 105.
4. Eisenstein 2012.
5. Emirbayer and Sheller (1999: 733) see, for instance, publicity as "the institutions of culture and communication."
6. Gluckman 1963; Granovetter 1973.
7. Lewis 1969; Aumann 1976.
8. Katz and Allport 1931. See also Merton 1968: 431.
9. Hamilton et al. 2014: 247
10. Sen 1967.
11. Chwe 2002: 15.
12. Ermakoff 2008: 202–3.
13. Geanakoplos 1992: 54.
14. Andersen 1996: 441.
15. Schoeman 1992.
16. Zerubavel 2006.
17. Walter Lippmann (1914: 6) pointed out correctly, "Often muckraking consists merely in dressing up a public document with rhetoric and pictures, translating a court document into journalese."
18. Knight 1933: 16.
19. Lang and Lang 1983: 310.
20. Lang and Lang 1983: 83.
21. For an extended treatment see Adut 2008: 99–128.
22. Lang and Lang 1983: 126.
23. Davison 1983.
24. Stephanopoulos 1999: 55.
25. Sewell 1996.
26. Hall 1966.
27. Swidler 2001: 168–9.
28. See, among others, especially Lévi-Strauss 1964.
29. Bourdieu 1979.
30. Geertz 1977.
31. Wittgenstein 1973. See also Morris 1938 for a more accessible overview.
32. Searle 1984.
33. An exception is the very important work of Ann Swidler (2001) on culture, which has many parallels and complementarities with my understanding.
34. Ball 1975; Elster 1989: 109.

35. Disraeli 2015: 34.
36. See the extended treatment of the Oscar Wilde case in Adut 2005.
37. Croft-Cooke 1972: 164; Ellmann 1988: 409; Harris 1916: 104; Marjoribanks 1932: 88.
38. Hamilton 1986: 236.
39. Greenberg 1988.
40. Wilde 1966: 894.
41. Queensberry 1949: 52.
42. Wilde 1928: 96–7.
43. Marjoribanks 1932: 230; Healy 1928: 416.
44. Ellmann 1988.
45. Ball 1975; Elster 1989.
46. Anderson 1983.
47. Bennett and Iyengar 2008.
48. Starr 2012.
49. Dayan and Katz 1992.
50. This mechanism is complementary to the mimetic isomorphism as theorized by Paul DiMaggio and Walter Powell (1983). The main motivation for imitation is uncertainty in both cases. The difference is that in the former uncertainty is about what others are doing, whereas in the latter it is about what is legitimate.
51. Strang and Macy (2001) show that this logic explains faddish cycles in the business community.
52. Ermakoff 2008. But this was only one factor in the fall of the Third Republic. That the German troops were only a mile away must have also mattered. See critical remarks in Adut 2010.
53. Turco and Zuckerman 2014.
54. Arendt 1981: 72.
55. Important exceptions are Cowen 2002 and Gamson 1994.
56. Boorstin 1961: 217.
57. Girard 1961.
58. Quoted in Thompson 2010: 210.
59. Alberro 2003.
60. Findlay 2014.
61. Findlay 2014: 40–1.
62. Art auctions are not without some opacity, though. It is not always clear who is actually bidding and how estimates and reserve prices are set. There may even be a lack of information about the bids. For lots that elicit no interest, auctioneers frequently pull fake bids "off the chandelier," and it is hard to know for sure which bids are real and which are not.
63. Findlay 2014: 88.
64. Quoted in Coppet and Jones 2002: 168.
65. Thompson 2010: 26.
66. Fried 1998: 48.
67. Hughes 1981: 369.
68. Baudelaire 1855: 712.
69. Adorno and Horkheimer 1986: 159.

70. Nietzsche 1967: 79.
71. Spierenburg 1984.
72. Bastien 2006: 40.
73. Collins 2009.
74. Huizinga 1955: 80.
75. Auguet 1972: 195.
76. Quoted in Sparks 2010: 425.
77. Quoted in Niven 1975: 22.
78. Thompson 2000.
79. Eisenstein 2012: 147–8.
80. Arendt 2007: 14. Similarly, the term fame comes from the Latin word *fama*, meaning "manifest deeds."
81. Compare this with Bourdieu's (1972) impoverished, incorrect understanding of the notion that has had a huge impact in social sciences. For him, *doxa* is ideology, some sort of false consciousness, the opinion of the masses. Yet *doxa* is not only opinion but also fame. And while for Bourdieu its main function is to limit the horizon of the powerless and neutralize them, *doxa*, in fact, affects mostly the behavior of the elite of the public sphere, who are seeking the attention and approval of the spectators.
82. Arendt 1982.
83. Geertz 1977.
84. Geertz gave short shrift to the visceral satisfaction that all gambling involves, whether it is individual or collective, private or public, deep play or shallow play.
85. Not even the seemingly selfless potlatch, a gift-giving feast that we find among many Pacific people, is immune from this logic. "The potlatch is in fact a game as well as a test," wrote Marcel Mauss (2002: 147).

Chapter 4. Politics in Public

1. Calhoun 1993: 273.
2. Chancer 2005.
3. Machiavelli 2005: 80.
4. Machiavelli 2005: 81.
5. Vacano 2007.
6. Schumpeter 1942: 258.
7. For an incisive take down of mainstream political theory that conceptualizes democracy as the voice of the people, see Greene 2010.
8. Merleau-Ponty 1960.
9. Kantorowicz 1957.
10. Foucault 1979: 29.
11. Spierenburg 1984.
12. Gambetta 1993.
13. Orgel 1975.
14. Bruyère 1880: 211.
15. Elias 1983: 118.
16. Apostolidès 1981.

17. Aquinas 1981: 2489.
18. Scott 1990: xvii.
19. Meyrowitz 1985.
20. Weber 1952: 286–7.
21. *Meet the Press*, September 20, 2015.
22. Goffman 1959.
23. Lowi 1985.
24. Kernell 1997: 70
25. The discussion in this and the following paragraphs draws heavily from Tullis 1988: 87–93.
26. Dahl 2010.
27. Dahl 2010: 33.
28. Brace and Hinckely 1992.
29. Cook 1998.
30. Greenberg 2016: 385; Altschuler 1990.
31. Summers 2000.
32. This attitude reached its apex during the Kennedy years. See Hersh 1997.
33. Schlesinger 2004.
34. Rozell 2002.
35. Neustadt 1997: 194–7.
36. Schlesinger 2004: 153–5.
37. Ibid.: 158.
38. Lowi 1985.
39. For an extended treatment of how distrust escalated the frequency of political scandals, see Adut 2008.
40. American National Election Studies poll. www.electionstudies.org/nesguide/toptable/tab5a_1.htm
41. Garment 1991.
42. Mayhew 2005.
43. Maltese 1992.
44. Grossman and Kumar 1981.
45. Edwards 1996.
46. Heclo 1996.
47. See www.theharrispoll.com/politics/Confidence_in_Congress_and_Supreme_Court_Drops_to_Lowest_Level_in_Many_Years.html
48. Cohen 2008; Ragsdale 1997, 1998.
49. Clayman and Heritage 2002.
50. Patterson 1994.
51. Cohen 2008.
52. Cook and Gronke 2001.
53. Thompson 2000.
54. Greenberg 2016.
55. *New York Times*, September 29, 1990, p. 8.
56. Edwards 2003.
57. See Adut 2004 for an extended treatment of the discussion in this and the next paragraph.
58. Smith 2011.

59. Kuran 1995. See Granovetter 1978 for a theoretical discussion of similar collective dynamics.
60. Warriner 1958.
61. Maxwell 1967; Ball 1975.
62. Darnton 1995; Popkin 1989.
63. Bentham 1843: 314.
64. Kant 1991: 93–130.
65. Elster 1998: 111.
66. Benhabib 1996: 71–2.
67. Garment 1991.
68. Schmidt 2007.
69. See, among others, Naurin 2008.
70. Quoted in Stasavage 2004: 20.
71. Elster 1995: 251.
72. Steiner et al. 2004.
73. Mill 1962: 204; Mill 1838, 87–8.
74. Quoted in Clark 1994: 148.
75. Anechiarico and Jacobs 1996.
76. Kuran 1995: 93.
77. Bentham 1843: 314.
78. Stasavage 2004.
79. The Freedom of Information Act was passed in 1966 in an effort by Congress to control the federal bureaucracy. See Schudson 2015.
80. Roberts 2006: 119.
81. See Adut 2008 for an extended analysis.
82. See *The Statistical Abstract of the United States 1978–2010*.
83. See figures in www.pollingreport.com/institut.htm
84. Thompson 1999: 183.
85. Harvey and Mukherjee 2006.
86. Sunstein 2001.
87. Berman 1997.
88. DiMaggio et al. 1996; Wolfe 1998.
89. Posner 2003.
90. DiMaggio et al. 1996.
91. Hampson 1988: 116.
92. Bourke and DeBats 1977–8: 259–88.
93. Mill 1873: 46.
94. Vincent 1998: 92–3.
95. Bensel 2004: 295.
96. McCook 1892: 1–13.
97. Evans 1917.
98. Heckelman 1995: 107–24. As the secret ballot replaced open voting, democracy also became less spectacular, again thanks to the efforts of the reformers. In nineteenth-century America, political campaigns involved intense partisanship in torchlight parades and mass rallies, with cheering crowds burning candles in their windows. As a historian (McGerr 1988: 28) writes,

Everywhere, parades marked the climax of the spectacular campaign. In small towns, a company or two marched down the main street. In New York, as many as 50,000 local and out-of-town marchers might turn out for a parade. Across the North, the more elaborate processions included special attractions along with the usual uniformed marching companies. Sometimes men rolled a giant ball or wheel to symbolize the inexorable progress of party principles. Occasionally, a live animal – a "coon" or a caged eagle – appeared in a procession. More often parades featured horse-drawn floats and giant wagons. The "ship of state," with girls and young women in white representing the states and the Goddess of Liberty, was particularly popular. Floats celebrated the varieties of labor, with men forging tools and making wheels.

99. Gueniffey 1993.
100. Mayer 1996.
101. Hersh 2012.
102. Parker and Parker 1998.
103. Coser 1974.

Chapter 5. Content Regulation

1. Gavison 1998: 43.
2. Posner 2001; Sunstein 1995.
3. Bourdieu 1982. Bourdieu's opinions on the issue largely reflect and systematize the common sense that I want to criticize here.
4. Language as structure, as *langue* in the Saussurian terminology, is deep but not always sociologically powerful, as William Sewell (1992: 24) points out. Language tends to become directly consequential in the form of *parole*.
5. Riesman 1942: 735.
6. Posner 2001. An early application of this approach can be found in Mill 1991.
7. Austin 1962.
8. Coleman 1990: 203–15.
9. Prosser 1984.
10. Posner 1981.
11. Friedman 2007: 41–2.
12. Shuger 1998.
13. Darnton 1984.
14. *Oxford English Dictionary* 1989: 573. For the history of English defamation laws see Veeder 1903.
15. Stone 2004.
16. Drew 2006.
17. Walker 1994.
18. Friedman 2007: 243.
19. Posner 2006: 108.
20. Twain 1907: 208.
21. Wolfe 1997.
22. Douglas 1966; Frazer 1994: 166–219.

23. Steiner 1956.
24. Freeman 1980: 52–3.
25. Malinowski 1926: 80.
26. Kennedy 2003.
27. Blackstone 1962: 242.
28. Adut 2008; Cocks 2009; Ellis 1912; Gilbert 1977; Greenberg 1988: 400; Harvey 1978: 940. Radzinowicz 1968: 330.
29. Cocks 2009: 45.
30. Jackson 1999: 18–22.
31. Cocks 2009: 65.
32. Cocks 2009: 37.
33. Quoted in Cocks 2009: 37–8.
34. Quoted in Hyde 1976: 84.
35. Gawthorne-Hardy 1979; Croft-Cooke 1967: 95–118; Grosskurth 1964: 33–40.
36. Hyde 1970: 181.
37. Quoted in Harvey 1978: 942.
38. See Adut 2008, ch, 2, for extended treatment.
39. Rey 1982; Merick 1998; Taeger 2000; Bastien 2006: 40.
40. Beisel 1997.
41. Gurstein 1998: 66.
42. Levine 1988.
43. Beisel 1997.
44. Waterman 1932: 11–12.
45. For a detailed account, see Fox 1999.
46. Kuru 2008.
47. Quoted in Poliakov 2003a: 36.
48. MacKinnon 1987.
49. Boling 1996.
50. McNally 2003.
51. Mahon 2005.
52. Clark 1972.
53. Julius 2003.
54. D'Emilio and Freedman 1988.
55. Sabato 2000: 82.
56. Gurstein 1998: 179–212.
57. Collins 1998; Summers 2000. There were, of course, the mistress and the illegitimate child of Warren Harding, but the issue only surfaced after the president died in office.
58. Lichter, Richter, and Rothman 1994.
59. Terrot 1979.
60. Marcus 1975; In effect, obscene images could be displayed in print-shop windows in many parts of London. See Nead 2000.
61. Kendrick 1987.
62. Adut 2008; Leckie 1999.
63. Leckie 1999: 62–111.
64. Spierenburg 1984; Gatrell 1994.

65. Nietzsche 1989: 66–7.
66. Friedman 1993: 26.
67. Sjoberg 1960: 248.
68. Quoted in Friedman 1993: 18.
69. Runciman 1952: 78.
70. This paragraph owes much to Pieter Spierenburg 1984, 1991. The Dutch historian also provides a cogent critique of Foucault. The execution of Damiens in 1757, involving quartering, was for the French thinker the perfect illustration of punishment in the Ancien Régime. It is not a coincidence that *Discipline and Punish* opens with a vivid description of the gruesome event. In fact, quartering had already become a rarity by then; it happened only twice in the entire eighteenth century, a period when many already regarded such cruelty as barbaric. Damiens was only quartered because he was convicted of attempted regicide, a most extraordinary and execrable crime. See also Bastien 2006.
71. Bleackley and Lofland 1977.
72. Elias and Dunning 1994; Crone 2012.
73. Elias 1982.
74. Ariès 1974.
75. Huizinga 1954.
76. Ariès 1974: 12.
77. Chanu 1978.
78. Spierenburg 1984: 20–5, 55–82.
79. Darnton 1984.
80. Ariès 1974: 25.
81. Elias 1982. See also Ariès 1974 and Spierenburg 1984.
82. Mandeville 1725. See discussion in Smith 2008.
83. Huizinga 1954: 1–2.
84. Mumford 1961: 277.
85. Quoted in Le Roy Ladurie 1979: 201.
86. Ariès 1989: 9.
87. Ariès 1989: 5.
88. Chartier 1989: 125.
89. Goulemot 1989.
90. Revel 1989: 188–9.
91. Corbin 1982.

Chapter 6. Visibility in Society

1. Organizations can be particularly intolerant. Schools, churches, and hospitals are very fastidious about what cannot be worn on their premises. Nowadays, states are not interested in what people wear on the streets, provided that they wear something. But it was not always so. Medieval and early modern governments controlled urban visibility by sumptuary codes. One's public appearance had to signal one's profession (Grace-Heller 2004). In the Middle Ages, dress communicated religious minority status as well: the Fourth Lateran Council in 1215 decreed that Jews and Muslims

should don special attire – yellow badges in some places, horned hats in others.
2. Rousseau 2004: 316.
3. Compare this with traditional Hindu women, who need to veil before close relatives, especially father-in-laws.
4. Marmon 1995: 8.
5. Campo 1991: 98.
6. Lesko 1987: 70.
7. Feldman and McCarthy 1983: 952.
8. Göle 1997.
9. Mernissi 1975.
10. Ammann 2006: 118.
11. Homer 2000: 11–12.
12. Clark 2001.
13. Beard 2014.
14. Thucydides 2013: 77.
15. Craveri 2005; Landes 1988.
16. Maza 1993.
17. Honneth 1996.
18. Said 1979.
19. Bourdieu 1999.
20. Butler 1997.
21. Chauncey 1995.
22. Hegel 1977.
23. Patterson 1985: 100.
24. Fanon 2008: 195.
25. Jakobson 1995.
26. Baldwin 1955.
27. Ellison 1995: 3.
28. For a devastating critique of Said, see Irwin 2006.
29. Katz 1961: 158.
30. Poliakov 2003b: 255.
31. Lofland 1985: 86.
32. Cited in Poliakov 1974: 64.
33. Friedlaender 1997: 73–80.
34. Wirth 1928; Baron 1928; Katz 1961.
35. Gregorovius 1948: 19.
36. Sennett 2011: 39
37. Katz 1961: 134, 138.
38. Cohen 2002: 745.
39. Mendelsohn 1999.
40. The rate of baptisms rose from 8.4 percent in 1901 to 21 percent in 1918. Mixed marriages between Jews and Gentiles increased from 8.4 to 29.86 percent from 1901 to 1915 in Berlin and from 11 to 52 percent from 1890 to during World War I in Breslau (Elon 2003: 229).
41. Arendt 2007: 99.
42. Katz 1961: 196.

43. Whitefield 1996: 4–5. See also Alexander (2007: 459–548) for an extended discussion of the Jewish problem in the American public sphere.
44. Leff 2005.
45. Quoted in Poliakov 2003c: 299.
46. Chauncey 1995.
47. Loftin 2007.
48. Quoted in Loftin 2007: 581.
49. Taylor and Fiske 1976.
50. Kanter 1977.
51. Elon 2003: 364.
52. Lippmann 1922: 575.
53. Quoted in Steel 1980: 194–5.
54. Gilman 1993: 193.
55. Abbott 1981.
56. Freeland and Zuckerman 2014.
57. Zelizer 2004.
58. Wilson 1956: 69.
59. Zelizer 2004: 212.
60. O'Neill 1987: 204.
61. Smith 1989.
62. Foucault 1979: 187.
63. A recent attack on surveillance and the culture of exposition is Harcourt 2015.
64. Alport 2000: 127.
65. Nock 1993.
66. Foucault 2006: xxviii.
67. For an excellent critique of Foucault's politics, see Walzer 2002.
68. Gauchet and Swan 1980: 491–2.
69. Parry-Jones 1971.

Chapter 7. Justice and Morality in the Public Sphere

1. Lytton 2008: 4.
2. For a difference between legal and popular justice, see Posner 1999.
3. Bérubé 1990: 3.
4. Farge and Foucault 1982.
5. Jousse 1771: 550.
6. But this does not always work, even for lawyers: one risks looking too much like a performer. Hence Jeffrey Toobin's evaluation of Brendan Sullivan, Oliver North's lawyer, in his trial following the Iran-Contra scandal: "He never gave an interview, he never held a press conference, never appeared to give a damn what was written about him and the case. He only cared about the judge and the jury. The press loved him" (1997: 168).
7. Huizinga 1955: 73.
8. Miller 1991.
9. Friedman 2015: 83.
10. Garment 1991; Johnson 2001.

11. Gormley 1999.
12. The best analysis of the scandal remains Posner 1999.
13. "The moment a good work becomes known and public, it loses its specific character of goodness, of being done for nothing but goodness' sake," stated Hannah Arendt (1958: 69).
14. Kundera 1984: 42.
15. Boltanski and Thévenot 1990.
16. Proust 1998: 232.
17. Goffman 1959.
18. Kant 1978: 39.

Chapter 8. A Defense of Spectatorship

1. Sennett 1977.
2. Rousseau 1979: 23. See Kohn 2008 for a thorough commentary.
3. Rousseau 2004: 17. He also claimed that theater degraded family values by displaying women and corrupted social life by putting a premium on artificial forms and precious phrases.
4. For the history of this tendency in Western thought, see Barish 1981.
5. Starobinski 1976: 119.
6. Scruton 1987: 13.
7. On the figures of the spectator, see Boltanski 1999.
8. In the best-case scenario, one turns the spectator into an actor – an impartial one bearing witness in the name of some general principle. Spectatorship is thus upgraded into a sort of action – or at least into a call or prolegomena to action. See also Rancière (2009: 13), who argues that the spectator acts as he "observes, selects, compares, interprets".
9. Feuerbach 2008.
10. Voltaire 2009: 48.
11. Quoted in Shaya 2004: 47.
12. Balzac 1901: 31–2.
13. Quoted in Benjamin 2006: 28.
14. Baudelaire 1995: 10.
15. Baudelaire 1995: 9.
16. Sartre 1947: 138.
17. Fournel 1867: 270.
18. Voltaire 1878: 527.
19. Benjamin 2006.
20. Updike 1996: 33.
21. Diego von Vacano, private communication.
22. That no one walks in America has become part of the national character. Here is a lament from a British expat:

> The fact is, Americans not only don't walk anywhere, they won't walk anywhere, and woe to anyone who tries to make them, as a town here in New Hampshire called Laconia discovered to its cost. A few years ago Laconia spent $5m on pedestrianizing its town centre, to make it a pleasant shopping

environment. Aesthetically it was a triumph – urban planners came from all over to coo and take photos – but commercially it was a disaster. Forced to walk one whole block from a car park, shoppers abandoned downtown Laconia for suburban malls. In 1994 Laconia dug up its pretty brick paving, took away the benches and tubs of geraniums and decorative trees, and put the street back to the way it had been in the first place. Now people can park right in front of the shops again and downtown Laconia thrives anew (Bryson 1999: 157).

23. Kunstler 1994.
24. See, for instance, Florida 2004.
25. Lévinas 1982.
26. Schumpeter 1942: 262. Some contemporary commentators have even argued that his ignorance should disqualify the typical citizen from voting. For a defense of epistocracy – the rule of the knowledgeable – see Brennan 2016.
27. Tetlock 2005.
28. Reuters/Ipsos poll, Nov 2–6, 2016.
29. Vacano 2015; Nightingale 2004.
30. Aristotle (2012: 1) writes in *Metaphysics*: "All men by nature desire to know. An indication of this is the delight we take in our senses; for even apart from their usefulness they are loved for themselves; and above all others the sense of sight. For not only with a view to action, but even when we are not going to do anything, we prefer seeing (one might say) to everything else."
31. Geertz 1977: 111.
32. As Adorno wrote, only a philistine "craves art for what he can get out of it" (1984: 25).
33. Bourdieu 1988. See the excellent criticism in Jon Elster 1981.
34. For a nonreductionist sociology of aesthetic experience see Ikegami 2005.
35. This holds for objects that we consume too. For a study of how aesthetics, as opposed to utility, matters in all consumer products, see Molotch 2005.

References

Abbott, Andrew. 1981. "Status and Status Strain in Professions." *American Journal of Sociology* 86 (4): 819–35.
Adorno, Theodor. 1984. *Aesthetic Theory*. London: Routledge & Kegan Paul.
Adorno, Theodor, and Max Horkheimer. 1986. *The Dialectics of Enlightenment*. London: Verso.
Adut, Ari. 2004. "Scandal as Norm Entrepreneurship Strategy: Corruption and the French Investigating Magistrates." *Theory and Society* 33 (5): 529–78.
    2005. "A Theory of Scandal: Victorians, Homosexuality, and the Fall of Oscar Wilde." *American Journal of Sociology* 111 (1): 213–48.
    2008. *On Scandal: Moral Disturbances in Society, Politics, and Art*. New York: Cambridge University Press.
    2010. "Interest, Collusion, and Alignment: A Critical Evaluation of Ruling Oneself Out." *Social Science History Journal* 34 (1): 83–9.
Alberro, Alexander. 2003. *Conceptual Art and the Politics of Publicity*. Cambridge, MA: MIT Press.
Alexander, Jeffrey C. 1989. *Structure and Meaning: Rethinking Classical Sociology*. New York: Columbia University Press.
    1998. "Civil Society between Difference and Solidarity: Rethinking Integration in the Fragmented Public Sphere." *Theoria* 12: 1–14.
    2008. *The Civil Sphere*. Oxford: Oxford University Press.
Allport, C. Fred. 2000. "What Would It Matter if Everything Foucault Said about Prison Were Wrong? Discipline and Punish after Twenty Years." *Theory and Society* 29: 125–46.
Altschuler, Bruce E. 1990. *LBJ and the Polls*. Gainesville: University of Florida Press.
Altschuler, Glenn C., and Stuart M. Blumin. 2001. *Rude Republic: Americans and Their Politics in the Nineteenth Century*. Princeton: Princeton University Press.
Ammann, Ludwig. 2006. "Private and Public in Muslim Civilization." In *Islam in Public*, edited by Nilufer Gole and Ludwig Amman, pp. 77–125. Istanbul: Istanbul Bilgi University Press.

Andersen, Hans Christian. 1996. *The Complete Hans Christian Andersen Fairy Tales*. New York: Gramercy.
Anderson, Benedict. 1983. *Imagined Communities: Reflections on the Origins and Spread of Nationalism*. London: Verso.
Anechiarico, Frank, and James B. Jacobs. 1996. *The Pursuit of Absolute Integrity: How Corruption Control Makes Government Ineffective*. Chicago: University of Chicago Press.
Apostolidès, Jean-Marie. 1981. *Le roi-machine: Spectacle et politique au temps de Louis XIV*. Paris: Éditions de Minuit.
Aquinas, Saint Thomas. 1981. *Summa Theologica*. New York: Christian Classics.
Arendt, Hannah. 1958. *The Human Condition*. Chicago: University of Chicago Press.
   1959. "Reflections on Little Rock." *Dissent* (6) 1: 45–56.
   1981. *The Life of the Mind*. New York: Harcourt, Brace & Jovanovich.
   1982. *Lectures on Kant's Political Philosophy*. Chicago: University of Chicago Press.
   2007. *The Promise of Politics*. New York: Schocken Books.
   2007. *The Jewish Writings*. New York: Schocken Books.
Ariès, Philippe. 1974. *Western Attitudes toward Death: From the Middle Ages to the Present*. Baltimore: Johns Hopkins University Press.
   1989. "Introduction." In *A History of Private Life, Volume III: Passions of the Renaissance*, edited by Roger Chartier, pp. 1–11. Cambridge, MA: Harvard University Press.
Aristophanes. *Clouds*. 2012. New York: Cambridge University Press.
Aristotle. 1996. *Politics and The Constitution of Athens*. New York: Cambridge University Press.
   2012. *Metaphysics*. CreateSpace Independent Publishing Platform.
Aronowitz, Stanley. 1993. "Is a Democracy Possible? The Decline of the Public in the American Debate." In *The Phantom Public Sphere*, edited by Bruce Robbins, pp. 75–92. Minneapolis: University of Minnesota Press.
Auguet, Roland. 1972. *Cruelty and Civilization: The Roman Games*. London: Routledge.
Aumann, Robert. 1976. "Agreeing to Disagree" *Annals of Statistics* 4 (6): 1236–9.
Austin, John. 1962. *How to Do Things with Words*. Cambridge, MA: Harvard University Press.
Baiocchi, Gianpaolo. 2003. "Emergent Public Spheres: Talking Politics in Participatory Governance." *American Sociological Review* 68: 52–74.
Baker, Keith. 1990. *Inventing the French Revolution: Essays on French Political Culture in the Eighteenth Century*. Cambridge: Cambridge University Press.
Baldwin, James. 1955. *Notes of a Native Son*. New York: Beacon Press.
Ball, Donald. 1975. "Privacy, Publicity, Deviance and Control." *Pacific Sociological Review* 18: 259–78.
Balzac, Honoré de. 1901. *Physiologie du mariage; ou, méditations de philosophie éclectique sur le bonheur et le malheur conjugal*. Paris: Société d'Éditions Littéraires et Artistiques.
Barish, Jonas A. 1981. *The Antitheatrical Prejudice*. Berkeley: University of California Press.
Baron, Salo W. 1928. "Ghetto and Emancipation." *Menorah Journal* 14: 515–26.

Barthes, Roland. 1967. *Système de la mode*. Paris: Seuil.
  1978. *Image-Music-Text*. New York: Hill and Wang.
Bastien, Pascal. 2006. *L'exécution publique à Paris au XVIIIe siècle: Une histoire des rituels judicaires*. Ceyzérieu: Champ Vallon Seyssel.
Baudelaire, Charles. 1995. *Le peintre de la vie moderne*. Paris: Fayard.
Baumgarten, Alexander. 1954. *Reflections on Poetry*. Berkeley: University of California Press.
Beard, Mary. 2014. "The Public Voice of Women." *London Review of Books* 36 (6): 11–14.
Beisel, Nicole. 1997. *Imperiled Innocents: Anthony Comstock and Family Reproduction in Victorian American*. Princeton: Princeton University Press.
Benhabib, Seyla. 1992. "Models of Public Space: Hannah Arendt, the Liberal Tradition, and Jürgen Habermas." In *Habermas and the Public Sphere*, edited by Craig Calhoun, pp. 73–98. Cambridge: MIT Press.
  1996. "Toward a Deliberative Model of Democratic Legitimacy." In *Democracy and Difference*, edited by Seyla Benhabib. Princeton: Princeton University Press.
Benjamin, Walter. 1999. *The Arcades Project*. Cambridge, MA: Harvard University Press.
  2006. *The Writer of Modern Life*. Cambridge, MA: Harvard University Press.
Bennett, W. L., and S. Iyengar. 2008. "A New Era of Minimal Effects? The Changing Foundations of Political Communication." *Journal of Communication* 58: 707–31.
Bensel, Richard Franklin. 2004. *The American Ballot Box in the Mid-Nineteenth Century*. New York: Cambridge University Press.
Benson, Rodney. 2004. "Bringing the Sociology of Media Back In." *Political Communication* 21: 275–92.
Bentham, Jeremy. 1843. *The Works of Jeremy Bentham*. Edinburgh: William Tait.
Berelson R. Bernard, Paul F. Lazarsfeld, and William N. McPhee. 1986. *Voting: A Study of Opinion Formation in a Presidential Campaign*. Chicago: University of Chicago Press.
Berman, Sheri. 1997. "Civil Society and the Collapse of the Weimar Republic." *World Politics* 49 (1997): 401–29.
Bérubé, Allan. 1990. *Coming out under Fire: The History of Gay Men and Women in World War II*. New York: Macmillan.
Birnbaum, Pierre, ed. 1994. *La France de l'affaire Dreyfus*. Paris: Gallimard.
Black, Donald. 1993. *The Social Structure of Right and Wrong*. New York: Academic Press.
Black Public Sphere Collective, ed. 1995. *The Black Public Sphere: A Public Culture Book*. Chicago: University of Chicago Press.
Blackstone, Sir William. 1962. *Commentaries on the Laws of England*. Boston: Beacon Press.
Bleackley, Horace, and John Lofland. 1977. *State Executions Viewed Historically and Sociologically*. Montclair, NJ: Patterson Smith.
Boling, Patricia. 1996. *Privacy and the Politics of Intimate Life*. Ithaca: Cornell University Press.
Boltanski, Luc. 1990. *L'amour et la justice comme compétence*. Paris: Métaillé.

1999. *La souffrance à distance: Morale humanitaire, médias, et politique*. Paris: Métaillé.
Boltanski, Luc, and Laurent Thévenot. 1990. *De la justification*. Paris: Gallimard.
Boorstin, Daniel J. 1961. *The Image: A Guide to Pseudo-Events in America*. New York: Harper and Row.
Bourdieu, Pierre. 1972. *Esquisse d'une théorie de la pratique*. Paris: Éditions Droz.
 1979. *La distinction. Critique sociale du jugement*. Paris: Les Éditions de Minuit.
 1982. *Ce que parler veut dire: L'économie des échangés linguistiques*. Paris: Fayard.
 1999. *Language and Symbolic Power*. Cambridge, MA: Harvard University Press.
Bourke, Paul F., and Donald A. DeBats. 1977–8. "Identifiable Voting in Nineteenth Century America: Toward a Comparison of Britain and the United States before the Secret Ballot." *Perspectives in American History* 11: 259–88.
Brace, Paul, and Barbara Hinckley. 1992. *Follow the Leader: Opinion Polls and the Modern Presidents*. New York: Basic Books.
Braudy, Leo. 1986. *The Frenzy of Renown: Fame and Its History*. New York; Oxford University Press.
Bredin, Jean-Denis. 1986. *The Affair: The Case of Alfred Dreyfus*. New York: George Braziller.
Brennan, Jason. 2016. *Against Democracy*. Princeton: Princeton University Press.
Breviglieri, Marc. 2002. "L'horizon du ne plus habiter et l'absence du maintein du soi." In *L'héritage du pragmatisme. Conflits d'urbanité et épreuves de civisme*, edited by D. Céfaie and I. Joseph, pp. 319–36. La Tour-d'Aigues, France: Éditions de l'Aube.
Bryson, Bill. 1999. *Notes from a Big Country*. London: Black Swan.
Buber, Martin. 1958. *I and Thou*. New York: Scribner.
Burke, Edmund. 2008. *A Philosophical Enquiry into the Origin of Our Ideas of the Sublime and Beautiful*. New York: Oxford University Press.
Burkhardt, Jacob. 1998. *The Greeks and Greek Civilization*. New York: St. Martin's Press.
Butler, Judith. 1997. *Excitable Speech: A Politics of the Performative*. London: Routledge.
Calhoun, Craig. 1992. *Habermas and the Public Sphere*. Cambridge, MA: MIT Press.
 1993. "Civil Society and the Public Sphere." *Public Culture* 5: 267–80.
Camp, John M. 1986. *The Athenian Agora: Excavations in the Heart of Classical Athens*. London: Thames & Hudson.
Campo, Juan Eduardo. 1991. *The Other Sides of Paradise: Explorations into the Religious Meanings of Domesticity in Islam*. New York: Columbia University Press.
Carothers, J. C. 1956. "Culture, Psychiatry, and the Written Word." *Psychiatry* 22 (4): 307–20.
Chanu, Pierre. 1978. *La mort à Paris, XVIe et XVIIe siècles*. Paris: Fayard.
Chancer, Lynne. 2005. *High Profile Crimes: When Legal Cases Become Social Causes*. Chicago: University of Chicago Press.

Chartier, Roger. 1989. "The Practical Impact of Writing." In *A History of Private Life, Volume III: Passions of the Renaissance*, edited by Roger Chartier, pp. 111–60. Cambridge, MA: Harvard University Press.
Chauncey, George. 1995. *Gay New York: Gender, Urban Culture, and the Making of the Gay Male World 1890–1940*. New York: Basic Books.
Chwe, Michael. 2002. *Rational Ritual*. Princeton: Princeton University Press.
Clark, Henry C. 1994. *La Rochefoucauld and the Language of Unmasking in Seventeenth-Century France*. Geneva: Droz.
Clark, Kenneth. 1972. *The Nude: A Study in Ideal Form*. Princeton: Princeton University Press.
Clark, Matthew. 2001. "Was Telemachus Rude to His Mother? Odyssey 1.356–59." *Classical Philology* 96 (4): 2001.
Clayman, Steven E., and John Heritage. 2002. *The News Interview: Journalists and Public Figures on the Air*. New York: Cambridge University Press.
Cocks, H. G. 2009. *Nameless Offences: Homosexual Desire in the 19th Century*. London: I. B. Tauris.
Cohen, Jean. 1997. "Rethinking Privacy: Autonomy, Identity, and the Abortion Controversy." In *Public and Private in Thought and Practice*, edited by Jeff Weintraub and Krishan Kumar, pp. 133–65. Chicago: University of Chicago Press.
Cohen, Jean, and Andrew Arato. 1992. *Civil Society and Political Theory*. Cambridge, MA: MIT Press.
Cohen, Jeffrey E. 2008. *The Presidency in the Era of 24-Hour News*. Princeton: Princeton University Press.
Cohen, Richard. 2002. "Urban Visibility and Biblical Visions." In *Cultures of the Jews: A New History*, edited by David Biale, pp. 731–98. New York: Schocken Books.
Coleman, James. 1990. *The Foundations of Social Theory*. Cambridge, MA: Harvard University Press.
Collins, Gail. 1998. *Scorpion Tongues*. New York: William Morrow.
Collins, Randall. 2000. *Sociology of Philosophies*. Cambridge, MA: Harvard University Press.
  2003. *Interaction Ritual Chains*. Princeton: Princeton University Press.
  2009. *Violence: A Micro-Sociological Theory*. Princeton: Princeton University Press.
Converse, Philip. E. 1964. "The Nature of Belief Systems in Mass Publics." In *Ideology and Discontent*, edited by David Apter, pp. 206–61. London: Free Press of Glencoe.
  1975. "Public Opinion and Voting Behavior." In *Handbook of Political Science, Volume IV*, edited by Fred I. Greenstein and Nelson W. Polsby, pp. 75–169. Reading: Addison-Wesley.
Cook, Timothy E. 1998. *Governing the News: The News Media as a Political Institution*. Chicago: University of Chicago Press.
Cook, Timothy E., and Paul Gronke. 2001. "Dimensions of Trust: Is Public Confidence in the Media Distinct from other Institutions?" Paper presented at the Annual Meeting of the Midwest Political Science Association, Chicago.

Coppet, Laura de, and Alan Jones. 2002. *The Art Dealers: The Powers behind the Scenes Tell How the Art World Really Works*. New York: Cooper Square Press.

Corbin, Alain. 1982. *Le miasme et la jonquille: L'odorat et l'imaginaire social, XVIIIe–XIXe siècles*. Paris: Aubier Montaigne.

Coser, Lewis. 1974. *Greedy Institutions: Patterns of Undivided Commitment*. New York: Free Press.

Council for Excellence in Government and the Center for Media and Public Affairs. 2003. *Government: In and Out of the News*. Washington, DC: Author.

Cowen, Tyler. 2002. *What Price Fame?* Cambridge, MA: Harvard University Press.

Craveri, Benedetta. 2005. *The Age of Conversation*. New York: New York Review of Books.

Croft-Cooke, Rupert. 1967. *Feasting with Panthers: A New Consideration of Some Late Victorian Writers*. London: W. H. Allen.

———. 1972. *The Unrecorded Life of Oscar Wilde*. London: W. H. Allen.

Crone, Rosalind. 2012. *Violent Victorians: Popular Entertainment in Nineteenth-Century London*. Manchester: Manchester University Press.

Dahl, Robert. 1961. *Who Governs? Democracy and Power in an American City*. New Haven: Yale University Press.

———. 2010. *The Pseudodemocratization of the American Presidency* (The Tanner Lectures on Human Values delivered at Harvard University, April 11 and 12, 1988). Acend.

Dahlgren, Peter. 1995. *Television and the Public Sphere: Citizenship, Democracy and the Media*. London: Sage Publications.

Darnton, Robert. 1984. *Great Cat Massacre and Other Episodes in French Cultural History*. New York: Basic Books.

———. 1995. *Forbidden Best-Sellers of Pre-Revolutionary France*. New York: Norton.

Davison, W. Phillips. 1983. "The Third-Person Effect in Communication." *Public Opinion Quarterly* 47: 1–15.

Dayan, Daniel, and Elihu Katz. 1992. *Media Events: The Live Broadcasting of History*. Cambridge, MA: Harvard University Press.

Debord, Guy. 1994. *Society of the Spectacle*. New York: Zone.

D'Emilio, John, and Estelle B. Freedman. 1988. *Intimate Matters: A History of Sexuality in America*. Chicago: University of Chicago Press.

Derrida, Jacques. 1967. *De la grammatologie*. Paris: Éditions de Minuit.

Dewey, John Dewey. 1946. *The Public and Its Problem: An Essay in Political Inquiry*. Chicago: Gateway Books.

DiMaggio, Paul, John Evans, and Bethany Bryson. 1996. "Have Americans' Social Attitudes Become More Polarized?" *American Journal of Sociology* 102: 690–755.

DiMaggio, Paul, and Walter Powell. 1983. "Iron Cage Revisited: Institutional Isomorphism and Collective Rationality in Organizational Fields." *American Sociological Review* 48 (2): 147–60.

Disraeli, Benjamin. 2015. *Tancred: Or, the New Crusade*. CreateSpace Independent Publishing Platform.

Douglas, Mary. 1966. *Purity and Danger: An Analysis of Concepts of Pollution and Taboo*. New York: Praeger.
Drew, Elizabeth. 2006. "Power Grab." *New York Review of Books* 53 (11): 10–15.
Dumont, Louis. 1980. *Homo Hierarchicus: The Caste System and Its Implications*. Chicago: University of Chicago Press.
Ebrey, Patricia Buckley. 1933. *The Inner Quarters: Marriage and the Lives of Chinese Women in the Sung Period*. Berkeley: University of California Press.
Edwards, George C., III. 1996. "Frustration and Folly: Bill Clinton and the Public Presidency." In *The Clinton Presidency: First Appraisals*, edited by Colin Campbell and Bert A. Rockman, pp. 234–61. Chatham, NJ: Chatham House.
  2003. *On Deaf Ears: The Limits of the Bully Pulpit*. New Haven: Yale University Press.
Eisenstein, Elizabeth. 2012. *The Printing Revolution in Early Modern Europe*. New York: Cambridge University Press.
Eley, Geoff. 1992. "Nations, Publics, and Political Cultures: Placing Habermas in the Nineteenth Century." In *Habermas and the Public Sphere*, edited by Craig Calhoun, pp. 289–339. Cambridge, MA: MIT Press.
  2013. *Nazism as Fascism: Violence, Ideology, and the Ground of Consent in Germany 1930–1945*. London: Routledge.
Elias, Norbert. 1978. *The History of Manners*. New York: Pantheon.
  1982. *Power and Civility*. New York: Pantheon.
  1983. *Court Society*. New York: Pantheon.
Elias, Norbert, and Eric Dunning. 1994. *Quest for Excitement: Sport and Leisure in the Civilizing Process*. London: Blackwell.
Eliasoph, Nina. 1998. *Avoiding Politics: How Americans Produce Apathy in Everyday Life*. New York: Cambridge University Press.
Eliot, T. S. 1968. *Four Quartets*. Mariner Books.
  1989. *Knowledge and Experience in the Philosophy of F. H. Bradley*. New York: Columbia University Press.
Ellis, Havelock. 1912. *The Task of Social Hygiene*. London: Constable.
Ellison, Ralph. 1995. *Invisible Man*. New York: Vintage Books.
Ellmann, Richard. 1988. *Oscar Wilde*. New York: Alfred A. Knopf.
Elon, Amos. 2003. *The Pity of It All: A Portrait of the German-Jewish Epoch, 1743–1933*. New York: Picador.
Elshtain, Jean Bethke. 1981. *Public Man, Private Woman*. Princeton: Princeton University Press.
Elster, Jon. 1981. Snobs. *London Review of Books* 3 (20): 10–12.
  1986. "The Market and the Forum." In *Foundations of Social Choice Theory*, edited by J. Elster and A. Hylland, pp. 103–32. Cambridge: Cambridge University Press.
  1989. *Social Norms: A Study in Social Order*. Cambridge: Cambridge University Press.
  1995. "Strategic Uses of Argument." In *Barriers to Conflict Resolution*, edited by Kenneth J. Arrow et al, pp. 236–57. New York: Norton.
  1998. "Deliberation and Constitution Making." In *Deliberative Democracy*, edited by J. Elster, pp. 97–122. New York: Cambridge University Press.

Emirbayer, Mustafa, and Mimi Sheller. 1999. "Publics in History." *Theory and Society* 28 (1): 145–97.

Ermakoff, Ivan. 2008. *Ruling Oneself Out: A Theory of Collective Abdications.* Durham: Duke University Press.

Evans, E. C. 1917. *A History of the Australian Ballot in the United States.* Chicago: University of Chicago Press. 1917

Fanon, Frantz. 2008. *Black Skin, White Masks.* New York: Grove Press.

Farge, Arlette. 1992. *Dire et mal dire, l'opinion publique au XVIIIe siècle.* Paris: Seuil.

Farge, Arlette, and Michel Foucault. 1982. *Le désordre des familles: Lettres de cachet des Archives de la Bastille.* Paris: Gallimard.

Feldman, Shelley, and Florence McCarthy. 1983. "Purdah and Changing Patterns of Women in Bangladesh." *Journal of Marriage and Family* 45(4): 949–59.

Ferree, Myra Marx, William A. Gamson, Jürgen Gerhards, and Dieter Rucht. 2002. *Shaping Abortion Discourse: Democracy and the Public Sphere in Germany and the United States.* New York: Cambridge University Press,

Feuerbach, Ludwig. 2008. *Essence of Christianity.* Dover Books.

Findlay, Michael. 2014. *The Value of Art.* New York: Prestel.

Finley, Moses. 1983. *Politics in the Ancient World.* New York: Cambridge University Press.

Fisher, Claude S. 1981. "The Public and Private Worlds of City Life." *American Sociological Review* 46: 306–16.

Florida, Richard. 2004. *Cities and the Creative Class.* London: Routledge.

Ford, Clellan, and Frank Beach. 1951. *Patterns of Sexual Behavior.* New York: Harper.

Foucault, Michel. 1979. *Discipline and Punish.* New York: Vintage Books.
  1980. *History of Sexuality.* New York: Vintage Books.
  2006. *History of Madness.* London: Routledge.

Fournel, Victor. 1867. *Ce qu'on voit dans les rues de Paris.* Paris.

Fox, Richard Wightman. 1999. *Trials of Intimacy: Love and Loss in the Beecher-Tilton Scandal.* Chicago: University of Chicago Press.

Fraser, Nancy. 1992. "Rethinking the Public Sphere: A Contribution to the Critique of Actually Existing Democracy." In *Habermas and the Public Sphere,* edited by Craig Calhoun, pp. 109–42. Cambridge, MA: MIT Press.

Frazer, James George. 1994. *The Golden Bough. A New Abridgement.* Oxford: Oxford University Press.

Freeland, Robert, and Ezra Zuckerman. 2014. "The Problems and Promise of Hierarchy: Voice Rights and the Firm." Unpublished manuscript. University of Wisconsin and the MIT Sloan School of Management.

Freeman, James M. 1980. *Untouchable: An Indian Life History.* New York: Allen Unwin

Fried, Michael. 1998. *Art and Objecthood.* Chicago: University of Chicago Press.

Friedlaender, Saul. 1997. *Nazi Germany and the Jews, Vol. I.* New York: HarperCollins.

Friedman, Lawrence M. 1993. *Crime and Punishment in American History.* New York: Basic Books.

2007. *Guarding Life's Dark Secrets: Legal and Social Controls over Reputation, Propriety, and Privacy.* Stanford: Stanford University Press.

2015. *The Big Trial: Law as Public Spectacle.* Lawrence: University Press of Kansas.

Gambetta, Diego. 1993. *Sicilian Mafia: The Business of Private Protection.* Cambridge, MA: Harvard University Press.

Gamson, Joshua. 1994. *Claims to Fame.* Berkeley: University of California Press.

Garment, Suzanne. 1991. *Scandal: The Culture of Mistrust in America.* New York: Random House.

Gatrell, V. A. C. 1994. *The Hanging Tree: Execution and the English People, 1770–1868.* Oxford: Oxford University Press.

Gauchet, Marcel, and Gladys Swan. 1980. *La pratique de l'esprit humain: L'institution asilaire et la révolution démocratique.* Paris: Gallimard.

Gavison, Ruth. 1998. "Incitement and the Limits of the Law." In *Censorship and Silencing: Practices of Cultural Regulation,* edited by Robert C. Post, pp. 43–65. Los Angeles: Getty Research Institute for the History of Art and the Humanities.

Gawthorne-Hardy, Jonathan. 1979. *The Public Schools Phenomenon, 1597–1977.* London: Penguin.

Geanakoplos, John. 1992. "Common Knowledge." *Journal of Economic Perspectives* 6 (4): 53–82.

Geertz, Clifford. 1977. *The Interpretation of Cultures.* New York: Basic Books.

1980. *Negara: The Theater State in Nineteenth-Century Bali.* Princeton: Princeton University Press.

Gilbert, Arthur N. 1977. "Buggery and the British Navy, 1700–1861." *Journal of Social History* 10: 72–98.

Gilman, Sander. 1993. *The Jew's Body.* London: Routledge.

Girard, René. 1961. *Mensonge romantique et vérité romanesque.* Paris: Grasset.

Gitlin, Todd. 2002. *Media Unlimited: How the Torrent of Images and Sounds Overwhelms Our Lives.* New York: Picador.

1981. *The Whole World is Watching: Mass Media in the Making & Unmaking of the New Left.* Berkeley: University of California Press.

Glazer, Nathan, and Mark Lilla, eds. 1987. *The Public Face of Architecture: Civic Culture and Public Spaces.* New York: Free Press.

Gluckman, Max. 1963. "Gossip and Scandal." *Current Anthropology* 4: 307–16.

Goffman, Erving. 1959. *Presentation of Self in Everyday Life.* New York: Anchor Books.

1963a. *Behavior in Public Places: Notes on the Social Organization of Gatherings.* New York: Free Press.

1963b. *Stigma: Notes on the Management of Spoiled Identity.* New York: Simon & Schuster.

Göle, Nilüfer. 1997. *Forbidden Modern: Veiling and Civilization.* Ann Arbor: University of Michigan Press.

2015. *Islam and Secularity: The Future of Europe's Public Sphere.* Durham: Duke University Press.

Goody, Jack. 1977. *The Domestication of the Savage Mind.* New York: Cambridge University Press.

Gormley, Ken. 1999. "Impeachment and the Independent Counsel: A Dysfunctional Union." *Stanford Law Review* 51 (2) 309–55.
Goulemot, Jean Marie. 1989. "Literary Practices: Publicizing the Private." In *A History of Private Life, Volume III: Passions of the Renaissance*, edited by Roger Chartier, pp. 363–96. Cambridge, MA: Harvard University Press.
Grace-Heller, Sarah. 2004. "Sumptuary Laws and the Roman de la Rose." *French Historical Studies* 27 (2): 311–48.
Granovetter, Mark. 1973. "Strength of Weak Ties." *American Journal of Sociology* 78 (6): 1360–80.
———. 1978. "Threshold Models of Collective Behavior." *American Journal of Sociology* 83 (6): 1420–43.
Greenberg, David. 2016. *The Republic of Spin: An Inside History of the American Presidency*. New York: Norton.
Greenberg, David F. 1988. *The Construction of Homosexuality*. Chicago: University of Chicago Press.
Greene, Jeffrey. 2010. *The Eyes of the People: Democracy in an Age of Spectatorship*. New York: Oxford University Press.
Gregorovius, Ferdinand. 1948. *The Ghetto and the Jews of Rome*. New York: Schocken Books.
Griffiths, Richard. 1991. *The Use of Abuse: The Polemics of the Dreyfus Affair and Its Aftermath*. Oxford: Berg.
Grosskurth, Phyllis. 1964. *John Addington Symonds*. London: Longman.
Grossman, Michael, and Martha Kumar. 1981. *Portraying the President: The White House and the News Media*. Baltimore: Johns Hopkins University Press.
Gueniffey, Patrick. 1993. *Le nombre et la raison: La Révolution française et les élections*. Paris: École de Hautes Études en Sciences Sociales.
Guidry, John A., Michael D. Kennedy, and Mayer N. Zald. 2000. *Globalizations and Social Movements: Culture, Power, and the Transnational Public Sphere*. Ann Arbor: University of Michigan Press.
Gurstein, Rochelle. 1998. *Repeal of Reticence*. New York: Hill and Wang.
Habermas, Jürgen. 1989. *The Structural Transformation of the Public Sphere*. Cambridge, MA: MIT Press.
———. 1996. *Between Facts and Norms: Contribution to a Discourse Theory of Law and Democracy*. Cambridge: Polity Press.
———. 1997. "The Public Sphere." In *Contemporary Political Philosophy*, edited by Robert E. Goodin and Philip Petit, pp. 105–8. Oxford: Blackwell.
Hall, Edward T. 1966. *The Hidden Dimension*. Garden City, NY: Anchor Books.
Hallin, Daniel. 1989. *The "Uncensored War": The Media and Vietnam*. Berkeley: University of California Press.
Hamermesh, Daniel, and Amy M. Parker. 2003, July. "Beauty in the Classroom: Professors' Pulchritude and Putative Pedagogical Productivity." NBER Working Paper No. 9853.
Hamilton, Alexander, James Madison, and John Jay. 2014. *The Federalist Papers*. New York: Dover Publications.
Hamilton, Sir Edward. 1986. *The Destruction of Lord Rosebery: From the Diary of Sir Edward Hamilton 1894–1895*. London: Historians Press.

Hampson, Norman. 1988. *Prelude to Terror*. New York: Basil Blackwell.
Harcourt, Bernard. 2015. *Exposed: Desire and Disobedience in the Digital Age*. Cambridge, MA: Harvard University Press.
Harris, Frank. 1916. *Oscar Wilde*. East Lansing: Michigan University Press.
Harvey, A. D. 1978. "Prosecutions for Sodomy in England at the Beginning of the Nineteenth Century." *Historical Journal* 21: 939–48.
Harvey, Anna and Bumba Mukherjee. 2006. "Electoral Institutions and the Evolution of Partisan Conventions, 1880–1940." *American Politics Research* 34: 368–98.
Healy, Kieran. 2017. "Public Sociology in the Age of Social Media." *Perspectives on Politics*.
Healy, Timothy Michael. 1928. *Letters and Leaders of My Day*. London: T. Butterworth.
Heckelman, Jac. 1995. "The Effect of Secret Ballot on Voter Turnout Rates." *Public Choice* 82: 107–24.
Heclo, Hugh. 1996, June. "Presidential Power and Public Prestige: A 'Snarly Sort of Politics.'" Paper presented at the Presidential Power Revisited Conference. Woodrow Wilson International Center for Scholars, Smithsonian Institute.
Hegel, G. W. F. 1977. *Phenomenology of the Spirit*. New York: Oxford University Press.
Hersh, Eitan. 2012. "Primary Voters versus Caucus Goers and the Peripheral Motivations of Political Participation." *Political Behavior* 34: 689–718.
Hersh, Seymour M. 1997. *The Dark Side of Camelot*. New York: Little, Brown & Company.
Hirschman, Albert O. 1982. *Shifting Involvements: Private Interest and Public Action*. Princeton: Princeton University Press.
Hobbes, Thomas. 1981. *Leviathan*. London: Penguin.
Hohendahl, Peter Uwe, and Marc Silberman. 1979. "Critical Theory, Public Sphere and Culture: Jurgen Habermas and His Critics." *New German Critique* 16: 89–118.
Homer. 2000. *Odyssey*. Indianapolis: Hackett.
Honneth, Axel. 1996. *Struggle for Recognition: The Moral Grammar of Social Conflicts*. Cambridge, MA: MIT Press.
Hoynes, William. 1994. *Public Television for Sale: Media, the Market, and the Public Sphere*. Boulder, CO: Westview Press.
Hughes, Robert. 1981. *The Shock of the New*. New York: Knopf.
Huizinga, Johan. 1954. *The Waning of the Middle Ages*. Garden City, NY: Doubleday.
    1955. *Home Ludens: A Study of the Play Element in Culture*. Boston: Beacon Press.
Huntington, Samuel. 1968. *Political Order in Changing Societies*. New Haven: Yale University Press.
Hyde, Montgomery H. 1970. *The Other Love*. London: Heinemann.
    1976. *The Cleveland Street Scandal*. New York: Coward, McCann & Geoghegan.
Ikegami, Eiko. 2005. *Bonds of Civility: Aesthetic Networks and the Political Origins of Japanese Culture*. New York: Cambridge University Press.

Irwin, Robert. 2006. *Dangerous Knowledge: Orientalism and Its Discontents.* New York: Overlook Press.
Jackson, Louise A. 1999. *Child Sexual Abuse in Victorian England.* London: Routledge.
Jacobs, Jane. 1992. *The Life and Death of Great American Cities.* New York: Random House.
Jakobson, Roman. 1995. *On Language.* Cambridge, MA: Harvard University Press.
Johnson, Charles A. 2001. *Independent Counsel: The Law and the Investigations.* Washington, DC: CQ Press.
Jonas, Hans. 1966. *The Phenomenon of Life: Toward a Philosophical Biology.* New York: Harper & Row.
Jousse, Daniel. 1771. *Traité de la justice criminelle, vol 2.* Paris: Debure.
Julius, Alexander. 2003. *Transgressions: The Offenses of Art.* Chicago: University of Chicago Press.
Kant, Immanuel. 1965. *Critique of Pure Reason.* New York: Saint Martin's Press.
    1978. *Anthropology from a Pragmatic Point of View.* Carbondale: Southern Illinois University Press.
    1991. *Political Writings.* Cambridge: Cambridge University Press.
Kanter, Rosabeth Moss. 1977. "Some Effects of Proportions on Group Life: Skewed Sex Ratios and Responses to Token Women." *American Journal of Sociology* 82 (5): 965–90.
Kantorowicz, Ernst H. 1957. *The King's Two Bodies: A Study in Medieval Political Theology.* Princeton: Princeton University Press.
Katz, Daniel, and Floyd H., Allport. 1931. *Student Attitudes.* Syracuse, NY: Craftsman.
Katz, Jack. 2001. *How Emotions Work.* Chicago: University of Chicago Press.
Katz, Jacob. 1961. *Exclusiveness and Tolerance: Studies in Jewish-Gentile Relations in Medieval & Modern Times.* London: Oxford University Press.
Kaufman, Jason. 2002. *For the Common Good? American Civic Life and the Golden Age of Fraternity.* New York: Oxford University Press.
Keller, Helen. 2010. *The Story of My Life.* New York: Signet.
Kendrick, Walter. 1987. *The Secret Museum: Pornography in Modern Culture.* Berkeley: University of California Press.
Kennedy, Randall. 2003. *Nigger: The Strange Career of a Troublesome Word,* New York: Vintage.
Kernell, Samuell. 1997. *Going Public: New Strategies of Presidential Leadership.* Washington: CQ Press.
Klapper, Joseph T. 1960. *The Effects of Mass Communications.* Glencoe, IL: Free Press.
Knight, Frank K. 1933. *The Dilemma of Liberalism.* Ann Arbor: Edwards Brothers.
Kohn, Margaret. 2008. "Homo Spectator: Public Space in the Age of the Spectacle." *Philosophy and Social Criticism* 34: 467–87.
Koopmans, Ruud. 2004. "Movements and Media: Selection Processes and Evolutionary Dynamics in the Public Sphere." *Theory and Society* 33: 367–91.
Koselleck, Reinhard. 1988. *Critique and Crisis.* Cambridge, MA: MIT Press.

Kundera, Milan. 1984. "In Defense of Intimacy: An Interview with Philip Roth." *Village Voice*, June 26, 42–44.
   1993. *Les testaments trahis*. Paris: Gallimard.
   1999. *Identity*. New York: Harper Perennial.
Kunstler, James Howard. 1994. *The Geography of Nowhere: The Rise and Decline of America's Man-Made Landscape*. New York: Free Press.
Kuran, Timur. 1995. *Private Truths, Public Lies*. Cambridge, MA: Harvard University Press.
Kurtz, Howard. 1998. *Spin Cycle: Inside the Clinton Propaganda Machine*. New York: Free Press.
Kuru, Ahmet. 2008. "Secularism, State Policies, and Muslims in Europe: Analyzing French Exceptionalism." *Comparative Politics* 41 (1): 1–19.
La Bruyère. Jean de. 1880. *Caractères*. Paris: Flammarion.
Laertius, Diogenes. 2014. *The Lives and Opinions of Eminent Philosophers*. Translated by C. D. Yonge. CreateSpace Independent Publishing Platform.
Laitin, David. 1995. "National Revivals and Violence." *Archives Européennes de Sociologie* 6: 3–43.
Lakoff, George, and Mark Johnson. 1980. *Metaphors We Live By*. Chicago: University of Chicago Press.
Landes, J. B. 1988. *Women and the Public Sphere in the Age of the French Revolution*. Ithaca: Cornell University Press.
Lang, Gladys, and Kurt Lang. 1983. *The Battle for Public Opinion: The President, the Press, and the Polls during Watergate*. New York: Columbia University Press.
Lash, Christopher. 1979. *Haven in a Heartless World: The Family Besieged*. New York: Basic Books.
Le Roy Ladurie, Emmanuel. 1979. *Carnival in Romans: Mayhem and Massacre in a French City*. New York: George Braziller.
Leckie, Barbara. 1999. *Culture and Adultery: The Novel, the Newspaper and the Law, 1857–1914*. Philadelphia: University of Pennsylvania Press.
Leff, Laurel. 2005. *Buried by the Times: The Holocaust and America's Most Important Newspaper*. New York: Cambridge University Press.
Lesko, Barbara. 1987. "Women of Egypt and the Ancient Near East." In *Women: Becoming Visible: Women in European History*, pp 41–77. Boston: Houghton Mifflin.
Lévinas, Emmanuel. 1982. *De l'évasion*. Montpellier: Fata Morgana.
Levine, Lawrence. 1988. *Highbrow/Lowbrow: The Emergence of Cultural Hierarchy in America*. Cambridge, MA: Harvard University Press.
Lévi-Strauss, Claude. 1964. *Le cru et le cuit*. Paris: Plon.
Lewis, David. 1969. *Convention: A Philosophical Study*. Cambridge, MA: Harvard University Press.
Lichter, Robert S., Linda S. Richter, and Stanley Rothman. 1994. *Prime Time: How TV Portrays American Culture*. Lanham, MD: Regnery Publications.
Lichterman, Paul. 1999. "Talking Identity in the Public Sphere: Broad Visions and Small Spaces in Sexual Identity Politics." *Theory and Society* 28: 101–41.
Lippmann, Walter. 1914. *Drift and Mastery: An Attempt to Diagnose the Current Unrest*. New York: Mitchel Kennerley.

1922. "Public Opinion and the American Jew." *American Hebrew*, April 14.
1965. *Public Opinion*. New York: Free Press.
Lipset, Seymour, and William Schneider. 1983. *The Confidence Gap: Business, Labor, and Government in the Public Mind*. New York: Free Press.
Lofland, Lyne H. 1985. *A World of Strangers: Order and Action in Urban Public Space*. New York: Basic Books.
Loftin, Craig M. 2007. "Unacceptable Mannerisms: Gender Anxieties, Homosexual Activism, and Swish in the United States, 1945–65." *Journal of Social History* 40 (3): 577–96.
Lowi, Theodore. 1985. *The Personal President: Power Invested, Promise Unfulfilled*. Ithaca: Cornell University Press.
Lytton, Timothy D. 2008. *Holding Bishops Accountable: How Lawsuits Helped the Catholic Church Confront Clergy Sexual Abuse*. Cambridge, MA: Harvard University Press.
Machiavelli, Niccolò. 2005. *The Prince and the Discourses*. Clayton: Prestwick House.
MacKinnon, Catherine A. 1987. *Feminism Unmodified*. Cambridge, MA: Harvard University Press.
Mahon, Alyce. 2005. *Eroticism and Art*. Oxford: Oxford University Press.
Malinowski, Bronislaw. 1926. *Crime and Custom in Savage Society*. New York: Humanities Press.
Maltese, John Anthony. 1992. *Spin Control: The White House Office of Communications and the Management of Presidential News*. Chapel Hill: University of North Carolina Press.
Mandeville, Bernard. 1725. *An Enquiry into the Causes of Frequent Executions at Tyburn*. London: J. Roberts.
Mansbridge, Jane. 1983. *Beyond Adversary Democracy*. Chicago: University of Chicago Press.
Marcus, Steven. 1975. *The Other Victorians: A Study of Sexuality and Pornography in Mid-Nineteenth-Century England*. New York: Basic Books.
Marjoribanks, Edward. 1932. *The Life of Lord Carson*. London: Camelot Press.
Marmon, Shaun. 1995. *Eunuchs and the Sacred Borders in Islamic Society*. New York: Oxford University Press.
Marx, Gary. 1988. *Undercover: Police Surveillance in America*. Berkeley: University California Press.
Masur, Louis. 1989. *Rites of Execution*. Oxford: Oxford University Press.
Maxwell, Robert J. 1967. "Onstage and Offstage Sex: Exploring a Hypothesis." *Cornell Journal of Social Relations* 1: 75–88.
Mauss, Marcel. 2002. *The Gift: The Form and Reason for Exchange in Archaic Society*. London: Routledge.
Mayer, W. G. 1996. "Caucuses: How They Work, What Difference They Make." In *Pursuit of the White House: How We Choose our Presidential Nominees*, edited by W. G. Mayer, pp. 105–57. Chatham, NJ: Chatham House.
Mayhew, David. 2005. *Divided We Govern: Party Control, Lawmaking, and Investigations, 1946–2002*. New Haven: Yale University Press.
Maza, Sarah. 1993. *Private Lives, Public Affairs: The Causes Célèbres of Prerevolutionary France*. Berkeley: University of California Press.

McCook, J. J. 1892. "The Alarming Proportion of Venal Voters." *The Forum.* 14: 1–13.
McGerr, Michael E. 1988. *The Decline of Popular Politics: The American North, 1865– 1928.* New York: Oxford University Press.
McLuhan, Marshall. 1962. *The Gutenberg Galaxy: The Making of Typographic Man.* Toronto: University of Toronto Press.
   1964. *Understanding Media: Extensions of Man.* New York: Signet.
McNally, Richard J. 2003. *Remembering Trauma.* Cambridge, MA: Harvard University Press.
Mendelberg, Tali 2002. "The Deliberative Citizen: Theory and Evidence." In *Research in Micropolitics, Volume 6: Political Decision Making, Deliberation, and Participation,* edited by Michael X. Delli Carpini, Leoni Huddy, and Robert Y. Shapiro, pp. 151–93. Amsterdam: Elsevier.
Mendelsohn, Ezra. 1999. *People of the City: Jews and the Urban Challenge. Studies in Contemporary Jews,* Vol. 15. New York: Oxford University Press.
Merleau-Ponty, Maurice. 1960. *L'oeil et l'esprit.* Paris: Gallimard.
Mernissi, Fatima. 1975. *Beyond the Veil.* New York: Shenkman Press.
Merick, Jeffrey. 1998. "Commissionaire Foucault, Inspector Noël and the 'Pederasts' of Paris, 1780–1783." *Journal of Modern History* 32: 287–307.
Merton, Robert K. 1968: *Social Theory and Social Structure.* New York: Free Press.
Meyrowitz, Joshua. 1985. *No Sense of Place: The Impact of Electronic Media on Social Behavior.* New York: Cambridge University Press.
Michelet, Jules. 1847. *Histoire de la Révolution française,* Vol. III. Paris.
Milbraith, Lester W. 1965. *Political Participation: How and Why Do People Get Involved in Politics.* Chicago: Rand McNally.
Mill, John Stuart. 1838. *On Bentham and Coleridge.* New York: G. W. Stewart.
   1873. *Thoughts on Parliamentary Reform.* London: Cosimo Classics.
   1962. *Considerations on Representative Government.* South Bend, IN: Gateway
   1991. *On Liberty.* London: Cox and Wyman.
Miller, Arthur. 1991. "Confidentiality, Protective Orders, and Public Access to the Courts." *Harvard Law Review* 105: 427–502.
Molotch, Harvey. 2005. *Where Stuff Comes From: How Toasters, Toilets, Cars, Computers, and Many Other Things Come to Be as They Are.* London: Routledge.
Morris, Charles W. 1946. *Signs, Language and Behavior.* New York: Prentice-Hall.
Morstein-Marx, Robert. 2004. *Mass Oratory and Political Power in the Late Roman Republic.* New York: Cambridge University Press.
Mumford, Lewis. 1961. *The City in History: Its Origins, Its Transformations, and Its Prospects.* New York: Harcourt, Brace & World.
Mutz, Diana. 2006. *Hearing the Other Side: Deliberative versus Participatory Democracy.* New York: Cambridge University Press.
Nagel, Thomas. 1986. *The View from Nowhere.* New York: Oxford University Press.

Naurin, Daniel. 2008. *Deliberation Behind Closed Doors: Transparency and Lobbying in the European Union*. Colchester, UK: European Consortium for Political Research Press.

Nead, Lynda. 2000. *Victorian Babylon; People, Streets and Images in Nineteenth Century London*. New Haven: Yale University Press.

Negt, Oskar, and Alexander Kluge. 1993. *The Public Sphere and Experience: Toward an Analysis of the Bourgeois and Proletariat Public Sphere*. Minneapolis: University of Minnesota Press.

Neuman, W. Russell. 1986. *The Paradox of Mass Politics: Knowledge and Opinion in the American Electorate*. Cambridge, MA: Harvard University Press.

Neustadt, Richard. 1997. "The Politics of Mistrust." In *Why People Don't Trust Government*, edited by Joseph S. Nye, Philip D. Zelikow, and David C. King, pp. 79–202. Cambridge, MA: Harvard University Press.

Nietzsche, Frederick. 1967. *The Birth of Tragedy*. New York: Vintage.

  1974. *Gay Science*. New York: Random House.

  1989. *On the Genealogy of Morals and Ecce Homo*. New York: Vintage.

Nightingale, Andrea Wilson. 2004. *Spectacles of Truth in Classical Greek Philosophy: Theoria in Its Cultural Context*. Stanford: Stanford University Press.

Niven, David. 1975. *Bring on the Empty Horses*. New York: Hodder.

Nock, Steven L. 1993. *The Costs of Privacy: Surveillance and Reputation in America*. Hawthorne, NY: Aldine de Gruyter.

Nye, Joseph S, Philip D. Zelikow, and David C. King, eds. 1997. *Why People Don't Trust Government*. Cambridge, MA: Harvard University Press.

Ober, Josiah. 1996. *The Athenian Democracy: Essays on Ancient Greek Democracy and Political Theory*. Princeton: Princeton University Press.

  1989. *Mass and Elite in Democratic Athens; Rhetoric, Ideology, and the Power of the People*. Princeton: Princeton University Press.

Oliver, Pamela E., and Daniel J. Myers. 1999. "How Events Enter the Public Sphere: Conflict, Location, and Sponsorship in Local Newspaper Coverage of Public Events." *American Journal of Sociology* 105: 38–87.

O'Neill, Thomas, Jr. with William Novak. 1987. *Man of the House: The Life and Political Memoires of Speaker Tip O'Neill*. New York: Random House.

Ong, Walter. 1967. *The Presence of the Word*. New Haven: Yale University Press.

Orgel, Stephen. 1975. *The Illusion of Power: Political Theater in the English Renaissance*. Berkeley: University of California Press.

Park, Robert. 1972. *The Crowd and the Public and Other Essays*. Chicago: University of Chicago Press.

Parker, Glenn R., and Suzanne L. Parker. 1998. "The Economic Organization of Legislatures and How It Affects Congressional Voting." *Public Choice* 95: 117–29.

Parry-Jones, William Llywelyn. 1971. *The Trade in Lunacy: A Study of Private Madhouses in England in the Eighteenth and Nineteenth Centuries*. London: Routledge & Kegan Paul.

Pastner, Carrol. 1974. "Accommodation to Purdah: The Female Perspective." *Journal of Marriage and the Family* 36: 408–14.

Pateman, Carol. 1983. "Feminist Critiques of Public/Private Dichotomy." In *Public and Private Social Life*, edited by Stanley Benn and Gerald Gauss, pp. 3–27. London: Croom Helm.
Patterson, Orlando. 1985. *Slavery and Social Death: A Comparative Study*. Cambridge, MA: Harvard University Press.
Patterson, Thomas E. 1994. *Out of Order*. New York: Vintage.
Peirce, Charles. 1931. *Collected Papers*. Cambridge, MA: Harvard University Press.
   1940. *The Philosophical Writings of Peirce*. New York: Dover Publications.
Plato. 1986. *Gorgias*. Indianapolis: Hackett Press.
Poliakov, Léon. 1974: *The History of Anti-Semitism, Volume I: From the Time of Christ to the Court Jews*. New York: Schocken Books.
   2003a. *The History of Anti-Semitism, Volume II: From Mohammed to the Marranos*. Philadelphia: University of Pennsylvania Press.
   2003b. *The History of Anti-Semitism, Volume III: From Voltaire to Wagner*. Philadelphia: University of Pennsylvania Press.
   2003c. *The History of Anti-Semitism, Volume IV: Suicidal Europe, 1879–1933*. Philadelphia: University of Pennsylvania Press.
Popkin, Jeremy. 1989. "Pamphlet Journalism at the End of the Old Regime." *Eighteenth Century Studies* 22: 351–67.
Posner, Richard. 1981. *The Economics of Justice*. Cambridge, MA: Harvard University Press.
   1999. *An Affair of State: The Investigation, Trial, and Impeachment of President Clinton*. Cambridge, MA: Harvard University Press.
   2001. "The Speech Market and the Legacy of Schenck." In *Eternally Vigilant: Free Speech in the Modern Era*, edited by Lee C. Bollinger and Geoffrey R. Stone, pp. 120–51. Chicago: University of Chicago Press.
   2003. *Law, Pragmatism, and Democracy*. Cambridge, MA: Harvard University Press.
   2006. *Not a Suicide Pact: The Constitution in a Time of National Emergency*. New York: Oxford University Press.
Prior, Markus. 2007. *Post-Broadcast Democracy: How Media Choice Increases Inequality in Political Involvement and Polarizes Elections*. New York: Cambridge University Press.
Prosser, William L. 1988. "Defamation." In *Prosser and Keeton on the Law of Torts*, edited by William Lloyd Prosser and W. Page Keeton, pp. 771–849. St. Paul, MN: West Group.
Proust, Marcel. 1998. *In Search of Lost Time, Volume II: Within A Budding Grove*. New York: Modern Library Classics.
Putnam, Robert. 2001. *Bowling Alone: The Collapse and Revival of American Community*. New York: Simon & Schuster.
Queensberry, Marquess of. 1949. *Oscar Wilde and Black Douglas*. London: Hutchinson.
Quéré, Louis. 1992. "L'espace public: De la théorie politique à la métathéorie sociologique." *Quaderni*. 18: 75–92.
Radzinowicz, Leon. 1968. *A History of English Criminal Law, Volume IV: Grappling for Control*. London: Stevens.

Rancière, Jacques. 2009. *Emancipated Spectator*. London: Verso.
Ragsdale, Lyn. 1997. "Disconnected Politics: Public Opinion and Presidents." In *Understanding Public Opinion*, edited by Barbara Norrander and Clyde Willcox, pp. 229–51. Washington, DC: CQ Press,
   1998. *Vital Statistics on the Presidency: Washington to Clinton*. Washington, DC: CQ Press.
Revel, Jacques. 1989. "The Uses of Civility." In *A History of Private Life, Volume III: Passions of the Renaissance*, edited by Roger Chartier, pp. 167–205. Cambridge, MA: Harvard University Press.
Rey, Michel. 1982. "Police et Sodomie à Paris au XVIIIe siècle. Du pêché au désordre." *Revue d'histoire moderne et contemporaine* 29: 113–24.
Riesman, David. 1942. "Democracy and Defamation: Control of Group Libel." *Columbia Law Review* 42: 727–80.
Robbins, Bruce, ed. 1993. *The Phantom Public Sphere*. Minneapolis: University of Minnesota Press.
Roberts, Alasdair. 2006. *Blacked Out: Government Secrecy in the Information Age*. New York: Cambridge University Press.
Rousseau, Jean-Jacques. 1959. *Confessions*. Paris: Gallimard.
   1979. *Emile or On Education*. New York: Basic Books.
   2004. *Letter to D'Alembert and Writings for the Theater*. Hanover, NH: University Press of New England.
Rozell, Mark J. 2002. *Executive Privilege: Presidential Power, Secrecy, and Accountability*. Kansas City: University Press of Kansas.
Rozenblit, Marsha. 1983. *The Jews of Vienna, 1867–1914: Assimilation and Identity*. Albany: State University of New York Press.
Runciman, Steven. 1952. "Christian Constantinople." In *Golden Age of the Great Cities*, pp. 56–81. London: Thames and Hudson.
Ryan, Mary P. 1990. *Women in Public: Between Banners and Ballots, 1825–1880*. Baltimore: Johns Hopkins University Press.
Sabato, Larry. 2000. *Feeding Frenzy: How Attack Journalism Has Transformed American Politics*. Baltimore: Lanahan Publishers.
Said, Edward. 1979. *Orientalism*. New York: Vintage.
Sartre, Jean-Paul. 1947. *Baudelaire*. Paris: Gallimard.
   1972. *Plaidoyer pour les intellectuels*. Paris: Gallimard.
Schickel, Richard. 1985. *Intimate Strangers: The Culture of Celebrity*. New York: Doubleday.
Schlesinger, Arthur. 2004. *The Imperial Presidency*. Boston: Mariner Books.
Schoeman, Ferdinand. 1992. *Privacy and Social Freedom*. New York: Cambridge University Press.
Schmidt, Carl. 2007. *The Concept of the Political*. Chicago: University of Chicago Press.
Schudson, Michael. 1998. *The Good Citizen: A History of American Civic Life*. New York: Free Press.
   2006. "Varieties of Civic Experience." *Citizenship Studies* 10 (5): 591–606.
   2015. *The Rise of the Right to Know: Politics and the Culture of Transparency, 1945–1975*. Cambridge, MA: Harvard University Press.

Schumpeter, Joseph A. 1942. *Capitalism, Socialism, and Democracy.* New York: Harper and Brothers.
Scott, C. James. 1990. *Domination and the Arts of Resistance: Hidden Transcripts.* New Haven: Yale University Press.
Scruton, Roger. 1987. "Public Space and the Classical Vernacular." In *The Public Face of Architecture: Civic Culture and Public Spaces*, edited by Nathan Glazer and Mark Lilla, pp. 13–25. New York: Free Press.
Searle, John. 1984. *Expression and Meaning: Studies in the Theory of Speech Theory.* New York: Cambridge University Press.
Sen, Armatya K. 1967. "Isolation, Assurance, and the Social Rate of Discount." *Quarterly Journal of Economics* 81: 112–24.
Sennett, Richard. 1977. *The Fall of Public Man.* New York: Knopf.
   1994. *Flesh and Stone: The Body and the City in Western Civilization.* New York: Norton.
   2011. *The Foreigner: Two Essays on Exile.* London: Notting Hill Editions.
Sewell, William H. 1992. "A Theory of Structure: Duality, Agency, and Transformation." *American Journal of Sociology* 98 (1): 1–29.
   1996. "Historical Events as Transformations of Structures: Inventing Revolution at the Bastille." *Theory and Society* 25 (6): 841–81.
Shaya, Gregory. 2004. "The *Flâneur*, the *Badaud*, and the Making of a Mass Public in France, circa 1860–1910." *American Historical Review* 109 (1): 41–77.
Shuger, Debora. 1998. "Civility and Censorship in Early Modern Europe." In *Censorship and Silencing: Practices of Cultural Regulation*, edited by Robert C. Post, pp. 89–110. Los Angeles: Getty Research Institute for the History of Art and the Humanities.
Silverstein, Michael. 2003. *Talking Politics: The Substance of Style from Abe to "W."* Chicago: Prickly Paradigm Press.
Simmel, Georg. 1969. "Sociology of the Sense: Visual Interaction." In *Introduction to the Science of Sociology*, edited by Robert E. Park and Ernest W. Burgess, pp. 356–60. Chicago: University of Chicago Press.
   1972. *On Individuality and Social Forms.* Chicago: University of Chicago Press.
Sjoberg, Gideon. 1960. *Preindustrial City.* New York: Free Press.
Skocpol, Theda. 2003. *Diminished Democracy: From Membership to Management in American Civic Life.* Norman: University of Oklahoma Press, 2003.
Skocpol, Theda, M. Ganz, and Z. Munson. 2000. "A Nation of Organizers: The Institutional Origins of Civic Voluntarism in the United States." *American Political Science Review* 94 (3): 527–46.
Smith, Adam. 1976. *An Inquiry into the Nature and Causes of the Wealth of Nations.* Chicago: University of Chicago Press.
   2011. *The Theory of Moral Sentiments.* Seattle, WA: Gutenberg Publishers.
Smith, Philip. 2008. *Punishment and Culture.* Chicago: University of Chicago Press.
Smith, Steven. 1989. *Call to Order: Floor Politics in the House and Senate.* Washington, DC: Brookings Institution.

Somers, Margaret R. 1993. "Citizenship and the Place of the Public Sphere: Law, Community, and Political Culture in the Transition to Democracy." *American Sociological Review* 58: 587–620.

Somin, Ilya. 2004. "When Ignorance Isn't Bliss: How Political Ignorance Threatens Democracy." *Policy Analysis* 525: 1–27.

Soysal, Yasemin Nuhoglu. 1997. "Changing Parameters of Citizenship and Claims- Making: Organized Islam in European Public Spheres." *Theory and Society* 26: 509–27.

Sparks, Jared. 2010. *The Life of Gouverneur*. Charleston, SC: Nabu Press.

Spierenburg, Pieter. 1984. *The Spectacle of Suffering*. Cambridge: Cambridge University Press.

  1991. *Broken Spell: A Cultural and Anthropological History of Preindustrial Europe*. New Brunswick, NJ: Rutgers University Press.

Stamatov, Peter. 2000. "The Making of a 'Bad' Public: Ethnonational Mobilization in Post-Communist Bulgaria." *Theory and Society* 29: 549–72.

Starobinski, Jean. 1976. *Jean-Jacques Rousseau: La transparence et l'obstacle*. Paris: Gallimard.

Starr, Paul. 2004. *The Creation of the Media: Political Origins of Modern Communications*. New York: Basic Books.

  2012. "An Unexpected Crisis: The News Media in Post-Industrial Democracies." *International Journal of Press/Politics*. 17: 234–42.

Stasavage, David, 2004." Open-Door or Closed-Door? Transparency in Domestic and International Bargaining." *International Organization* 58(4): 667–704.

Steel, Ronald. 1980. *Walter Lippmann and the American Century*. New York: Little Brown & Co.

Steiner, Franz. 1956. *Taboo*. Harmondsworth: Penguin.

Steiner, Jurg, André Bächtiger, Markus Spörndli, and Marco R. Steenbergen 2004. *Deliberative Politics in Action: Analyzing Parliamentary Discourse*. New York: Cambridge University Press.

Steiner, Wendy. 1997. *Scandal of Pleasure: Art in an Age of Fundamentalism*. Chicago: University of Chicago Press.

Stephanopoulos, George. 1999. *All Too Human: A Political Education*. Boston: Little Brown.

Stillman, Sarah. 2016. "The List." *New Yorker*, March 14.

Stone, Geoffrey. 2004. *Perilous Times: Free Speech in Wartime from the Sedition Act of 1798 to the War on Terrorism*. New York: W. W. Norton.

Strang, David, and Michael W. Macy. 2001. "In Search of Excellence: Fads, Success Stories, and Adaptive Emulation." *American Journal of Sociology* 107 (1): 147–82.

Summers, John. 2000. "What Happened to Sex Scandals? Politics and Peccadilloes, Jefferson to Kennedy." *Journal of American History* 87: 825–854.

Sunstein, Cass. 1995. *Democracy and the Problem of Free Speech*. New York: Free Press.

  2001. *Republic.com*. Princeton: Princeton University Press.

Swidler, Ann. 2001. *Talk of Love: How Culture Matters*. Chicago: University of Chicago Press.

Taeger, Angela. 2000. "Du péché à la peccadille; la sodomie et la rationalisation des mœurs en France et au XVIIIe siècle. Du sexuel à la sexualité." *Francia* 27 (2): 103–18.
Tarrow, Sidney. 1998. "The Very Excess of Democracy: State Building and Contentious Politics in America." In *Social Movements and American Political Institutions*, edited by Anne Costain and Andrew McFarland, pp. 20–38. New York: Rowman & Littlefield.
Taylor, Charles. 1995. *Philosophical Arguments*. Cambridge, MA: Harvard University Press.
Taylor, Shelley, and Susan Fiske. 1976. "The Token in the Small Group: Research, Findings and Theoretical Implications." In *Psychology and Politics: Collected Papers*, edited by J. Sweeney. New Haven: Yale University Press.
Terrot, Charles. 1979. *The Maiden Tribute*. London: Frederick Muller.
Tetlock, Philip E. 2005. *Expert Political Judgment*. Princeton: Princeton University Press.
Thompson, Denis F. 1999. "Democratic Secrecy." *Political Science Quarterly* 114 (2): 181–93.
Thompson, Don. 2010. *The $12 Million Stuffed Shark: The Curious Economics of Contemporary Art*. New York: St. Martin's Griffin.
Thompson, John. 2000. *Political Scandal: Power and Visibility in the Media Age*. Cambridge: Polity.
Thucydides. 2013. *The History of the Peloponnesian War*. CreateSpace Independent Publishing Forum.
Tilly, Charles. 1992, April. "Civil Society and Revolutions." Paper delivered at Conference on Civil Society, New School for Social Research.
Toobin, Jeffrey. 1997. *The Run of His Life: The People v. O. J. Simpson*. New York: Touchstone Books.
Tullis, Jeffrey. 1988. *The Rhetorical Presidency*. Princeton: Princeton University Press.
Turco, Catherine, and Ezra Zuckerman. 2014. "So You Think You Can Dance: Lessons from the U.S. Private Equity Bubble." *Sociological Science* 1: 81–101.
Twain, Mark. 1907. *Complete Works of Mark Twain*. New York: Harper and Brothers.
Updike, John. 1996. *Rabbit at Rest*. New York: Random House.
Vacano, Diego von. 2007. *Art of Power: Machiavelli, Nietzsche, and the Making of Aesthetic Political Theory*. Lanham, MD: Rowman & Littlefield.
———. 2015. "The Scope of Comparative Political Theory." *Annual Review of Political Science* 18: 465–80.
Veeder, Van Vechten. 1903. "The History and Theory of the Law of Defamation." *Columbia Law Review*. 3: 546–73.
Veyne, Paul. 1987. "The Roman Empire." *In A History of Private Life, Volume I: From Pagan Rome to Byzantium*, edited by Paul Veyne, pp. 5–235. Cambridge, MA: Harvard University Press.
Vincent, David. 1998. *The Culture of Secrecy: Britain, 1832–1998*. New York: Oxford University Press.
Voltaire. 1878. *Œuvres complètes de Voltaire*. Volume 17. Paris.
———. 2009. *Works of Voltaire*. Ithaca: Cornell University Press.

Walker, Samuel. 1994. *Hate Speech: The History of an American Controversy.* Lincoln: University of Nebraska Press.
Walzer, Michael. 2002. *Company of Critics: Social Criticism and Political Commitment in the Twentieth Century.* New York: Basic Books.
Warner, Michael. 1990. *Letters of the Republic: Publication and Public Sphere in Eighteenth-Century America.* Cambridge, MA: Harvard University Press.
Warriner, Charles K. 1958. "The Nature and Functions of Official Morality." *American Journal of Sociology* 64:165–68.
Waterman, Willoughby Cyrus. 1932. *Prostitution and its Repression in New York City 1900–1931.* New York: Columbia University Press.
Weber, Max. 1952. *Ancient Judaism.* Glencoe: IL: Free Press.
Weintraub. Jeff. 1997. "The Theory and Politics of the Public/Private Distinction." In *Public and Private in Thought and Practice: Perspectives on a Grand Dichotomy,* edited by Jeff Weintraub and K. Kumar, pp. 1–42. Chicago: University of Chicago Press.
Westin, Alan. 1967. *Privacy and Freedom.* New York: Atheneum.
Whitfield, Stephen. 1996. *American Space, Jewish Time: Essays in Modern Culture and Politics.* London: Routledge.
White, Edmund. 2009. *City Boy: My Life in New York during the 1960s and '70s.* New York: Bloomsbury.
Wilde, Oscar. (defendant) (1911) 1928. *Three Times Tried* (Account of the trial in a libel action brought against Lord Queensberry in the Marlborough Street Police Court, London, and the trials of Oscar Wilde and Alfred Taylor held in the Central Criminal Court of London.). Paris. Private Print.
    1966. *The Complete Works of Oscar Wilde.* London: Collins.
Wilson, Woodrow, 1956. *Congressional Government.* New York: Meridian.
Wirth, Louis. 1928. *The Ghetto.* Chicago: University of Chicago Press.
Wittgenstein, Ludwig. 1973. *Philosophical Investigations.* New York: Pearson.
Wolfe, Alan. 1997. "Public and Private in Theory and Practice: Some Implications of an Uncertain Boundary." In *Public and Private in Thought and Practice: Perspectives on a Grand Dichotomy,* edited by J. Weintraub and K. Kumar, pp. 182–203. Chicago: University of Chicago Press.
    1998. *One Nation after All: What Middle-Class Americans Really Think about, God, Country, Family, Racism, Welfare, Immigration, Homosexuality, Work, the Right, the Left, and Each Other.* New York: Viking.
    2007. "Social Skills: The Civil Sphere." *New Republic*, April 23, 56–60.
Woodward, Bob. 2005. *The Secret Man: The Story of Watergate's Deep Throat.* New York: Simon & Schuster.
Young, Michael. 2003. "Before the Shooting Started: Civic Engagement and Culture War in Tocqueville's America." Unpublished manuscript.
Zaller, John R. 1992. *The Nature and Origins of Mass Opinion.* New York: Cambridge University Press.
Zaret, David. 2000. *Origins of Democratic Culture: Printing, Petitions, and the Public Sphere in Early-Modern England.* Princeton: Princeton University Press.

Zelizer, Julian. 2004. *On Capitol Hill: The Struggle to Reform Congress and Its Consequences, 1948–2000*. New York: Cambridge University Press.
Zelizer, Viviana. 2007. *Purchase of Intimacy*. Princeton: Princeton University Press.
Zerubavel, Eviatar. 2006. *The Elephant in the Room: Silence and Denial in Everyday Life*. New York: Oxford University Press.

Index

Abbott, Andrew, 131
ACLU, 5, 99, 100
acquaintances, 26–7, 116
aesthetics, 33, 38, 60, 67, 71, 156–7
African Americans, 103, 123–4, 130–1
agonal spirit, 21, 22, 23, 78, 139, 162n
agora, 2, 21–3, 34, 40, 153, 162n
Alexander, Jeffrey, 4, 160n, 161n, 164n, 174n
Alford, Fred, 133
Andersen, Hans Christian, 47–9
André, Carl, 62
anonymity, 26–7, 36–7, 41, 63, 67–9: in urban life, 113, 116, 149–52, 156, 164n
anti-Semitism, 126–30
Arab Spring, 10, 20
arcana imperii, 2, 86
archives, 25, 26, 69
Arendt, Hannah, 21–3: on *doxa*, 67; on appearances, 71; on agonal spirit, 162n; on goodness, 175n
Ariès, Philippe, 114, 116
Aristophanes, 22, 23
Aristotle, 155, 176n
art, 38, 96, 112–13, 125, 132, 136, 172n: scandal in, 56–7; pricing in, 60–2
asylum, 133, 135
asymmetry, 11–12, 48, 63–4, 66–7, 123
audibility, 15, 18, 19, 24, 34, 40, 48, 147
authenticity, 37, 77–8, 156

badaud, 151–2
Baldwin, James, 123

Balzac, Honoré de, 150
Barthes, Roland, 40
Baudelaire, Charles, 150–1
Baudrillard, Jean, 148
Baumgarten, Alexander, 38
Bazin, Anaïs, 150
Beecher-Tilton affair, 105–6
Benhabib, Seyla, 2, 86–7
Benjamin, Walter, 151
Bentham, Jeremy, 68, 86, 89, 119, 133
betrayal, 24, 42, 66, 134, 143
Bible, 99, 111
birth, 114
Blackstone, William, 104
Blumenfeld, Kurt, 129
Bolsheviks, 20, 76
Boston Globe, 136
Bourdieu, Pierre, 52, 122, 157, 167n, 170n
bourgeoisie, 1–3, 7, 27, 114
British Royal family, 121
bubble, 59
Buber, Martin, 42
Buñuel, Luis, 32
Burke, Edmund, 33
Burkhardt, Jacob, 22
Bush, George, W., 98

Carlyle, Thomas, 63
Catholic Church, 64, 74, 116
Catholicism, 34, 74, 116
celebrities, 11, 12, 33, 60–1, 66–7
Chappaquiddick affair, 111

201

Charlie Hebdo, 100–1
Chauncey, George, 122
Christianity, 107, 109, 112, 116, 125–6, 128
Chwe, Michael, 46
city, 19, 63, 186, 116, 135, 148: difference from suburb, 26–7, 152–4
civil disobedience, 6, 85
civil society, 2, 4, 8, 10, 69–70, 84
civilizing process, 32, 114–15
Clinton, Bill, 82, 98, 108, 140, 141–2
Clinton, Hillary, 77, 78, 141, 155
CNN, 51
cockfight, Balinese, 67–8, 73
coffeehouses, 15, 20, 21, 34
Cold War, 9, 79
Committee of the Whole, 92, 132
common belief, 47, 54
common knowledge, 47–8, 54, 57, 59, 84
common law, 96, 97, 100, 104, 105, 139
Comstockery, 105–6
Comte de Mirabeau, 138
Confederate flag, 101, 107
confession, 114, 121
Congress, 69, 78–82, 85, 88, 98, 101, 105, 108, 122, 131–2: oversight by, 82; voting in 92, 132; speech on the floor of, 102
conspicuous consumption, 20
corruption, 12, 84, 89, 92
courage, 65, 66, 68, 70, 73, 84–5, 87–9, 91, 142
Cromwell, Oliver, 66
Cronkite, Walter, 57
curiosity, 67, 124, 149–51, 154, 156

Dahl, Ronald, 10, 80
dandy, 63
death, 25, 47, 64, 112, 114–15
Debord, Guy, 29, 148
deep play, 68
defamation, 94, 96–7, 164n
denunciation, 13, 48, 54, 55, 83, 84, 85
Derrida, Jacques, 42
Dhimmis, 107
dialogue: civic, 2, 4, 7, 8, 9: as private phenomenon, 28–30, 41, 121, 143
Dickens, Charles, 150
discretion, 20, 23, 27, 36, 53, 111, 127, 138
disfigurement, 112
Disraeli, Benjamin, 53

distrust, 13, 77, 81, 83, 89, 144–5
domination, 9, 30, 108, 118, 122, 133
doxa, 67, 155, 167n
Dreyfus affair, 13–14, 127, 137, 142
driving, 38, 153
Drumont, Édouard, 128
Durkheim, Émile, 58
dyad, 25, 29, 30, 142, 163n

Electoral college, 79
Elias, Norbert, 74, 114–15
Eliot, T. S., 40
elites, 7, 11–12, 53, 63, 155
Ellison, Ralph, 123
Elster, Jon, 86, 88
emperor's clothes, 47–9
Erasmus, 67, 116
Ermakoff, Ivan, 58–9
Europe: medieval, 22, 64, 73, 114–16, 124–5, 149, 172: Renaissance, 97, 116; early modern, 1, 64, 73, 97, 115–16, 172; Ancien Régime, 105, 122, 172n; Enlightenment, 1, 21; eighteenth century, 1–3, 7, 113–14, 121, 126, 134–5, 138, 146, 172n; nineteenth century, 91, 113–14, 117–18; twentieth century, 126
executive privilege, 20, 81–2, 98
experts, 135, 155

Facebook, 27, 31
fame, 60, 61, 63, 67, 70, 155, 167n
family, 27, 93, 97, 120, 131, 138: conversations in, 25, 30, 52; reputation, 97, 138; nuclear, 116
Fanon, Frantz, 123
Federal Register, 44
feminism, 3, 18, 72, 102, 108
Feuerbach, Ludwig, 149
fitna, 119
flâneur, 63, 150–2
Foucault, Michel, 72–3, 132–5, 172n
France: prerevolutionary, 65, 105, 114, 121, 122, 138; revolutionary, 76, 77, 86, 88, 91–2, 125; nineteenth century, 13–14, 128, 137; twentieth century, 58–9, 84–5, 100, 106; twenty-first century, 100–1, 106
Frankfurter, Felix, 128
free speech, 11, 94, 99–100
freedom, 134, 149, 152
friendship, 143

Gable, Clark, 66
gay rights, 108–9
Geertz, Clifford, 29, 30, 32, 52, 67–8, 156–7, 163n
Gentiles, 126, 127, 130, 173n
Gentleman's Agreement, 127–8
gentrification, 154
ghetto, 124, 126–7
gladiators, 33, 65, 68
glory, 23, 66, 70, 87–8
Goffman, Erving, 37
Google, 43, 45, 134
gossip, 39, 46, 48, 97, 121
Government in the Sunshine Act, 82, 89
Greeks, 22–3, 60, 139, 155

Habermas, Jürgen, 1–2, 7, 9, 11, 34, 63, 121, 146: conventional critique of, 3–4; on public opinion, 20
Hamilton, Alexander, 88
hanging, 16, 64, 113
Hawthorne, Nathaniel, 112
Hegel, Friedrich, 57, 70, 123
Heine, Heinrich, 127
hijab, 119
Hirschman, Albert, 9
Hobbes, Thomas, 21, 33
Hollywood, 31, 39, 110, 111, 127
home, 19, 23, 38, 127, 152, 153: as quintessential private sphere, 27; boundary with street, 116
homosexuality, 53–6, 108, 122, 138–9
honor, 65, 68, 76, 138
Hughes, Robert, 62
hypocrisy, 143

Ibn Taymiyyah, 119
ignorance, 9, 48, 155, 176n
image, 16, 17, 19, 35, 36, 73, 95, 96, 99, 102, 148: meaning of, 39–40; objectivity of, 41; sexual, 98, 101
Impressionists, 14, 56–7
inauthenticity, 71, 82, 142, 152
independent counsels, 82, 140–2
Inquisition, 112, 125, 136
internet, 11, 18, 22, 24, 26, 27, 35, 37, 57, 154: porn in, 45; anonymity on, 67, 147
intimacy, 24–7, 29, 32, 34, 37–8, 66, 115, 142–3, 156
invisibility, 122–4, 133
Islam, 101, 106–7, 120

Jacobs, Jane, 17
Jakobson, Roman, 123
James, Henry, 54
Jews, 103, 107, 123–30, 172–5n
Jousse, Daniel, 138
jury, 139

Kant, Immanuel, 35, 86, 144
Kantorowich, Ernst, 73
Keller, Hellen, 42
Kennedy, John F., 81, 168n
Knight, Frank, 6, 49
Koons, Jeffrey, 61
Kundera, Milan, 32, 142–3

La Bruyère, Jean de, 74
La Rochefoucauld, François de, 88
langue, 30, 170n
leaks, 25, 69, 83–5, 139
Lennon, John, 34
lettres de cachet, 138
Lévi-Strauss, Claude, 52
Lewinsky affair, 14, 98, 140–2
libel, 54–5, 56, 96–7, 100, 101, 122
Lincoln, Abraham, 79
Lippmann, Walter, 130, 165n
Louis XIV, 74, 97, 114
Lucretius, Titus, 147
Luther, Martin, 67
lynching, 58, 113

Machiavelli, Niccolò, 70–1
Madison, James, 46, 88
madness, 134–5
Mahler, Gustav, 127
Malesherbes, Chrétien de, 45
Mandeville, Bernard, 115
Manet, Édouard, 57, 109
Marquis de Sade, 138
media, 16, 25, 35–6, 38, 57–8, 60, 83–4, 100, 101, 114, 133, 147: American, 8; as site of action, 19; electronic, 26, 75; commentary on, 40; influence of, 50–1, 83; social, 57; audience segregation in, 75; personalization of politics in, 77; trust in, 83; sexual content in, 110
Megan's Law, 45
Mendelssohn, Felix, 127
Merleau-Ponty, Maurice, 72
Mill, John Stuart, 86, 88, 92
minorities, 91, 125

mob, 6, 151
modesty, 23, 109–11, 115
Montaigne, Michel, 45
Mumford, Lewis, 116, 162n
muthos, 121
mutilation, 73, 112–13

nationalism, 36, 157
Nazis, 58, 100, 125, 128
Necker, Jacques, 86
New York Times, 17, 20, 81, 83, 100, 128, 141
Nietzsche, Friedrich, 23, 64, 112
Nixon, Richard, 49–50, 81, 140, 161n
nobility, 74, 86
notoriety, 63, 65
nudity, 11, 36–7, 103, 109

O'Neill, Tip, 132
Obama, Barack, 75, 78, 115
objectification, 28–31, 35, 48, 64, 72–3, 75, 142–3, 150–2, 156: publicity and, 28, 51; and domination, 30; meaning of, 31; in writing, 41–2; of public opinion, 50–1; glorification and, 67
obscenity, 99, 101, 105, 110–11, 116, 147, 171n
Odyssey, 120–1
Orientalism, 122, 124

Panopticon, 133
parole, 30, 170n
participation, 7–11, 20, 37, 59, 63–4, 67, 91, 110, 148–9, 153, 156: civic, 2–3, 10, 92, 146; motivations for, 9–10; in scandals, 13
Pascal, Blaise, 87
patriarchy, 9, 18
Peirce, Charles, 16, 35
Pentagon Papers, 82, 100
performance, 63, 70, 73–7, 116, 129, 155, 164n: interaction and, 37–8; status and, 65–6; and power, 73–4, 76; of politicians, 70, 75, 77; public denunciation as, 85
Perikles, 121
pillory, 28, 64, 113
Plato, 29, 42, 149
pluralistic ignorance, 46–8, 50
polarization, 6, 90–1
polygamy, 120
pornography, 26, 45, 57, 102, 105, 108, 110, 111

Posner, Richard, 96
prices, 34, 59, 61–2, 166n
prison, 25, 112, 133
privacy, 18, 20, 27, 33, 45, 63, 93, 102, 116, 138, 163: collective and organizational, 24–5; auditory, 34; social status and, 67; in politics, 82, 94, 98; of public figures, 100; and feminism, 108; in prison, 133
profiling, 38, 118
Protestantism, 36, 42, 64, 116
Proust, Marcel, 144
provocation, 13, 37, 55, 85, 109
public debate, 3, 6, 20
public domain, 4, 18–19
public events, 12–15, 20, 40, 51, 68, 69, 77, 132, 137, 147
public executions, 73, 76, 112–13, 116, 138, 149
public opinion, 1, 20, 50, 58, 80, 88, 121
punishment, 56, 64–5, 96, 112–13, 125, 132, 136, 172n
purdah, 119–20

Rabelais, François, 116
radio, 15, 16, 40, 63–4, 80, 83, 99, 103–4, 143
raison d'État, 2, 133
rape, 33, 108, 111, 133
Rathenau, Walter, 129
Reagan, Ronald, 82, 83, 140
recognition, 2, 60, 70, 85, 123, 151
Reign of Terror, 91
relationality, 122–3
Renaissance, 97, 109, 116
representation, 39, 41–2, 48, 108, 114, 137, 144, 147–8, 154: types of 16–17; of violence, 33; of sex, 33, 102, 108, 130; and signification, 35; creativity of 42, 71–2; of power, 73; of taboos, 103
resentment, 12, 66, 148
reserve, 105
reticence, 110–11, 115
rhetoric, 5, 8, 23, 29, 64, 87, 94
ritual, 44, 46, 58, 64, 68, 74, 107, 116, 132, 161–2n
Romans, 23, 33, 45, 65
Romney, Mitt, 75
Roosevelt, Franklin, Delano, 80, 81, 83, 128
Roth, Philip, 19

Rothko, Mark, 61
Rousseau, Jean-Jacques, 42, 45, 119,
  146–7, 149, 175n
rumor, 46, 53–4, 56
Rumsfeld, Donald, 32

Saatchi, Charles, 61
Saddam Hussein, 77
Sade, Marquis de, 138
Said, Edward, 122, 124
salons, 2, 121
sambenito, 125
Sartre, Jean-Paul, 7, 150–1
Saussure, Ferdinand de, 42, 52, 170n
scandal, 24, 38–9, 98, 155, 161n: as public
  event, 12–13; public sphere and, 14–15;
  in art, 57; according to Thomist ethics,
  75; in politics, 83–5; logic of, 84–8; in
  Renaissance England, 95–7; strategic use
  of, 109; trials and, 137
Schudson, Michael, 10
Schumpeter, Joseph, 72, 155
Scruton, Roger, 147
Searle, John, 52
secrecy, 86–90, 97, 133, 139: in Masonic
  lodges, 3; in voting, 7, 72, 86, 91–2,
  169n; in economic life, 20; sharing of,
  24; in family, 25; in government, 25, 86,
  87, 100; open, 46–7, 53, 104; of
  deliberations, 88, 89–90; in Congress,
  132; of jury activity, 139
secret ballot, 7, 86, 91–2
secularism, 106
Sennett, Richard, 146
Serrano, Andrew, 39
sexual abuse, 136
sexual liberalization, 100–1
sexual politics, 108–10, 124
Sharī'a law, 120
Shakespeare, William, 33, 111
shame, 33, 103, 108, 115, 117
Silverstein, Michael, 5
Simmel, Georg, 46, 151, 164n
Simpson, O. J., 137–8
slander, 96, 97
slaves, 30, 66, 119, 121, 123
Smith, Adam, 20, 28, 64–5, 85
Socrates, 42
sodomy, 54, 65, 104
Sontag, Susan, 31–2
spectacle, 12, 22: logic of, 29–31, 68; in
  politics, 71–2; power of, 73–6, 112, 113;

insane as, 135; Rousseau and, 146–7;
  spectator and, 148–52
speech, 37, 38, 41, 44, 48, 72, 94–101, 106,
  107, 119–22
Star Chamber, 95
Starr, Kenneth, 140–2
strangers, 26–7, 28, 31, 38, 40, 63, 72, 116,
  118
sublime, 33, 154
suburb, 26, 43, 44, 152, 154, 176n
Supreme Court, 50, 82, 89, 99, 100, 101,
  111, 128
Swidler, Ann, 51, 165n
swishes, 129

taboo, 32, 47, 53, 103–4, 114, 149
television, 2, 6, 16, 18, 21, 40, 57, 70, 92,
  111, 132, 148, 150: cable, 9; images of
  combat on, 39; presidential visibility
  and, 80; censorship of, 98, 100
text, 40–2, 48, 52, 95: objectivity of, 41–2,
  143
The Daily Show, 130
theater, 94, 96, 104, 119, 147, 148, 155,
  175n
Tilly, Charles, 15
Tocqueville, Alexis de, 6, 8, 10
token, 38, 128, 129, 130
torture, 73, 76, 113
totalitarianism, 7, 93, 137
transcendence, 154, 156–7
triad, 30, 163n
Tropic of Capricorn, 110
Truman, Henry, 81
Trump, Donald, 5, 71, 76, 77–8, 155
trust, 82–3, 98, 131, 144–5
Twain, Mark, 102
Twitter, 6, 11, 71, 134

Ulysses, 111
Umar Pact, 107
United States: colonial, 11, 112;
  antebellum, 6, 8, 10, 105; Civil War, 79,
  105; post-Civil War, 105; Progressive
  Era, 6; nineteenth century, 3, 75, 69;
  New Deal, 79; Cold War, 9, 79;
  twentieth century, 10, 79–81, 99, 101,
  104–5, 123, 127
Updike, John, 153
utilitarianism, 86, 96, 99, 100–1,
  157
utterance, 30, 41, 52, 95, 121

veil, 107, 119–20, 173n
Victorians, 54–6, 104–5, 111–12
Vietnam War, 82, 83, 87, 100
violence, 7, 91–2, 132, 169n, 176n
voice, 16, 29, 35, 40, 58, 69, 80, 120, 124, 131, 136
Voltaire, 149, 151
voting, 7, 91–2, 132, 169n, 176n

Wall Street Journal, 26
Walmart, 153
Washington, George, 79

Watergate scandal, 12, 14, 49–50, 82–3, 140, 161n, 162n
Weber, Max, 73, 77
wedding, 116, 119
White, Edmund, 31–2
Wikileaks, 133
Wilde, Oscar, 53–6, 104
Wilson, Woodrow, 80, 81, 131
Wittgenstein, Ludwig, 30, 52
World War II, 39, 81, 110, 128, 129

YouTube, 75